Translation Flows

# Benjamins Translation Library (BTL)
ISSN 0929-7316

The Benjamins Translation Library (BTL) aims to stimulate research and training in Translation & Interpreting Studies – taken very broadly to encompass the many different forms and manifestations of translational phenomena, among them cultural translation, localization, adaptation, literary translation, specialized translation, audiovisual translation, audio-description, transcreation, transediting, conference interpreting, and interpreting in community settings in the spoken and signed modalities.

For an overview of all books published in this series, please see
benjamins.com/catalog/btl

### General Editor
Roberto A. Valdeón
University of Oviedo

### Associate Editor
Franz Pöchhacker
University of Vienna

### Honorary Editors
Yves Gambier
University of Turku
& Immanuel Kant Baltic Federal University

Gideon Toury
Tel Aviv University

### Advisory Board
Cecilia Alvstad
Høgskolen i Østfold

Georges L. Bastin
University of Montreal

Dirk Delabastita
University of Namur

Daniel Gile
Université Paris 3 - Sorbonne Nouvelle

Arnt Lykke Jakobsen
Copenhagen Business School

Krisztina Károly
Eötvös Lorand University

Kobus Marais
University of the Free State

Christopher D. Mellinger
University of North Carolina at Charlotte

Jan Pedersen
Stockholm University

Nike K. Pokorn
University of Ljubljana

Luc van Doorslaer
University of Tartu & KU Leuven

Meifang Zhang
University of Macau

### Volume 163
Translation Flows. Exploring networks of people, processes and products
Edited by Ilse Feinauer, Amanda Marais and Marius Swart

# Translation Flows

Exploring networks of people, processes and products

*Edited by*

Ilse Feinauer
Amanda Marais
Marius Swart
Stellenbosch University

John Benjamins Publishing Company
Amsterdam / Philadelphia

The paper used in this publication meets the minimum requirements of the American National Standard for Information Sciences – Permanence of Paper for Printed Library Materials, ANSI Z39.48-1984.

DOI 10.1075/btl.163

**Cataloging-in-Publication Data available from Library of Congress:**
LCCN 2023031217 (PRINT) / 2023031218 (E-BOOK)

ISBN 978 90 272 1424 9 (HB)
ISBN 978 90 272 4940 1 (E-BOOK)

© 2023 – John Benjamins B.V.
No part of this book may be reproduced in any form, by print, photoprint, microfilm, or any other means, without written permission from the publisher.

John Benjamins Publishing Company · https://benjamins.com

# Table of contents

Foreword      VII

**PART 1. Historical flows**

CHAPTER 1. A naïve inquiry into translation between Aboriginal languages in pre-Invasion Australia      3
   *Anthony Pym*

CHAPTER 2. The circulation of knowledge vs the mobility of translation, or how mobile are translators and translations?      23
   *Philipp Hofeneder*

CHAPTER 3. A transatlantic flow of Spanish and Catalan *romans-à-clef*: Translators, publishers, and censors from Argentina to Franco's Spain      43
   *Sofía Monzón Rodríguez*

CHAPTER 4. Recognition versus redistribution? Translation flows and the role of politically committed publishers in Spain      69
   *Fruela Fernández*

CHAPTER 5. From intersection to interculture: How the classical Ottoman intercultural scene came to be      87
   *Sare Rabia Öztürk*

**PART 2. Current flows**

CHAPTER 6. Recirculated, recontextualized, reworked: Community-driven video game fan translation practices in Turkey      107
   *Selahattin Karagöz*

CHAPTER 7. Nollywood and indigenous language translation flows: A systems perspective      129
   *Maricel Botha*

CHAPTER 8. Maryse Condé and the Alternative Nobel Prize of 2018      149
   *Yvonne Lindqvist*

CHAPTER 9. The role of literary agents in the international flow of texts: A case study      163

*Duygu Tekgül-Akın*

CHAPTER 10. Flowing to the reception side: A trade-off model of translation acceptance                                              183
   *Bei Hu*

CHAPTER 11. The tidalectics of translation: On the necessity of rethinking translation flows from the Caribbean                                              207
   *Laëtitia Saint-Loubert*

CHAPTER 12. Combining translation policy and imagology: The case of Dutch literature in Italy                                              225
   *Paola Gentile*

Notes on the authors                                              247

Index                                              251

# Foreword

## Background

The 9th Congress of the European Society for Translation Studies was held in Stellenbosch, South Africa, in September 2019. This was the first time that this event took place outside Europe. The theme for the 9th Congress was "Living Translation – People, Processes, Products". The Congress included numerous current topics, such as the role of translation in the lived experience of the Other, in fake news, mass communication, power and ideology, oral histories, the hegemony of English, accessibility, inclusivity, education, gender and transformation.

Translation Studies is by its very nature a living, shifting and vibrant discipline which has shown its flexibility over the past decades. Congress presentations accordingly focused on numerous aspects of the field, including (inter)disciplinary, methodological, conceptual, professional, historical and geographical approaches, all relating the central Congress theme. A common thread that came to the fore, whether as a methodological or analytical feature, as a descriptive framework or as a subject in itself, was that of "flows" and the "flowing" nature of translation. This was the genesis of the present volume, starting with a call for papers to Congress participants as well as a general call to submit abstracts for consideration.

Initially, suitable abstracts for the volume were selected. After completion of each chapter, the full chapter was double-blind peer reviewed and authors who received provisional approval for publication had the opportunity to incorporate the suggestions from the reviewers. Following this, the draft manuscript was compiled, and the full manuscript was again peer double-blind reviewed and revised prior to publication.

## Ordering

It would seem logical to use the original sub-headings of the Congress theme – people, processes and products – as thematic subdivisions for the chapters selected for this book. However, many of the contributions could fit into more than one of these sections.

Therefore, the editors instead opted for clustering the chapters into two sections loosely based on the temporality of the given case study. The first five chapters can be seen as dealing broadly with historical flows – ranging from translation-historical to geopolitical. The second cluster is comprised of seven chapters that consist of more current case studies.

## Historical flows

In the first chapter in this section, **Anthony Pym** looks at the communicative flows between Aboriginal languages in Australia prior to the European invasion of 1788. He points out that when asking whether translation occurred in a given time and place, it is vital to conceptualise what exactly we mean by "translation", taking into account our existing positions, orientations and assumptions. Pym reconsiders the clear divide between languages and cultures, as well as the implicit assumption of congruence between a language and a culture in any given translational situation, which are all tenets of much of Western translation scholarship. This investigation of an as yet largely unknown set of interlingual communicative practices gives scholars of translation studies much food for thought, as it brings into focus the situatedness of language, in the process broadening the very nature of translation to include numerous natural phenomena and other communicative modalities. Pym reiterates the importance of indigenous knowledge, not merely as material or data, but also for all its rich and turbulent methodological potential.

In his contribution, **Philipp Hofeneder** works to reconstruct patterns of mobility of agents and objects in translation which together constitute what he dubs the so-called translatorial space. In doing so, he adopts a spatial approach towards translation flows, meaning that he focuses not only on translations as physical objects, but also on the agents enabling them, namely authors, translators and finally readers. His methodology leads to research questions involving the living and working spaces of these agents, as well as the locality of publications and their readers. He examines three different cases of translation spaces, all from the 19th century and with Russia as their epicentre, and studies the dissemination of the works beyond their initial place(s) of origin. This approach allows for a more in-depth analysis of translation history.

**Sofía Monzón Rodríguez** turns to the substantial flow of Argentinian-made translations that were scrutinized and often denied publication in the 1960s by the Francoist censorship board in Madrid. While Spanish and Catalan publishers as a result sought to get their own editions published, local translations were also affected and shaped by the agents appointed by the regime. The act of translation and the translation processes thus became arduous for translators and publishers who had to deal with the regime's censorship apparatus. The author sets out to investigate the consequent flows of translations and the network of agents that facilitated the translations. She explores the editions of *romans-à-clef* written by Henry Miller, Anaïs Nin and Lawrence Durrell that travelled from South America to the Iberian Peninsula in the 1960s, and the Spanish and Catalan translations produced domestically in Spain. The outcome is an illustration of how the agents – translators, publishers and censors – involved in this translation flow between North America, Argentina and Francoist Spain interacted to shape the reception of these novels among the Spanish and Catalan readership.

The chapter by **Fruela Fernández** points out that although contemporary characterisations of book translation flows within the global structure tend to proceed from a hierarchical basis, looking at the interplay between centres and peripheries, there is also a need to look at the internal, national field. Consequently, he unpacks the notion of the "politically-committed" publisher in the Spanish context by looking at the role of six such publishers over a period starting with the global financial crisis in 2008 and going up to 2021. Fernández positions these publishers as the intellectual home for pursuing the issues and causes first raised by the so-called 15M protest movement. In recent years, there have been concerns that the post-15M left in Spain are overly concerned with causes such as sexual and racial identity, and not concerned enough with causes relating to labour and political strategy. Using a thematic analysis of publications from the six politically-committed publishers, Fernández shows that the evidence does not support this view, but that there is also a great need for further studies along these lines.

Inspired largely by Pym's idea of transfer maps, **Sare Rabia Öztürk** employs a historical survey to map the flow of people, knowledge, customs, practices and centres of power across the Middle East between the 5th and 14th centuries. The chapter proceeds from the premise that the historical flow between the three sites associated with Arabic, Persian and Turkish cultures gave way to the classical Ottoman setting of interculture. From here, the author investigates how Ottoman translators within this space engaged with both Persian and Arabic not only as source languages, but also as components of an Ottoman epistemic discourse. The chapter shows how intercultural transfers can influence cultural input in several domains such as science, literature, bureaucracy, education and religion.

## Current flows

Just as translation evolves, the objects of its study evolve as well, broadening the scope of translation studies. In the first chapter in this section, **Selahattin**

**Karagöz** draws on a sociological analysis to investigate flows in the practice of non-commercial and non-professional translation of video games, and the flows resulting from these practices. Karagöz introduces the concept of "gaming capital" to foreground how translators create new language patches for games that have been in circulation for some time. To do so, these translators draw especially on their gaming knowledge and, ostensibly, their identity and position as gamers to do this work. The work they do leads to older video games being recirculated and recontextualised, forming an alternative production flow to the better-known commercial distribution channels. These translators, just like their work, are deeply embedded within a particular gaming community, and they utilise paratextual spaces both to aid them in their selections and to showcase what they have done. The production of these language patches is not driven by commercial considerations, but rather by the personal choices, history and preferences of the translators themselves.

Secondly, we have a contribution from and about Africa. **Maricel Botha** examines the role of subtitling in Nigeria's film industry (informally known as Nollywood) in stimulating translation from and into indigenous African languages. Here Botha shows that translation in Africa does not necessarily involve horizontal flows between English and/or French and the indigenous languages, but that vertical flows between various indigenous languages also occur. Although the subtitling is usually done non-professionally and informally, Botha states that it has represented an important mechanism for communication flows within Nigeria and to other countries. Botha's sociologically informed research employs Niklas Luhmann's social systems theory (SST), as described by Tyulenev. Luhmann's SST sees society as consisting of communication networks, rather than people or actions. This communication in the form of subtitling provides significant information flows between different language groups in Nigeria, but also between different countries where developing economies do not always offer the means for creating information flows. Botha has highlighted an excellent application for Luhmann's SST. Nollywood's ability to project a relatable African identity and to address pan-African themes lead to the export of indigenous-language films. The fact that these films are then subtitled into other indigenous languages highlights Africa and the African presence.

Inspired by the methodological framework of "histoire croisée" (intersecting events influencing history), **Yvonne Lindqvist** reconstructs four major intersecting flows of events that led up to the nomination and selection of the French Caribbean author Maryse Condé for the 2018 Alternative Nobel Prize in Literature. Each of these flows is presented in a compelling analysis, namely the translation bibliomigrancy of French Caribbean fiction to Sweden during the past 40 years; the authorship of Maryse Condé and her reception in Sweden; the effects and repercussions of the cancellation of the Nobel Prize in Literature in 2018 and in particular the consequences of the reorganization of the Royal Swedish Academy; the last series of events entails the foundation of the "New Academy" and the Alternative Nobel Prize in Literature. The question still remains open as to whether Maryse Condé's chances of being awarded the regular Nobel Prize in Literature were spoilt by being awarded the Alternative Nobel Prize in Literature.

The role of international literary agents in the flow of texts and the network of relations of the global literary market is the focus of **Duygu Tekgül-Akın**'s chapter. She uses a case study from Kalem Agency, Turkey's largest literary agency, and investigates the acts of translation that are undertaken and commissioned by literary agents, as well as acts of image building through such translation. Primary data (including interviews with the co-founder of the agency, as well as published news items and promotional material produced by Kalem) were analysed making use of content and discourse analysis in order to address questions regarding the types of translation that are undertaken or commissioned by international literary agents, and how these are related to the overall flow of texts. Furthermore, the role of these acts of translation in transnational cultural intermediation are considered, ultimately providing a perspective on the place of international literary agents in the broader network of the literary translation industry.

**Bei Hu** investigates the transnational flow of Chinese texts in translation. She draws on empirical evidence from a quasi-experiment in which a group of 22 readers in Australia responded to various English translations of foreign affairs discourses. Her findings illustrate how a nonlinear trade-off model could be used to explain the readers' judgements where they weigh linguistic and ethical considerations against each other. The trade-off is between what seems mutually contradictory, namely faithfulness vs fluency, explicitation vs implicitation, and distance vs proximity. Hu views translation reception as a continuum, ranging from a position where a translation is definitely refused to where a text is absolutely accepted. According to these findings, the readers tend to take into account a pair of two seemingly mutually contradictory expectations (e.g. faithfulness vs. fluency) and, at some point, reach a compromise. Hu therefore regards translation reception as a trade-off, being optimal when it yields the maximum desired effects with minimum risks. She also suggests that the extent to which the translation is accepted is subject to the degree to which the readers trust the translator. The more trust the translator gains, the more open the reader is to accepting a wider range of translator interventions resulting in, for example, a more fluent translation with more explication and moving further away from the meaning of the source text.

**Laëtitia Saint-Loubert** analyses literary circulation in the Caribbean from a more fluid, decentred perspective in order to reveal horizontal, submarine (translation) flows, and to connect Caribbean Studies and Translation Studies. Saint-

Loubert claims that the Caribbean literary ecosystem and Caribbean Studies as a discipline are central to a decolonial approach to translation and literary circulation. Translation flows are analysed as tidal movements that focus primarily on literary (non-)circulation within the insular Caribbean. Kamau Brathwaite's term "tidalectics" is used as theoretical lens to describe Translation Studies from the perspective of Caribbean Studies. The research has shown that existing models of analysis for the transnational circulation of literature are not suitable for the region. Case studies such as libraries and book kiosks examined in this chapter, all individual and community-based initiatives, demonstrate solidarity and resourcefulness that resist mainstream circulation flows. Saint-Loubert's conclusion is that a more integrated approach is urgently needed to address issues of bibliodiversity and epistemological justice in regions such as the Caribbean. This requires decolonizing the mainstream book market, as well as the theory and praxis of translation.

**Paola Gentile** investigates the transnational imagology at play during cultural transfers between the Netherlands and Italy, two cultural peripheries within the global flow of translated literature. She considers the reasons and motivations behind the selections made by institutional agents when it comes to both the production and the reception of literary translations. The literary and cultural image of a country, in this case the Netherlands, is formed in large part by the selection of translations made of its literature. Therefore, in forming translation policies and supporting translation, agents such as the Dutch Foundation for Literature and Flanders Literature play an important role in shaping the representation of a culture abroad. Gentile builds on these principles in a case study showing how Italian publisher Iperborea has utilised the Nordic image of Dutch literature as promoted by the Dutch Foundation for Literature to promote translated Dutch literature in the Italian market. The benefits as well as the potential dangers of this situation are also pointed out.

## In conclusion

The 12 chapters in this volume are a clear illustration of the wide scope of Translation Studies, indicating the way in which the discipline has started moving away from its traditionally European situatedness. Whereas the first cluster of chapters consists mainly of work on and from the Global North, the second cluster complements this by bringing the Global South into the picture as well.

This kind of methodological distinction is, of course, not a fact out in the real world. Dividing up the globe into two halves, deciding on which continent a study is based, and the like, are all attempts to simplify the complexities related to delineating nations and nation states, continents, identities, ideologies and other aspects of being-in-the-world. The junction between the two sections, for example, is formed by two contributions reaching from the Ottoman Empire right into modern-day Turkey. As the title states, however, *translation flows*, not just in the conventional sense, between languages and cultures, but over artificial borders, into new spaces, between non-traditional agents and actors, and through various genres and mediums.

The contributions in this volume open up new avenues for further research, while extending the range of perspectives on the basis of which the discipline can be expanded. Translation as a social practice forms a golden thread throughout the various chapters that each provide novel points of departure, whether it be by incorporating non-traditional language pairs, materials, datasets or geographical and temporal spaces.

We foresee that this volume of state-of-the-art research will stimulate robust discussions as we map our way forward as a living discipline.

Ilse Feinauer, Amanda Marais and Marius Swart

PART 1

# Historical flows

CHAPTER 1

# A naïve inquiry into translation between Aboriginal languages in pre-Invasion Australia

Anthony Pym
The University of Melbourne

Was there translation between Australian Aboriginal languages prior to the European Invasion dated from 1788? The evidence from archeological research and the accounts of early European settlers would suggest that there were no specialized translators as such between Aboriginal languages, no specific communicative solution that could be called translation in the post-Renaissance Western sense of the term, and no evidence of a dominant lingua franca that might have acted as an alternative communication solution. Instead, we find ample reference to polyglot speakers, to multilingual meeting places for trade, ceremony and dispute resolution, to multilingual narratives, and the use of local sign languages, smoke signals, bush tracks and message sticks, all of which could help in the performance of communication across language borders. Taken together, these practices suggest interlingual communication flows based not on conveying a message clearly or quickly, but on multilayered interlingual practices based on respect for the territorial embeddedness of languages and the active, informed interpretation of data. Unlike Western calls for ever more translations across ever more languages, Indigenous practices might enhance sustainability by teaching us to respect linguistic diversity, translate less, and think more.

**Keywords:** translation flows, borders, Indigenous languages, code-switching, language contact, interpreting, multilingualism, sign languages, message sticks, multimedia communication

This is an inquiry into possible translation flows between Australian Aboriginal languages (not including Torres Strait Islander languages) in the period prior to 1788, which would nominally mark the beginning of the European Invasion. The inquiry is not based on any personal specialized knowledge, but instead draws on readings of Europeans' early contacts with Aboriginal cultures as well as on discussions with academic colleagues who work on Aboriginal languages, mostly at the University of Melbourne. To that extent, the inquiry is consciously naïve, written from the perspective of an outsider who thinks in terms of translation in the European sense of the word, which may be an entirely different discipline drawn from an entirely different set of cultures. I have been a learner grappling with a deceptively simple question.

**Why the inquiry?**

The question arose when I made a beginner's mistake. Looking for an extreme case where a society would in theory not need any translators or interpreters (in Pym 2020), I referred to the northern Australian island of Warruwi, where some 400 people use nine Indigenous languages, plus English as a lingua franca (Singer and Harris 2016). In the enclosed space of the island, each person reportedly speaks at least three languages. In theory, there would thus be almost no need for translators, or rather, everyone could be their own translator, translating themselves when necessary. My colleague Ruth Singer, whose work I was drawing on, corrected me soon thereafter, indicating that spoken translation does indeed occur. Further, "there are a lot of practices in any case that involve mediated communication – not only translation between languages but also 'prompting' where somebody whispers in another person's ear and they repeat it to a third party" (Singer, personal communication, 30 May 2017). These forms of mediation are not necessarily due to the presence of an unknown language, but have more to do with the cultural need to observe "avoidance relations", prohibiting unmediated conversation between certain members of the group, as when a man should not speak directly to his mother-in-law or indeed any woman in the same family position as his mother-in-law (I refrain from praising too loudly the wisdom of the measure). When such communication is necessary, the prohibition is circumvented by use of a mediator, or in the absence of a mediator, sometimes by people speaking back-to-back. Since the mediation may or may not concern different languages, we cannot really classify the social practice as any kind of clearly necessary interlingual translation. What matters in such cases is not so much the languages involved as who has the right to speak with whom.

From that kind of observation, one starts to rethink the assumptions we make when we opine that all societies need translation and nothing but translation. Even to ask about translation flows might be to impose a foreign view. One learns to become naïve.

I then went looking for anything that might resemble a translation practice in pre-Invasion Aboriginal cultures – and here I include spoken translation, or interpreting, as an aspect of the term "translation". I searched through glossaries and dictionaries for words for translation in Aboriginal languages, both in the early accounts – *namalelama* is "to translate" (*verdolmetschen, übersetzen*) in Strehlow's 1909 dictionary of Arrernte (Kenny 2018: 279) – and in more recent compilations – "to translate" is listed as *akngarte-iweme* (to turn something over, change, translate) in a wordlist of Eastern and Central Arrernte and as *kngartiwuma* (translate, change) in a glossary of Western Arrernte. There are clearly differences and various major metaphors at work,[1] yet the evidence is inherently unreliable simply because the European compilers were all, by definition, translating: there is no guarantee that they themselves did not select or create the apparent equivalents for their own action "to translate". And beyond that, the most worrying thing is the *absence* of entries for translation in most of the early wordlists. There is no guarantee that the words alone show us much of what was happening pre-Invasion.

I then searched for words for translation in contemporary linguists' descriptive accounts of Aboriginal languages and language contacts, and then I went through reports written by a few of the early amateur anthropologists, who were chronologically closer to pre-Invasion data. In all cases I consulted, the only use of "translation" or "to translate" was in relation to Malayan or European languages; I found nothing that might pass as an account of translation practices as such between Aboriginal languages.

My initial reaction was to accuse the linguists and anthropologists of ingrained blindness to translation. That would be essentially the same kind of blindness we find in our traditionally immersive language teachers or in our national literary historians, indeed in anyone who goes looking for pure systems and thus only finds pure systems – they often systematically overlook translation as perturbance to system. That is, I thought the absence of translation might be due to the blindness of the settler-culture observers and those who inherited their nationalist epistemologies. But then it dawned on me that the absence might actually be in the object of knowledge itself. Could it be that pre-Invasion Aboriginal cultures really had no established translation practices? Or perhaps the practices they had simply did not look like anything that the linguists and anthropologists would use the word "translation" to describe?

---

1. The most intriguing semantic overlap might be in the Burarra Lexicon, where *burrgurdanyja* is glossed as "to give in exchange, to translate" and contains *gurdanyja* ("to return in kind"). In the Wordlist of Eastern and Central Arrernte, *akngarte-iweme* is "to turn something over, change, translate". In the Western Arrarnta Lexicon, *kngartiwuma* is described as meaning "to translate, to change" but morphological comparison suggests a possible compounding of *wuma* (sound) and *knharta* (become, grow). There is more to be discovered here.

Hence the simple question: Was there anything like translation in pre-Invasion Aboriginal cultures? Before giving some answers, I should sketch out why the question might be of some importance.

## Assumptions about translation flows

There is a certain tendency in translation studies to assume that the world needs ever more translations, of all kinds and in all directions. Some highly unequal flows between languages are read as signals of hegemony, as in the never-ending misreadings of a "3 percent problem" where some are scandalized by apparently few translations coming into English (an assumption corrected in Pym and Chrupała 2004, Ginsburgh and Weber 2011). One kind of response to that problem is to call for increases in translations from the subaltern language or country (cf. Sapiro 2014, 2019). Ever more translations will bring ever more resistance to hegemony! Translation flows are thus seen as weapons in a global struggle between languages, such that each translation in a direction opposing hegemony becomes an act of potential liberation. A paroxysm of this assumption is reached in a catalogue of literary translations from French into German (Jurt, Ebel and Erzgräber 1989) that lists the works that "should" have been translated but were not, resulting in page after page of empty white space on the German side. Why would anyone ever think that everything should be translated? After all, if there were really so many great works to access in French, surely the learning of French would be the most cost-effective solution for all German readers? Yet the apparent need to translate ever more persists, along with a logical correlative in the bemoaned shortage of (good) professional translators. Happily, electronic communication and online machine translation now help us over that apparent hurdle, making translations ever more attainable and potentially democratized to the extent that they can be user-driven. When fewer than 1% of the words being translated in the world are actually rendered by professional translators (Pym and Torres-Simón 2021), free online translations might even seem to be flowing in response to something like raw human needs, at least for as long as we assume that no one can never have too many translations.

That kind of crude but quite widespread assumption is being questioned in view of the environmental costs of the production and storage of electronic data (cf. Cronin 2017; Moorkens and Rocchi 2021). If the training of one online machine-translation engine costs the equivalent of five cars for the entire lifetime of the cars (Strubell, Ganesh, McCallum 2019), we would perhaps want to make sure that the cost is justified in terms of actual human benefits. This argument can be made, I think, if and when we train people to use machine translation intelligently. But what would that mean, exactly? Most forays into machine translation literacy (notably in Bowker and Buitrago Ciro 2019) indicate the need to distrust raw machine translation, to compare different translations, to think through the message in terms of context, in short to play an active role in message construction. The same lessons basically apply when we become aware of the massive circulation of intentional misinformation via electronic means, to say nothing of the violence done by profiling and trolling. The proposition that all translation is good translation deserves to be questioned, now more than ever.

An alternative ethics might then be based on *limiting* the modes and intensities of translation flows. This would ideally not be in order to cultivate ignorance, but might instead work in the interests of promoting more ecologically sustainable modes of communicating across languages. Perhaps we should only invest effort in high-stakes communication, limiting our labour to what is important for cross-cultural cooperation (Pym 1997, 2004). A more ambitious strategy, though, is to seek alternatives to a narrow Western concept of translation, especially when it comes to challenging the assumed "commissive promise" that a translation should offer a full representation of some aspects of an anterior text (cf. Chesterman 2001: 149). If we forget about fulfilling that kind of promise, what happens?

So when I ask whether there were translation practices in pre-Invasion Australia, the question is not formulated out of mere academic curiosity. It is part of a wider search for alternative ways of thinking about translation. And when the initial answers seem to be that there was little or no translation going on, that in itself suggests there might be other ways of solving communication problems.

That said, when I first asked the question, I was not at all sure there was any substantial knowledge to be gained from Aboriginal language practices. The case for learning from the Indigenous seems not as clear-cut as it is in the highly intelligent ways in which Aboriginal family structures imposed intricate relations across moieties to bind people to country and regulate complex solidarity, or in the ways efficient land management was carried out by the use of controlled fires (Gammage 2012) – as contemporary Australians discover when enormous bushfires result from our contemporary lack of land management. In those aspects, there is undoubted interest in learning from First Nations. But in the sphere of interlingual communication, I can only start from a naïve question.

## What can lines on a map tell us?

Translation, in the traditional Western view, is between languages. So if we are going to find that kind of translation in pre-Invasion Australia, we first have to know what the languages were and how they were distinguished.

Maps of Australian languages show most of them belonging to the Pama-Nyangan family, except for those in the very north. Estimates vary as to how many mutually unintelligible varieties there might have been in the late 18th century, but the consensus seems to be upward of 250 languages for a population of perhaps 350,000 people. The numbers involve a lot of guesswork, but if you divide one by the other, the suggestion is that the average language might have had some 1,400 speakers. That is, there were many languages, some with relatively small numbers of speakers. There is no evidence of any lingua franca or territorially dominant language prior to Europeanized Kriol – there was no language that could be called "Aboriginal Australian". These few indications suggest that language was being used for something other than the communication of messages to large numbers of people or over long distances. The maps instead show a mishmash of language borders across the continent, providing no shortage of language contact points for translators to work across. But if the prime purpose of language was something other than to communicate across the contact points, there would be a reduced need for translation.

Within and across the lines on the standard language maps, there is evidence of much else going on. If one considers language *varieties* that have some degree of mutual intelligibility, the count goes from 250 up to some 800 (Vaughan and Loakes 2020). You can explore this online (https://50words.online/). For example, in the Wadjak Noongar region, where I grew up, "welcome" is *wandjoo* and "hello" is *kaya*. If I move 540 km south, to the country my mother is from, I find other varieties of Noongar but those words are the same. However, some 750 km to the north-east, where I did mining work, I am in Ngalia country and the words are *wutayi* and *yuwa palunya* respectively. And in Wajarri country, 850 km to the north, they are *barndi yanayi* and *nyinda barndi*. So although almost all varieties do belong to the same language family, that is not going to help you much if you want to travel more than a few hundred kilometers.

In addition to the language maps, there is ample evidence of trade routes or "chains of connection" by which goods and knowledge travelled and were exchanged (Mulvaney 1976; Paton 1994; Smith 2013). The reconstruction of the routes mostly comes from archeological identification of material and cultural products found far from where they were produced, such as items from the sea that are found far inland. Among the accounts close to the first European settlements, Roth, for example, observed in inner Queensland objects that had come from the coast some 1,000 km to the north: "Thus it happens that ideas are interchanged, superstitions and traditions handed from district to district, and are more or less altered in transit, that new words and terms are picked up, and that corrobborees are learnt and exchanged, just like any other commodities" (1897: 136). The routes themselves are sometimes associated with dreaming lines, held to follow the primal movements of creator beings, and with songlines, where series of geographical features are committed to memory and become maps in the mind – to learn the song is to know one's way across country, so the song may be chanted as one moves. Since these lines can sometimes go for more than a thousand kilometers, some hard language boundaries had to be crossed and there had to be some way to cross them. So the lines running across the language boundaries suggest that there should have been occasions for translation.

There are several ways of conceptualizing these lines that cross languages. In some of my earlier musings about translation, I was much intrigued by Bruce Chatwin's populist view of what Aboriginal songlines might mean:

> Suppose you had a tribal area like that of the Central Aranda. Suppose there were weaving in and out of it some six hundred Dreamings [or connected places that sacred songs describe as the routes travelled by creator beings]. That would mean twelve hundred 'hand-over' points dotted around the perimeter. Each 'stop' had to be sung into position by a Dreamtime ancestor: its place on the song-map was thus unchangeable. But since each was the work of a different ancestor, there was no way of linking them sideways to form a modern political frontier. Each 'stop' was the point where the song passed out of your ownership; where it was no longer yours to look after and no longer yours to lend. You'd sing to the end of your verses, and there lay your boundary. (Chatwin 1987: 66)

I tried to use this model to reverse the epistemological priority of culture over translation. A translation is traditionally charged with having to represent one side of a cultural divide. But if we see the songlines as routes by which messages travel, then these "handover" points would be not just the limits of a culture, but also the points where translation has to take place. Where does a culture stop? At the point where translation becomes necessary – at a series of separate hand-over points in time and space, without any need to join the points up with a continuous line. Thus translations define cultures; cultures do not define what translations have to do (Pym 1992: 139; 2003; 2004; 2014).

The problem with that model, politically appealing as it may still be, is that the songs and artefacts it sought to be based on did not include actual observations of what happens at the end of one's song. Following Chatwin, it assumed that when you came to the end of your song, you were at the end of your language, in physical space and time. But that need not be the case. My appropriation of the songlines unfairly attached it to the notion of one individual bearer of knowledge magically giving way to another, as in the space configured by two texts in different languages on a translator's computer screen. That model clearly needs to be rethought on the basis of better evidence.

Now, why would anyone want to go walking along a pre-established route to the end of an area where a language is spoken, possibly for a hundred kilometers or more? Surely not just to see what is at the end. If we go back to Roth, we find him describing the hand-over points as specially arranged meeting places: "comparatively large numbers of people of both sexes may be congregated sometimes at these local markets" (Roth 1897: 136). Elsewhere we find descriptions of up to 300 people meeting in "neutral ground" for ceremonies and trade (Robinson 1841, in McBride 1986: 89; Howitt 1904: 709). That is, when language contacts were necessarily involved because of exchanges over long distances, the place for those contacts could be collective rather than individual, and the exchange itself could be for social or ceremonial purposes rather than immediate economic advantage (cf. Thomson 1949).

Given the absence of any dominant lingua franca, those meeting places were likely to work in series. Studying the dissemination of blades mined in the western Northern Territory, Paton (1994) identifies one exchange site 325 km north-west of the place of production, then another a further 275 km to the north-west, where fewer blades reached. The local informant gave the ritual names of the blades in three different languages (1994: 179), which might suggest they were meaningful across a restricted multilingual space. McBride (1986) notes trade patterns extending up to 800 km and describes the distribution of mined blades in Victoria, with artefacts crossing language boundaries and potentially leaving traces in loan words: similar words describe just the blade in the language area where it is mined, but refer to a whole tomahawk in the language area where it was received.

Rather different evidence of contact zones comes from accounts of "law grounds", which were firstly places where young men were initiated into the law of their extended group. These places were normally within the group's country, but could also reportedly be on borders between groups, creating spaces for intra-Indigenous dispute resolution by elders (Olive 1997: 76, cit. Korff 2020).

These few indications suggest that dynamic language contacts were likely to occur in a series of places for *collective* language contact, rather than in a one-on-one cultural location defined by any specially tasked translators.

**Polyglot speakers as a translation solution**

What do we know about contacts between Aboriginal languages? Pidgins and creoles may have existed prior to Invasion, but I find no record of them – they would perhaps not be what any linguist was particularly looking for. In their survey of contact solutions between Australian languages, Vaughan and Loakes (2020) only list transitory varieties used for contact with the Malay of Macassans in the north and then the various pidgins and creoles developed in contact with Europeans. They then list the whole gamut of communication solutions that are available when speakers are polyglots, especially code-switching, receptive multilingualism (intercomprehension), and translanguaging. All of these appear in relation to European languages, however, and the word "translation" remains strangely absent from the inventory. Their survey does nevertheless indicate a certain Aboriginal disposition to multilingual conversations, the mixing of languages and for new varieties to develop from those mixes. The koines or simplified mixes of languages are all dated from the period of colonization, but the fact that they developed quite easily might suggest a relatively relaxed degree of language loyalty.

All and any of these solutions may have been used in the Aboriginal trading encounters, since the one general condition we can be reasonably sure of is the widespread presence of polyglot speakers. The complex exogamic rules of some Aboriginal family structures meant that everyone could have several languages (McConvell and Bowern 2011). This is noted in an early account by Dawson in Victoria (1881: iv): "their general information and knowledge of several distinct dialects – in some instances four, besides fair English – gratified as well as surprised me."

This is by no means a thing of the past. At a conference in Melbourne in 2006, I and many others were fascinated by a speaker from the very north of Australia who recounted how she learned her mother's language as a small child, then her father's language as she grew up, and at puberty she began to learn *her* language, the language of her skin or totem. That is, three languages in the process of gaining identity, although one then becomes the speaker's language of skin or totem identity, associated with country (independently of how well or badly one actually speaks that language).

In some accounts, the learning of languages is associated not just with family relations but also with country, in a way that unites identity with land. The following is from Rhonda Inkamala (2018: 12):

> I am an Aboriginal Australian woman of central Australia. I am multilingual and so a fluent speaker of Western Aranda, Luritja and Pitjantjatjara. I also read and write in these languages and understand other Arandic and Western Desert dialects. My language connections are through my parents and grandparents.
> My mia (mother) speaks Western Aranda and Luritja. My mia kanha pmara nama (mother's country), tjamia kanha pmara nama (mother's father's country) and my lyurra kanha pmara nama (mother's mother's country) are on Tjoritja (also known as West MacDonnell National Park). My karta (father) spoke Western Aranda and Pitjantjatjara. My mamaku ngurra (father's country) and tjamuku ngurra (father's father's country) lies on Pitjantjatjara territory in the south-west Petermann Ranges. My father spoke Western Aranda because he was adopted by the Inkamalas who grew him up as an Aranda and as their own.

Family structure, language and country are thus intermeshed but do not map onto each other: there is no unitary identity where ethnicity, land, family relations and language all coincide in something like the Western "nation". In explaining these relations, Rumsay (1993) notes that the direct relation is between language and land (or "country", land with identity), with the human speaker then being the indirect and variable element in the relation:

> It is not the case that, for example, Jawoyn country is called that because it is or was occupied by people who speak the Jawoyn language. Rather, it is called Jawoyn country because it is the region in which that language was directly instilled or 'planted' in the landscape by Nabilil 'Crocodile', a Dreamtime creator figure who moved up the Katherine River, establish sites and leaving names for them in the Jawoyn language. (Rumsay 1993: 199–200)

The relation with country is such that a speaker might switch languages not because of the person they are speaking to, but out of respect for the land they are travelling across: "it is a regular practice to change the language one is speaking when entering a new territory, to address particular locales (wells, or dangerous places) in the local language" (Evans 2007: 29). This may be out of respect as well as fear: "certainly when formally dealing with many totemic and other extra-human features of the landscape, it is appropriate to speak the language which belongs there. Other Aboriginal languages would not be effective in ritual matters; indeed use of another language may well bring forth hostility from totemic forces" (Trigger 1987: 217–218). Further, the creator figures themselves are held to have switched languages as they moved from one country to another (examples are given in Trigger 1987: 219).[2]

The important point here is that multilingualism was clearly not seen as a problem that had to be overcome by resorting to a common language. In the system of small, interlocking languages, each person could use their languages as parts of their identity, and understand the neighboring languages that could be used in the same conversation. Multilingualism was a positive thing since the language you spoke indicated your place not just in the conversation, but also in the extended family structures and in country. To replace one language with another through a Western translation practice would potentially be to replace all those identity relations.

If the presence of polyglot speakers can be generalized to any extent, we begin to see why exchange processes might not need a special mediator – except in the case of the avoidance relations mentioned above. Polyglot speakers are also able to use significant intercomprehension (bilingual or multilingual conversations)

---

2. My thanks to my colleague Rachel Nordlinger for the references in this paragraph.

to overcome communication gaps. They might also engage in the code-switching and translanguaging described on the basis of post-Invasion evidence. And they can create loan words, as traced in the case of the blades that become tomahawks in a receptor language. None of these solutions requires intervention by a translator as a special mediator. Or rather, everyone might be able to translate themselves, to at least come extent.

Can we really assume that all speakers knew several languages? Much of the evidence that we have comes from the arid areas of the interior, following displacement of Aboriginal people from the more fertile parts of the continent. We know rather less about what happened in pre-Invasion communities in areas that supported greater population densities. I do not know how much credence to give to claims about such communities made by the scholar of knowledge management Karl-Erik Sveiby, who worked on law stories told to him by the Aboriginal elder Tex Skuthorpe in the 1990s. The stories are from the Nhunggabarra, who lived along the Darling River in the north-western part of New South Wales, in relatively fertile river lands, and thus perhaps to be contrasted with what we know from the interior of the continent. Sveiby and Skuthorpe (2006) estimate the population of the Nhunggabarra and surrounding language groups as having been 15,000 in an area the size of Belgium. Sveiby makes much of an economy where the provision and preparation of food required only two to five hours per person per day, which left considerable time for the production and circulation of intangible cultural goods. The claim that most intrigues me is the following:

> Particularly the demands on the men were considerable. During some 18 years, from around 14 years of age, the men lived literally as 'journeymen', travelling around all 26 neighbouring countries to learn each others' law stories, lands, songs, ceremonies, habits, resources *and languages*, and to build personal networks. After an investment of half their productive life, the men were finally considered adults at the age of 32 and capable to take on their role in society.
>
> (Sveiby 2009: 349–50, italics mine)

This extreme mobility was apparently not accorded to the women, who had to learn from the men who married into their group, says Sveiby. So would we want to say that these men had all been trained to be translators? One should not rush to judgement. If credence is to be given to the narration, then *all* men would be trained to be potential translators, and the general solution to interlingual communication would indeed be a system where all polyglots translate themselves.

Such a rash generalization is nevertheless contradicted by some early European accounts of each language group having one or several specially selected messengers. Howitt (1889: 315) notes that "the messenger was usually one of the younger men, and if possible one whose sister was married to some one in that part of the tribe to which the messenger was to go, for under such circumstances a man could go and return in safety, being known to and protected by the people he visited." The various early mentions of messengers that are collected in Frankel and Major (2017: 83–85) concur that they were usually young men of light build, able to travel across long distances with little food, and with potentially propitious family relations. They might be selected "for their intelligence and their ability as linguists" (Dawson 1881: 74; Howitt 1904: 690; cf. Frankel and Major 2017: 83), but one might also surmise that the selection was made from among a more or less polyglot population.

**Non-linguistic semiotic resources**

In addition to the accounts of Aboriginal languages, there is ample evidence of a range of semiotic resources that could have also enabled some degree of communication across languages. I mention a few of the most salient.

Sign languages

In his account of the Aboriginal groups in Victoria, Howitt (1904) records the signs of "gesture language" that could be used to communicate. At the simplest level, these would be metonymic gestures that offer a certain universality: given that Aboriginal languages tend to have no morphemes for numbers above three, the exact numbers would be indicated with figures, or distance would be expressed by placing figures on the upper arm to indicate the number of days walking. But Howitt discovers that there is also system in the signs: "I came to see that these gestures were part of a complete system of hand signs, by which a person might be interrogated, informed, welcomed, or warned" (1904: 749). Howitt records some 65 signs in all. For example, *to hear* is "to point to the ear with the forefinger of the right hand" among the Wurundjeri (1904: 757), whose land I trespass on whenever I ride my bike along the Yarra River around Melbourne. That sign would seem to make intuitive sense and could perhaps be understood by any speaker of any language. Howitt nevertheless notes much local variation in the signs used, as indeed is the case in many signed languages today. He therefore surmises that "gesture language could not be made use of at a distance excepting in rare cases" (1904: 757). This conclusion has generally been backed up by later research: unlike the Native American sign language that was used as a lingua franca over a wide area of North America (Campbell 2000), Australian gestures did not operate systematically across language borders. Kendon (1988: 17–18, 48) and Green (2021) nevertheless give cases where signs have crossed borders between languages. The use of more or less codified gestures could offer potential support where language differences challenged mutual cooperation. In such cases, once again, there need be no resort to specialized translators.

## Multimedia narratives

Beyond the signed languages, there are also movements and gestures that are part of traditional narratives. In her study of the "sand stories" told by the Arandic women of central Australia, Green (2014: 27) insists on the multimodality of the narratives, which are recounted with hand gestures, body movements, sand drawings and movements of objects, as well as a particular spoken language. Green notes that some of the gestures are found across the borders between Arandic languages, so we might suppose that they too could be supports for understanding across language boundaries. That, however, is the least of her interests. She uses the rich multimodality of the narratives to question the putative central role of a spoken language system, insisting that the meaning-making depends on semiotic resources at all levels, in a way where no one medium is considered as replacing or representing any other. There is no question of the spoken language having a "meaning" that is then illustrated or annotated in the other media. Instead, all modes of expression create affordances by which meaning can be constructed.

This view does not help much with my question about translation. It does, however, start to suggest why the question itself might be irrelevant, at least to the extent that our concept of translation assumes that there is one identifiable meaning that is to be reproduced.

## Message sticks

Something similar might be gleaned from the traditional use of message sticks. These are short pieces of wood that bear carved marks indicating items such as the sender, the addressee, features of a message, and perhaps some decorative or ceremonial marks (Frankel and Major 2017: 85–87; Kelly 2020). A messenger carries the stick to the addressee and then speaks the message; the stick is not normally the sole bearer of the message. For this reason, Roth (1897: 136–7) and Howitt (1889, 1904: 735) believed that message sticks basically acted as passports, allowing the bearer safe passage across others' countries and attesting the right to tell the message. Howitt (1904: 709) gives an example where notches are decoded as identifying the addressees, inviting them to a corroboree, presumably in an implicit way, with the obverse side of the stick being for decorative marks. Roth (1897) was nevertheless able to identify several stable meanings for references to people and geographical features.

Despite the general practice of the messenger speaking the message, there is some evidence that message sticks could be deciphered on their own. Kelly tells of an experiment conducted by Bishop Gilbert White near the beginning of 20th century:

> Having been entrusted with both a message stick and an oral message by an Indigenous sender in Darwin, White agreed to deliver it to Daly Waters [about 600 km away]. Yet, after he had dispatched the stick to its rightful addressee, the bishop decided to withhold the verbal message and was astonished to discover that the recipient interpreted the motifs accurately: a request to deliver boomerangs and headbands. (Kelly 2020: 140)

This suggests not only that the message sticks could communicate as a medium in themselves, but also that they could do so across language borders, given the distances involved. If this is so, then the sticks could constitute a set of semiotic resources of some help when language borders have been crossed.

To the extent that the marks on the sticks can be meaningful in themselves, the obvious burning question is whether Australian Indigenous cultures had a system of writing, at least as a system of marks that replace and represent speech. Addressing this question, Kelly (2021) argues that it is the wrong question, framed by an evolutionist mindset that makes it hard to see the evidence for what it is – "writing is over-rated; it has only been invented four times". The marks are more like gestures that can trigger meaning affordances in specific situations and between specific communication partners. As such, they would not be translations in the sense of replacing any anterior text; they would be part of communication acts that could work across language borders. Kelly (2020: 138) aptly notes that Roth (1897) described message sticks in the context of communicative practices that also included sign language, smoke signals and track signs. They are one of a range of semiotic resources.

Of course, for my inquiry here, the importance of the message sticks is not so much the nature of the marks as it is the supposition that the stick requires a messenger. This remits to the early mentions of messengers being selected because of their language and ability to travel long distances: when language boundaries were crossed (as was presumably the case in the story from Bishop White), then the messenger would be telling the message in another language, that is, translating.

Taken together, local sign languages, narrative gestures, body movements and images, and carved message sticks would all be semiotic resources of use in situations where a language system is not fully shared. It might help to think of them as acting in the way that hand gestures became an enhanced semiotic resource in Italy prior to the late nineteenth century, developed to help communication cross dialect chains in the absence of a lingua franca. In Australian contexts where there were overlapping language varieties and probably a fair presence of polyglot speakers, these could all be part of communicative acts that could take place without translators, occurring in situations where a European might expect to find translators.

## Interlingual flows in an economy of interpretative restriction

One of the idealistic assumptions that Westerners make, myself included, is that all knowledge should be as public as possible. This is a basic tenet of modernity: informed citizens are needed for participative democracies. It is from that position that one reaches the idea that all translation is good translation, since there can never be too much distribution of information.

Australian Indigenous cultures tend not to make that assumption. Narratives may be distributed widely, but the ability to *interpret* their meanings tends to be restricted to various levels of initiates. Sveiby (2009) gives the example of a Nhunggabarra story from which the initiated interpreter can identify seven laws and three sacred levels of meaning. A crane tells a crow to cook raw fish before eating it. We would say this is sound advice, since the crane is the expert in dealing with fish. The skilled interpreter nevertheless sees that this is a contravention of the law that one should not impose one's view on others. And so on. A similar example recounted by Hymes (1974: 99–100) concerns an American Chinook narrative where the guilty party is not the transgressor of a rule but the actor that formulates the prohibition. In both these cases, the language of the story is simple enough and should not pose a problem for most linguistic translation processes, but the hermeneutics, the rules for interpreting the story, must be learned as a part of a culture-specific process of initiation. There are stories told by women and others by men, but the Australian Indigenous knowledge of law interpretation would seem to remain the preserve of male elders – who are also the ones charged with high-level negotiations across cultural divides. Stories can thus flow freely and be translated, but interpretative knowledge does not.

This raises the question of what exactly we mean by a "translation flow". The movement of narrative may not be the movement of knowledge.

## So, what can we learn?

I am reluctant to idealize Indigenous cultures. There is certainly wisdom to be sought in that space, but I cannot pretend to have gained any deep understanding of it or any right to speak on such matters. There is the constant risk of blinkered informants, false generalizations, truths that remain concealed by culturally imposed silence, and overstatements formulated in the Indigenous cause.

The one thing that does result from this inquiry nevertheless seems to be that my initial question is badly formulated: it makes little sense to ask if translation was used in communication between Australian languages if and when we assume that translation is a socially specialized language operation, that it produces a text that replaces an anterior text, that it somehow separates meaning from expression, and that meaning can thus be dislocated from its place of production, from linguistic formulation, and from interpretation. Instead of translation in that post-Renaissance Western sense, I find practices that rely not just on a more or less generalized presence of polyglot speakers but also on a range of semiotic resources that are non-coterminous with discrete language systems, as well as complex interpretative skills that have to be learned. In all these practices, participants actively construe semiotic clues on the basis of the elements available in each situation. One could, of course, claim that our term "translation" should now cover all those practices, in the name of an ever-expanding Western discipline. That would be merely slick and self-serving, however, as if we were immediately experts in everything – at least until we find something passably new and insightful to say about all those practices. In the meantime, it makes more sense to track, as best we can, a wide range of mediation strategies, including much language learning (cf. Pym 2018).

Of all the aspects just named, perhaps the role of hermeneutic interpretation is the most suggestive. Our contemporary calls for ever more translations carry an implicit plea for faster production and consumption: more texts in the same time means there is less time to be spent on each. The Indigenous practices we have been looking at, on the other hand, indicate a far slower kind of movement, where information hops from exchange place to exchange place, working through chains of translation processes, through the overlaps of languages and semiotic skills, with each step requiring time to be spent on understanding incoming text and finding it a place in each new cultural context. That would be a far more tangled communicative process, perhaps like a few of the slower receptive processes that can be found within our own cultural ambit: one thinks of the dynamic online discussions where prosumers of audiovisual products these days not only express opinions and debate incoming text, but also produce and discuss their own translations. Where fast translation seeks immediate construal, clarity and adaptation where necessary, slower cultural practices spend longer on collective sense-making across several media.

To summarize: translate less and think more.

## Postscript: The lesson of the river

The Birrarung, also known as the Yarra River, along which I ride my bike these days, meanders across Wurundjeri country as it flows down towards Port Phillip Bay. When European settlers set up farms along its banks in the 1830s and 1840s, they removed tree trunks from the river to make it more navigable, as a fast means of communication. The river's turbulence diminished; the speed of communication increased. Rivers nevertheless need all those impediments to free flow: "without turbulence, drifting in a canoe on the Yarra River would happen at a hair-raising 2,000 km per hour, instead of a lazy one km per hour" (Marusic, Damousi and Broomhall 2018). Europeans thus removed turbulence precisely where the Wurundjeri had created it: those tree trunks in the river had been put there on purpose to slow the water down, creating ecosystems for eels, shellfish, and freshwater lobsters that have not been seen in the Birrarung for more than a hundred years.

## References

Bowker, Lynne, and Jairo Buitrago Ciro. 2019. *Machine Translation and Global Research: Towards Improved Machine Translation Literacy in the Scholarly Community*. Bingley: Emerald Publishing.

Burarra Lexicon. Accessed April, 2022. https://ausil.org.au/Dictionary/Burarra/lexicon/main.htm.

Campbell, Lyle. 2000. *American Indian languages*. New York: Oxford University Press.

Chatwin, Bruce. 1987. *The Songlines*. London: Picador.

Chesterman, Andrew. 2001. "Proposal for a Hieronymic Oath." *The Translator* 7(2): 139–54.

Cronin, Michael. 2017. *Eco-Translation: Translation and Ecology in the Age of the Anthropocene*. Abingdon: Routledge.

Dawson, James. 1881. *Australian Aborigines. The Languages and Customs of Several Tribes of Aborigines in the Western District of Victoria, Australia*. Melbourne: George Robertson.

Evans, Nicholas. 2007. "Warramurrungunji Undone: Australian Languages in the 51st Millennium." In *Endangered Languages*, ed. by Peter K. Austin and Andrew Simpson, 19–44. Hamburg: Helmut Buske.

Frankel, David and Janine Major (eds). 2017. *Victorian Aboriginal Life and Customs through Early European Eyes*. Melbourne: La Trobe University.

Gammage, Bill. 2012. *The Biggest Estate on Earth. How Aborigines made Australia*. Crows Nest: Allen and Unwin.

Ginsburgh, Victor and Shlomo Weber. 2011. *How Many Languages Do We Need? The Economics of Linguistic Diversity*. Princeton, NJ: Princeton University Press.

Green, Jennifer. 2014. *Drawn from the Ground: Sound, Sign and Inscription in Central Australian Sand Stories*. New York: Cambridge University Press.

Green, Jennifer. 2021. "Mothers, Mountain Devils, and Pointing to Eternity: The 'Horns' Handshape in Australian Indigenous Sign Languages." *Sign Language Studies* 22(1), 5–41.

Howitt, Alfred William. 1889. "Notes on Australian Message Sticks and Messengers." *The Journal of the Anthropological Institute of Great Britain and Ireland* 18: 314–332.

Howitt, Alfred William. 1904. *The Native Tribes of South-East Australia*. London: Macmillan.

Hymes, Dell. 1974. *Foundations in Sociolinguistics: An Ethnographic Approach*. Philadelphia: University of Pennsylvania Press.

Inkamala, Rhonda. 2018. "Working on the dictionary." In *Carl Strehlow's 1909 Comparative Heritage Dictionary*, ed. by Anna Kenny, 15–22. Transcribed and translated from the German by Anna Kenny. Translated from Aranda and Loritja to English by the Inkamala families and members of the Western Aranda community. Acton ACT: Australian National University Press.

Joseph Jurt, Martin Ebel, and Ursula Erzgräber. 1989. *Französischsprachige Gegenwartsliteratur 1918–1986/87. Eine bibliographische Bestandsaufnahme der Originaltexte und der deutschen Übersetzungen*. Tübingen: Max Niemeyer.

Kelly, Piers. 2020. "Australian message sticks: Old questions, new directions." *Journal of Material Culture* 25(2): 133–152.

Kelly, Piers. 2021. "The linguistics of message sticks." *Webinar*, November 5. The University of Melbourne.

Kendon, Adam. 1988. *Sign Languages of Aboriginal Australia: Cultural, Semiotic and Communicative Perspectives*. Cambridge: Cambridge University Press.

Kenny, Anna (ed.). 2018. *Carl Strehlow's 1909 Comparative Heritage Dictionary*. Transcribed and translated from the German by Anna Kenny. Translated from Aranda and Loritja to English by the Inkamala families and members of the Western Aranda community. Acton ACT: Australian National University Press.

Korff, Jens. 2020. *Tribal punishment, customary law and payback*. Accessed January 1, 2022. https://www.creativespirits.info/aboriginalculture/law/tribal-punishment-customary-law-payback.

Marusic, Ivan, Joy Damousi, and Susan Broomhall. 2018. "Turbulence isn't just a science problem." *The Conversation*, June 20, 2018. https://theconversation.com/turbulence-isnt-just-a-science-problem-97171

McBride, Isabel. 1986. "Artefacts, language and social interaction: A case study from south-eastern Australia." In *Stone Age Prehistory*, ed. by G. N. Bailey and P. Callow, 77–93. Cambridge: Cambridge University Press.

McConvell, Patrick and Claire Bowern. 2011. "The Prehistory and Internal Relationships of Australian Languages." *Language and Linguistics Compass* 5(1): 19–32.

Moorkens, Joss and Marta Rocchi. 2021. "Ethics in the Translation Industry." In *The Routledge Handbook of Translation and Ethics*, ed. By Kaisa Koskinen and Nike K. Pokorn, 320–37. Abingdon: Routledge.

Mulvaney, Derek John. 1976. "The chain of connection. The material evidence." In *Tribes and Boundaries in Australia*, ed. by Nicolas Peterson, 72–94. Canberra: Australian Institute of Aboriginal Studies.

Olive, Noel (ed.). 1997. *Karijini Mirlimirli: Aboriginal histories from the Pilbara*. Fremantle: Fremantle Arts Centre Press.

Paton, Robert. 1994. "Speaking through Stones: A Study from Northern Australia." *World Archaeology* 26(2): 172–184.

Pym, Anthony. 1992. *Translation and text transfer. An essay on the principles of intercultural communication.* Frankfurt am Main: Peter Lang.

Pym, Anthony. 1997. "Transferre non semper necesse est." *Quaderns. Revista de traducció* 1(1): 88–93.

Pym, Anthony. 2003. "Alternatives to borders in translation theory." In *Translation Translation*, ed. by Susan Petrilli, 451–463. Amsterdam/New York: Rodopi.

Pym, Anthony. 2004. "Propositions on Cross-Cultural Communication and Translation." *Target.* 16(1): 1–28.

Pym, Anthony. 2014. *Negotiating the frontier. Translators and intercultures in Hispanic history.* London/New York: Routledge.

Pym, Anthony. 2018. "Introduction: Why mediation strategies are important." *Language Problems and Language Planning* 42(3): 255–266.

Pym, Anthony. 2020. "For a sociology of translator training." In *Translator Training*, ed. by Junfeng Zhao, Defeng Li, Lu Tian, 9–19. Singapore: Springer Nature.

Pym, Anthony and Ester Torres-Simón. 2021. "Is automation changing the translation profession?" *International Journal of the Sociology of Language.* 270: 39-57.

Pym, Anthony and Grzegorz Chrupała. 2004. "The Quantitative Analysis of Translation Flows in the Age of an International Language." In *Less Translated Languages*, ed. by Albert Branchadell and Lovell Margaret West, 27–38. Amsterdam/Philadelphia: John Benjamins.

Robinson, G.A. 1841. "Vocabulary and census of the Manemeet Station. May 24. Portland Bay." *Papers* 54(2): 136–65.

Roth, W.E. 1897. *Ethnological Studies among the north-west Queensland Aborigines.* Brisbane: Government Printer.

Rumsey, Alan. 1993. "Language and territoriality in Aboriginal Australia." In *Language and Culture in Aboriginal Australia*, ed. by Michael Walsh and Colin Yallop, 191–206. Canberra: Aboriginal Studies Press.

Sapiro, Gisèle. 2014. "Translation as a Weapon in the Struggle Against Cultural Hegemony in the Era of Globalization." *Bibliodiversity* 3: 31–40.

Sapiro, Gisèle. 2019. "Translation and Translation as a Weapon'." *Oxford Research Encyclopedia of Literature*

Singer, Ruth and Salome Harris. 2016. "What Practices and Ideologies Support Small-scale Multilingualism? A Case Study of Unexpected Language Survival in an Australian Indigenous Community." *International Journal of the Sociology of Language* 241: 163–208.

Smith, Mike. 2013. *The Archeology of Australia's Deserts.* Cambridge: Cambridge University Press.

Strubell, Emma, Ananya Ganesh, and Andrew McCallum. 2019. "Energy and Policy Considerations for Deep Learning in NLP." Paper presented to the 57th Annual Meeting of the Association for Computational Linguistics, Florence, Italy. July 2019. https://arxiv.org/abs/1906.02243.

Sveiby, Karl-Erik. 2009. "Aboriginal Principles for Sustainable Development as Told in Traditional Law Stories." *Sustainable Development* 17 (6): 341-356.

Sveiby, Karl-Erik and Tex Skuthorpe. 2006. *Treading lightly: The hidden wisdom of the world's oldest people.* Crows Nest: Allen and Unwin.

Thomson, Donald F. 1949. *Economic Structure and the Ceremonial Exchange Cycle in Arnhem Land.* Melbourne: Macmillan.

Trigger, David S. 1987. "Languages, Linguistic Groups and Status Relations at Doomadgee, an Aboriginal Settlement in North-West Queensland, Australia." *Oceania* 57 (3): 217–238.

Vaughan, Jill and Debbie Loakes. 2020. "Language contact and Australian languages." In *The Handbook of Language Contact*, second edition, ed. by Raymond Hickey, 717–40. Hoboken NJ: John Wiley and Sons.

Western Arrarnta Lexicon. Accessed April, 2022. http://ausil.org.au/Dictionary/Western-Arrarnta/lexicon/index.htm.

Wordlist of Eastern and Central Arrernte. Accessed April, 2022. https://arrernte-angkentye.online/.

CHAPTER 2

# The circulation of knowledge vs the mobility of translation, or how mobile are translators and translations?

Philipp Hofeneder
Karl-Franzens-University

One way of doing research on translation history is to measure and analyse translations (for a classic example see Pym and Chrupała 2005). This quantitative approach normally focuses on published translations between different languages and as such is limited in several respects. First, it focuses primarily on translations as products of translatorial activities. Secondly, translation flows are mostly structured along particular source and target languages, which are more than often not equated with particular political entities. In my contribution I would like to adopt a spatial approach to these translation flows. In doing so, I focus not only on translations as physical objects but also on the agents enabling them, that is authors, translators and finally readers. My aim is to reconstruct patterns of mobility of relevant agents and objects in translation which together constitute a so-called translatorial space. Where do these agents live and work? Where are these works published and where are the readers of these works located? Is the mobility of ideas automatically connected to the mobility of people or objects? In this respect it is not important that a certain language or literature circulates, but how it disseminates beyond its initial place(s) of origin.

**Keywords:** translation history, space, mapping, visualizing translation, thematic maps

## Introduction

Translation history, understood here as a social practice, covers a wide array of different activities. This includes agents enabling a translation as well as the processes involved, and finally the products emerging from these activities (D'hulst 2015). At the centre of such an understanding are the social factors that guide translation at every stage of its emergence (Simeoni 2007; Buzelin 2018). Translation is no longer understood as a singular and isolated event, but as being closely connected to other social phenomena.

In the present paper I would like to contribute to this understanding of translation history by adopting a spatial turn and as such increase the possibilities of reconstructing historical translation phenomena. This heightened interest in space as an epistemological category developed at the end of the 1980s and from then on can be observed in different academic disciplines (Crang and Thrift 2000). Space is no longer understood as the mere precondition of all human action, but as mutually influencing each other. As such a spatial turn is very much characterized by a practical approach and asks, amongst other things, how places of knowledge are influenced by certain knowledge practices (such as translation) and "how knowledge moves from its point of construction and out into the world of general intellectual commerce" (Livingstone 2010, 4). In translation studies space as an epistemological category has been of minor importance. If elements with reference to the natural space were mentioned, they either were of minor importance or used mainly in a figurative sense (Guldin 2016).

With respect to translation history, this leads to the following questions: Where are the agents who enable translation? What places do they enter and along which paths do they move? A spatial approach does not stop at identifying the exact geographic position. What is important is rather the spatial relationships between these whereabouts. Do the relevant agents meet in one and the same place? Do they work together? Or is there a spatial relationship characterized by exclusion, even to the extent that these agents do not meet at all? It is also of interest to note for whom a translation is intended. It of course makes a difference where a translation is initiated and where it is subsequently produced. Furthermore, the place of application influences the way a text is translated. By revealing certain spatial relationships between agents (and their subsequent life cycles) as well as objects and their history of production and later dissemination, certain translation spaces are uncovered. These spaces can range from close proximity to greater distance. Their meaning and significance have to be evaluated on a case-by-case basis.

The history of translation benefits from this combined approach in several respects. Diachronic translation phenomena are often characterized by very limited availability of data. Not much is known about the circumstances under which the translations were undertaken, and even less in many cases about translators as historical agents. This means that every bit of accessible information should be worked with. Beyond that, spatial information received and still receives very little attention. But it can be a valuable source for a thorough reconstruction. Movement patterns and spatial relations between agents and objects tell us a lot about how translation functioned as a social practice and can, accordingly, help us better understand the past. Finally, this raises the possibility of questioning our prevailing understanding of translation. Even in strict academic discourses (written or spoken), we tend to use a whole series of expressions in a figurative sense when we talk about translation as a social phenomenon. Such discourses often make use of geographical units such as translation zones (Apter 2006), translation landscapes (Kershaw and Saldanha 2013) or translation sites (Simon 2019), without automatically focusing on the geographical aspects of translation in detail. In other cases, such metaphors do not directly refer to translation or are not associated with it.

One such case is the understanding of translation as the circulation of knowledge. Interestingly, in Translation Studies this understanding is mostly used to describe translatorial activities in a general way. As a consequence, it is not a conceptual approach which is based on theoretical or methodological considerations, but rather a general understanding in a figurative sense; see Belle and Hosington (2017), who go into detail about communication circuits.

While the usage of such figurative phrases is often derived from the general academic discourse and the possibility of conveying complex social processes in the shortest possible way, we should be cautious in using them too often, especially without questioning their usefulness and appropriateness in advance by asking how and why circulation takes place (Secord 2004: 144f.). It is also necessary to ask to whom we should address such questions – to agents or to objects (or to both of them)? Additionally, we should include all kinds of institutions – be they political, cultural or social – which also play a significant role in that respect. This allows us to reconstruct the circumstances of the production and further dissemination of a translation. Understood literally, circulation points to the fact that the processes described move along more or less immutable trajectories or orbits. It is sufficient to think of the movements of air or blood, which we normally describe as a kind of circulation. We should now ask the question of how useful it is to understand translation as a social activity whose movements can be characterized this way. More often than not, agents, objects and institutions hardly move at all and as a consequence translation is characterized as having very limited mobility.

The present paper describes three different instances of translation spaces. They are all taken from the 19th century and can be traced back to Russia as their epicentre from which further activities evolved. These three different approaches taken together make up a translation space which consists of different aspects and is not confined to the actual act of translation, but also includes the activities before and after the act of translating. In the first case, the life cycle of an important cultural mediator, Nikolay Karamzin, is analysed in spatial terms. How mobile was this mediator at that time? When it comes to translation, do people move or is it mainly objects (in the form of texts) which are transferred (or both)? A second example deals with the emergence of some translations of Karamzin's works and their subsequent locations, such as the place of translating, printing and publishing. Normally, only some of these places are mentioned at all and barely attract any attention. Their places of production and later dissemination tell us a lot about the activity of translation. Officially, they are often characterized by a high degree of distance, while in fact most of the activities are carried out by relevant agents at one and the same place and as such are characterized by a high degree of proximity. Finally, a third example touches upon the readers of these translations from Karamzin's works. For which readers are these translations intended? Where are the readers of these translations located and what can this tell us about the translation itself? All too often the intended readers of a translation are simply equated with the target language and even more with the political entity governing this target language. As we will see, this only partly reflects historical reality.

## Theoretical and methodological requirements

The present contribution aims at a practical application of this spatial approach towards translation. For this purpose, several thematic maps visualize places and connections between them. This practical understanding is even more necessary as theoretical works about space (for an overview see Günzel 2010: 77–109) are often difficult to apply in practice as they offer an initial orientation, but "no practical value as a means of constructing human-scientific explanations" (Mejstrik 2006: 11).

It was Anthony Pym (2000: 2) who stated that an idealized understanding of translation "eclipses or at best misrepresents the place of the translator, and thereby almost all human mediation between cultures". Consequently, he draws attention to a so-called frontier space and, within it, to the physical movement of agents and objects related to translation. This was probably the first call within Translation Studies to engage directly in the actual physical environment of translation as a social phenomenon and to look more closely at those places where translation is initiated, produced and distributed.

Lawrence Venuti took the next step in differentiating between certain places of translation. If translation cannot be limited to a predefined political space, differences between individual spaces and places occur in a consistent further development of this idea. In this context, Venuti (2005: 192) refers to local contexts through which translation is decisively shaped. According to him, communicative effectiveness depends on the social situation or environment within which the translator works. In a consistent application of this approach, a distinction must be made between the place(s) of production and the place(s) of dissemination of a translation.

Consequently, Sherry Simon proposed to take a closer look at those places where translation is made possible and, by so doing, to map translation practices. She underlined that "the space where this translation occurs is to be taken seriously – à la lettre – defined by the figures and trajectories that make translation possible" (Simon 2006: 17). It is these trajectories of translation and thus a material understanding of space that are examined by Simon. Space only becomes a relevant category when it is perceived as changeable and mutable, and no longer exclusively as a material prerequisite and, as it were, an unchanging shell of human activity. Simon consequently focuses on "areas of negotiation, the spaces where connections are created through translation" (Simon 2012: 2).

In this context, finally, a case study by Lieven D'hulst and Heleen van Gerwen (2018) shows in a very convincing manner how a strict spatial approach allows us to broaden our understanding of translation as a historical phenomenon. The starting point for their considerations is no longer one particular language or a language pair but all translatorially relevant activities within one political entity, namely Belgium in the 19th century. With translation understood in a broader sense, they manage to uncover a broad series of direct and indirect influences and interactions, and thereby identify a complex system of transfer and translation directions.

The spatial turn can be characterized as having a truly interdisciplinary character and it is difficult to assign space to one specific academic discipline as the epistemological category. What's more, it developed across a series of disciplines over a period of time (Dünne and Günzel 2006). As such, it shows different manifestations, depending on the relevant discipline. As far as translation is concerned, it is therefore useful to formulate several theoretical premises that function as a theoretical point of departure and whose practical application has to be proven afterwards.

The first premise deals with the fact that a spatial turn always encompasses the natural space. Although trivial in content, many approaches focus on social and metaphorical aspects and as such do not refer to the natural or geographic space. We should speak of a spatial turn only when space in its physical form is also the subject of investigation. It was Henri Lefebvre who developed this thought extensively (Lefebvre 1991). This is a starting point according to which space is understood as a medium that does not exclusively represent an objectification. This means that several spaces can be located at a specific and physically determinable place at the same time. Different social groups experience this location in the form of different spaces, which is why a distinction must be made between physical, social and mental spaces (for a critical account of Lefebvre's position see

Goonewardena, Kipfer, Milgrom, Schmid 2008 and Schmid 2010). These are in a reciprocal relationship to be defined; they are mutually dependent and never exist in isolation. At the same time, for Lefebvre the production of space was of special interest, contrary to its later significance. The focus of such an approach is, therefore, on the emergence of a certain space.

It is this kind of relativization which leads to another important premise of the spatial turn, namely that (social) space is a social product. It was again Henri Lefebvre who formulated a major contribution to this understanding of space. His monograph on social place makes manifest several important aspects of a spatial turn. Space as a social category underlies social attributions and as such is influenced by them (and in turn influences social actions). Space in this understanding is subject to a recurring attribution of meaning, the validity of which, however, is subject to a process of decay (Löw 2016). In this understanding, space becomes a "relational (arrangement) of bodies that are incessantly in motion, whereby the arrangement itself is constantly changing" (Löw 2016: 131). Space, therefore, arises only through human action.

A third premise states that space does not have absolute value, but can be understood only through its internal relations. It was Michel Foucault (2005: 931–942) who referred to space in a new sense. For him, space is no longer a static container, but a variable which is being changed over time. It is the relational position of agents and objects in space which is of importance and not their absolute position. Consequently, t5he dimension of inclusion or exclusion with regard to certain places is of fundamental importance.

These premises are to be understood as a first step towards a concrete methodology of spatial-critical thinking. They are intended to show the extent to which space in critical perception also affects a fundamental understanding of the study of culture. This space-critical approach is in turn part of an overarching and broad cultural-scientific development and at the same time complements it. Hence, space ceases to be a merely neutral medium, but becomes a concept for the practical revision of theoretical considerations (Crang and Thrift 2000: 3).

## Three examples of a cartography of translation

In what follows I am going to reconstruct a number of places that are relevant for this translation study. Prior to this reconstruction, some basic considerations of how to localize translation will be discussed. Maps, just like cartography in general, tend to be perceived as providing an objective view of the world. But they, regardless of their accuracy, also depict a subjective understanding of the world that is characterized by the inclusion as well as the exclusion of certain information. It is, therefore, important to underline their immediate purpose. The thematic below maps are composed to show the spatial relationships of certain agents and objects towards Russia. At the centre are a Russian author, his works and his readers at the turn of the 19th century. I would like to examine how his works disseminated from their place of origin and what role translators and translations played in that respect. Traditionally, this kind of cultural transfer is seen as a bridging between two or more cultural spaces that include a vast area of interaction as well as the activity of important representatives of these two cultural spaces. That is why these maps focus on Russia in particular.

Information about movements in space regarding translational phenomena is highly fragmented and scattered across different sources. Very often we have only limited knowledge about the translatorial activity, not to mention about the translator's lives in general. Consequently, the movements of agents and objects can only be depicted in a schematic way. Nevertheless, relevant patterns can be shown, which means this approach still has value.

My aim is to produce a general methodology of a translation space that can be easily realized. I therefore take a macro-perspective, which focuses on the more general movements of agents and objects, that is in and between certain countries, areas and cities. Where possible, this approach can be broadened by additional information that draws on a micro-perspective, including certain districts of a city, streets, rooms, buildings and places of the relevant activities. The concrete place of translation activities is a mere starting point, which includes questions about the place of translating as well as printing and publishing. In many cases, most of this information can be obtained and as such is normally the official information accessible at the time of publication. In addition, what happened before and after these activities shall be examined as well. This includes the activities of the translators as well as the authors. Where were they before, how and where did they come into contact with each other? Finally, what happened after a translation was published? Where does it spread, and can we reconstruct its place of application? This investigation includes the authors and the translators as well. Do they leave the place of translating? These different approaches allow us to reconstruct a translatorial space in its entirety – from the very beginning up to its termination, as every space has a certain temporal period of existence.

This brings us to the point at which we ask: How does one prepare such a thematic map? What is to be taken into account? Basically, several cartographic principles must be observed. These include questions about the colours, contrast, legibility and comprehensibility of the pictograms used (for a still valuable account, see Hake 1985 and Robinson, Morrison, Muehrcke, Kimerling and Guptil 1995). These questions must be adapted to the needs of one specific place and therefore cannot be determined in advance. The following maps are based on a blank map indicating the borders of Russia in 1815. Minor changes before and after are of little significance as the places of interest were always located within the borders shown on the map. The dark pink area was officially part of Russia, the light pink areas became part of Russia only during the 19th century (they are the Kingdom of Poland, the Grand Duchy of Finland, and parts of present-day Kazakhstan). The aim of the following four maps is to show the spatial relationships of some agents and objects connected to relevant historical translation phenomena in Russia.

### Do mediators move as well?

My first example is Nikolay Karamzin (1766–1826), an influential person in Russia at the turn of the 19th century (Lotman 1997). Karamzin was one of the most distinguished writers of his time in Russia (Cross 1971) and one of the few whose works were extensively translated into other languages as well. He was also widely known for his work as an editor of influential journals (where he published his own translations and reforms of the standard Russian of his day) (Uspenskij 1985; Zhivov 2009). Karamzin is a paradigmatic representative of the cultural and political ties between Russia and the rest of Europe at that time, which had become stronger since the 17th century. He is proof that Russia not only received knowledge from abroad, but also actively participated in the public discourse (especially around a Russian culture that had to be newly defined in the light of Russia's increasing political importance in Europe at the beginning of the 19th century). Karamzin, therefore, represents a turning point, after which Russia became an active part of a Europe-wide public. Karamzin is generally seen as one of the most important cultural mediators of his time in Russia. He not only translated some 300 texts (mainly from German and French originals) and as such provided Russia's society with the latest political and cultural news, but he also actively tried to influence the image of Russia abroad, mainly by translations and articles in newspapers or journals (see Kafanova 1989, 1991).

What does the life journey of such an important mediator look like? Where does he spend most of his time? And with whom is he in contact as a substitute for direct contact in one place? As we can see on the following thematic map, Karamzin's life journey stands in sharp contrast to his social and cultural standing as one of the leading mediators in Russia at the time.[1] He was born 1766 in the province of Simbirsk, some 700 kilometres south-east of Moscow. There he was

---

1. Information about his life is taken from several biographies: Pogodin (1866), Kochetkova (1975) and Lotman (1997). See also the following website for archival information: http://karamzin.rusarchives.ru.

educated by home teachers and attended a private boarding school for some time. At the age of 14 he went to Moscow, where he continued his education. When he started focusing on his literary career, he spent one year in St. Petersburg as an officer, but withdrew from his commission immediately and returned to Moscow. He left Moscow again only in 1789 for one and a half years to travel to different countries in Europe. Much like the Grand Tour of the 17th and 18th centuries, he visited several German states, Switzerland, France and England (but not Italy!). After his return to Russia, he spent the next 25 years more or less in Moscow again. He remained in the city during the winter months, but left Moscow in the warmer months of the year and moved to Ostafyevo, a well-known estate of the Vyazemsky family and at the same time an important centre of Moscow's cultural life. The only exception in these years was during Napoleon's attack on Russia in 1812, when Karamzin was forced to leave Moscow in the face of the approaching army. He returned from his exile in Yaroslavl and Nizhny Novgorod a year later. In 1816 he moved to St. Petersburg at the invitation of the Tsar, and died there in 1826. There too he spent only the colder months of the year in the city and he moved to Tsarskoye Selo, the Tsar's residence some 25 kilometres away, during the warmer months. There the Tsar provided an entire residence for him in his immediate vicinity. Regardless of his social status as a leading cultural mediator of his time, Karamzin spent most of his life in Moscow, a city which – in contrast to St. Petersburg – was rather sceptical about importing Western ideas (for details see Lotman and Uspenskij 1975). Beyond that, Karamzin left Russia only once in his life. While he did get to see an impressive number of influential people and places, this journey probably played a more important role for his construction of a new Russian culture than in establishing personal contacts, which he did not maintain for extended periods of time.

Karamzin's own movement patterns throughout his life are in sharp contrast to his position as one of the leading cultural mediators (as well as translators) of his time. While he was transferring and assimilating a huge amount of information, he resided mainly in and around Moscow. Furthermore, he did not try to overcome the barriers of geographical distance by any other communicational means. Many other cultural agents of the 18th and 19th centuries relied heavily on letters instead of traveling throughout Europe. One need only recall Voltaire or Benjamin Franklin, whose letters spread all over Europe.[2] With respect to Karamzin, no similar activities are known (see the latest edition of his Collected Works, Karamzin 1998–2009). Most of his letters are addressed to people living in Russia. The only exception is Johann Caspar Lavater (1741–1891), a Swiss

---

2. For further information on their activities see the project "Mapping the Republic of letters" at Stanford University, http://republicofletters.stanford.edu.

philosopher, with whom Karamzin exchanged several letters during his journey through Europe (see Grot 1893).

As a mediator, and this is an important point here, his broad cultural activities stand in sharp contrast to his own limited mobility. In fact, he spent most of his life in Moscow, the second largest city in Russia at that time, which was known for its cultural conservativism and at the same time scepticism towards cultural influences from Western Europe. Despite, or possibly precisely because of, his close connection to Moscow, Karamzin can be regarded as one of the most important people conveying European cultural history at the turn of the 19th century. As the spatial analysis of his life and his generally central location in Moscow shows, this mediation activity was only partially accompanied by extensive travel activities. Karamzin was not interested in actively bringing together various agents from different cultures in a network for the purpose of a permanent and mutual exchange, but rather to adapt those ideas and models that were important to the cultural and historical development of Russia to the given circumstances and for their own purposes in Russia itself. His intensive cultural-historical mediation work thus contrasts sharply with his own limited physical mobility.

Map 1.

The second example presented here deals mainly with the mobility of Karamzin's works and as such focuses on physical objects. Prior to his work as a historiographer (starting officially in 1803), he was a well-known author of mainly sentimental stories. Works like "Poor Liza" (1792), "Julia" (1794) and "Marfa the Mayoress" (1804) centre on female protagonists whose psychological inner life is depicted. Karamzin emphasizes their emotions and how they deal with everyday problems. With this he overcame the abstract and dry observations of the classical period that preceded his own time and at the same time he joined a literary trend that spread across Europe. Probably one of his most important fictional works was the *Letters from a Russian traveller*, published for the first time in 1791/92 in a Moscow-based journal (Lotman and Uspenskij 1984; Panofsky-Soergel 2010). In it, he describes the journey of a young Russian nobleman to different countries in Europe. Based on his own experiences and observations during his journey around Europe in the years 1789 and 1790, this gave him the opportunity to describe Europe from a Russian point of view and at the same time to participate in a pan-European discourse about culture and politics in general.

The following two maps display Karamzin's works (only those independently published) and their known places of publication. Map 2 includes publications up to 1803, the year Karamzin was appointed historiographer to the Tsar and when he quit being an author of fictional works. Map 3 shows his publications from 1804 onwards up to 1818, when the first edition of his *History of the Russian State* was published in St. Petersburg. Comparing these two maps we can draw some important conclusions: as an active writer, Karamzin's fictional works were published mainly for an audience in Northern Europe. We see translations into English, French, German and Danish, which are published in cities such as Copenhagen, Hamburg, Leipzig, London, Moscow, Riga, St. Petersburg and Vilnius. What is of interest here is that almost 40% of all translations (7 out of 18), independently of their language of publication, were published in Russia. It is no coincidence that they were published in cities such as Riga, Vilnius, and St. Petersburg, cities which were characterized at that time by a high degree of ethnically and linguistically diverse population. While in central Russia censorship often prevented the publication of politically objectionable works, this was possible in cities like Riga and Vilnius, which were ethnically and culturally diverse. They functioned as places where translations from Russian were published and thus where Russian culture was projected. After 1803, when Karamzin quit writing fictional literature, this situation changes. Translations were published all over Europe, including cities such as Bologna, Geneva, Lausanne, Paris and Venice. The mere spatial broadening of the scope of these places of publication is accompanied by greater linguistic diversification. Nevertheless, still around 30% of these translations were published in Russia.

However, these translations are often not the result of an increased interest in Karamzin or even in Russian literature abroad (Cross 1971: 93ff.; Bartel and Lindemann 1992: 480), but were initiated and financed by Karamzin and relevant agents in Russia. Translations of his own works were often supervised by Karamzin himself in Moscow. A good example in this respect is Johann Gottfried Richter (1763–1829), who was responsible for most of the translations of Karamzin's work into German and is considered an important mediator of Russian literature and culture in German-speaking countries (Hexelschneider 2000: 61–80). Richter remained in Russia for sixteen years (1787–1803). During this time, he came into close contact with important cultural agents such as Karamzin, whose *Letters* he translated under the supervision of the author himself. As a result of censorship restrictions in Russia at that time, the translation itself proved to be the first extensive publication of the *Letters* in any language (even before the Russian edition) and was published in Leipzig in the years 1799 and 1800 (Marchenko 1984). Beside some reprints in the following years, it became the basis for several indirect translations into Danish (1801), English (1803, 1804), Dutch (1804), Swedish (1806) and even French (1808). A closer look at different translatorial subspaces reveals that the publication of Karamzin's works and their translations were written, translated and published in the same place. The translatorial space is thus characterized by a high degree of proximity. Translation in that respect predominantly emanates from the author himself, who either translated his own works or supervised other agents in translating his works. These activities around the act of translating were often concentrated in Moscow, while the official places of publications are spread all over Europe.

Map 2.

Chapter 2. The circulation of knowledge vs the mobility of translation 35

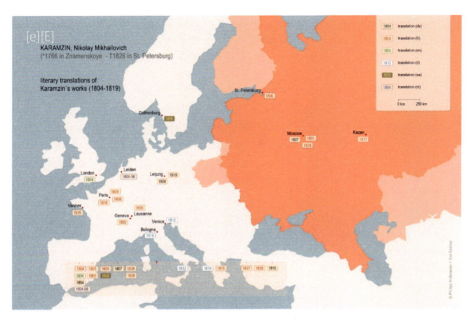

Map 3.

## Where are the readers?

The third and last example presented here deals with the readers of a given translation and therefore with the question of the geographical distribution or the range of places where a translation is read and used. The *History of the Russian State*, written by Karamzin himself, will serve as an example. One of the most influential historiographical works of his time (Afiani and Kozlov 1989; Offord 2010), the *History* was planned to be translated and distributed within Russia, but was also aimed at influencing the pan-European discourse on Russia. While the first edition of the *History* was initiated and financed by Tsar Alexander I himself, subsequent editions as well as translations had to be financed by private individuals. To secure the financing and thus also the printing of the extensive work, publishers tried to find subscribers in advance. These subscription lists were commonly published in newspapers and magazines and were intended to demonstrate social interest, as efforts were made to win over significant actors in social life. Subscription lists thus offer the opportunity to gain an insight into the social reach as well as the geographical scope of a work. There are at least two such lists for the *History*: for the 2nd edition in Russian (1818–1829) and the edition in French (1819–1826). In both these cases the lists were not published as separate lists in newspapers or magazines, but in the publication itself. In particular, the comparison between the source and the target texts allows much more precise information to be obtained as to who ordered the *History*, in which language and where. The lists indicate the full name, often the place of residence and a job title and, in the Russian version, also of a reference to their social position.

The list of subscribers in the 2nd edition of the *History* in Russian is spread over a total of six volumes (2, 3, 4, 5, 6, 8) and includes 214 people. Almost three quarters of all orders come from St. Petersburg, the city where Karamzin published his *History* and where he spent the last ten years of his life. This makes the *History* first of all a cultural phenomenon of the capital, from where it spread. Apart from Moscow (26 entries), the other orders are spread over the entire European part of the Tsarist Empire. Only Irkutsk, an important city on Lake Baikal, is located in Siberia. Three other orders do not come from the Tsarist Empire: Jernej Kopitar ordered a copy as court librarian in Vienna, another was ordered in Halych (Russian: Galich), which was located in the then crown land of Galicia and is one of the oldest East Slavic settlements mentioned by name. The third order came from Wallachia. The list mentions a total of 26 larger and smaller towns, which, significantly, cover the entire European part of Russia. There are no orders from the Kingdom of Poland, which had only recently been integrated into the Tsarist Empire, or from what is known nowadays as the Baltic States. Among the people who ordered the book are several who can be assigned to the network of the *History*, among them foreign minister and chancellor Nikolay Rumyantsev, a certain Baron Sacken, who was probably the second translator of the *History* into German, Aleksey Arakcheyev, influential statesman and responsible for the final publication, and Nikolay Grech, important publisher who published the second and third editions of the *History*. The selection of subscribers indicates that the aim was also to support the publication financially and to contribute to its popularisation.

The orders received often came from people who could be counted as part of the inner circle associated with the writing of the *History* anyway. Thus, it is not surprising that the frequently mentioned interest in the *History* is mainly concentrated in the European part of Russia and, specifically, in the Russian or East Slavic areas. However this does not apply to other areas such as Poland or the Baltic States. Of the 214 people named, 182 came from the nobility, while only 30 were not of noble origin. The *History* in the Russian language was predominantly a phenomenon of the capital city in which the nobility participated.

The extent to which it was an inner-Russian – and specifically a discourse of the capital city – can be seen in a comparison with the French edition, which was ordered by a total of 206 people. In contrast to the Russian-language list, the French version is sorted in alphabetical order and supplemented with complete information on place of residence as well as social origin. Of the 206 orders, 124

## Chapter 2. The circulation of knowledge vs the mobility of translation

Map 4.

are from Russia and only 82 from various countries in the rest of Europe. The majority of these orders placed outside of Russia are from Paris, with 61 orders. Other cities were in France or in French-speaking areas (such as Bordeaux, Marseille, but also Ghent or Liège). A few other orders came from Hamburg, London or Vienna. The distribution in Russia itself is equally interesting. There are 92 orders from St. Petersburg, which also makes the French version of the *History* very much a phenomenon of the capital. The Russian and the French editions show a complementary distribution. Only the translation into French is ordered in what is today known as the Baltic States – Dorpat (today's Tartu), Riga, Vilna (today's Vilnius), Warsaw or in Turku (or Åbo at that time), which was until 1812 the capital city of the Grand Duchy of Finland. Only twelve different cities are named in Russia, and fifteen outside. Another clue is provided by the order quantities. In most cases, the original is ordered only once; there are no collective orders in the subscription list. This shows that the original was ordered largely for reasons of loyalty. The translation, on the other hand, is ordered several times much more often. Of a total of 472 copies, 287 are ordered abroad, which shifts the imbalance somewhat. Of the orders that were placed outside Russia, many can be attributed to the Tsar's entourage as well as state offices such as embassies and the like. The names of the appointments from the Tsarist empire itself can in turn often be traced back to the network of *History*. In addition to Tsar Alexander I, these include his mother Maria Fedorovna (Sophie Dorothea of Württemberg), his wife Elizaveta Alexeievna (Princess Louise of Baden), Dmitry Bludov, the editor of the twelfth and last original volume, Friedrich Hauenschild, the first translator of the *History* into German, and Sergey Uvarov, then President of the Academy of Sciences and a key player in the *History* network.

## Conclusion

Translation history is essentially about the movement of agents, objects and institutions in the natural space. It is their relative position towards each other which determines not only the initial idea of a translation, but in consequence influences who translates and in what way. Finally, it is significant to note for which places a translation was intended and where it was finally read. In the present article I tried to highlight three different aspects of such a spatial approach towards translation history. The aim of this methodological approach is twofold. First, we get to know certain movement patterns and the spatial relations of relevant agents as well as objects. This allows us to analyse translation history more in depth and to gain a deeper understanding of historical processes as translation is fundamentally influenced by its immediate spatial environment. Secondly, we question our existing understanding of translation. As metaphors of translation heavily influence our understanding of translation, there is still a need to go beyond them and question their relevance. One of these is the metaphor of translation as a "circulation of knowledge". The question is how translation moves and which paths and places it touches upon. Does it really form a bridge between different cultures? And who or what is connected by translation? These questions are relevant as could be shown by Nikolay Karamzin, firstly, in addressing the issue of whether translation is mainly the movement of agents or of objects. Karamzin, despite his role as one of the most influential mediators in Russian culture at the turn of the 19th century, spent most of his life in Moscow. Beyond that, he did not communicate with other cultural or political agents by means of letters in order to compensate for his limited mobility. The fact that his mediating activities are predominantly focused on the transfer of ideas (in the shape of objects such as texts) tells us a lot about the functionality of translation in detail and the status of Russian culture at this time in general, as Karamzin was interested in adopting Western ideas for his immediate aims in Russia and not establishing a Europe-wide network of influential agents.

Secondly, it was my aim to show how the actual places of translation sometimes widely differed from those mentioned officially. This normally manifests with the official place of publication of the translation, which purposefully differs from the place of publication of the original and as such should point to the intended audience of the translation. As such, translations are presented as differing from their originals not only in a cultural but also in a geographic sense as the places of publication (of the source and the target texts) generally differ from each other. A spatial approach allows us to uncover the real places of translation, which in the present case are much more confined to one place than official sources would often lead us to believe. It is this romanticized understanding of translation that equates the language of translation with its main area of distribution, while the actual act of translating during those times was often characterized by a high degree of proximity, with authors and translators working in the same place and often together.

Finally, the (official) place of publication should not be automatically seen as the major place of application for which a translation was intended. As can be seen in the third example, where readers of an original were compared with the readers of the respective translation, the places of dissemination often differed from the romanticized understanding of language distribution. Translations (as well as originals) do not automatically develop alongside political entities; they may first spread in one country homogenously and exclusively, but then later the same texts are read in other countries. They rather spread as a result of certain political social and cultural circumstances, which all have their own characteristic developments, often simultaneous, erratic and geographically as well as socially limited. In the present case, the translation was more influential in large cities such as St. Petersburg and Paris than in smaller cities beyond the two capitals. Secondly, originals and translation sometimes act as complementary elements of one and the same kind of information. This is why the French version of Karamzin's *History* was read in the Kingdom of Poland and what is nowadays known as the Baltic states, while the Russian version was preferred in other areas of Russia. Sometimes originals and translations are overlapping in one and the same place. In any case, both the original and the translations were mainly read in St. Petersburg and there they were disseminated predominantly among the nobility.

# References

Afiani, Vitalii and Vladimir Kozlov . 1989. "Ot zamysla k izdaniiu "Istorii gosudarstva rossiiskogo", in: Karamzin, Nikolai, *Istoriia gosudarstva rossiiskogo*. Bd. 1, Moscow: Nauka, 514–550.

Apter, Emily. 2006 *The Translation Zone. A New Comparative Literature*. Princeton/Oxford: Princeton University Press.

Bartel, Heinrich and Mechthild Lindemann . 1992. "Karamzin entdeckt Deutschland", in: Herrmann, Dagmar and Kopelev, Lev (eds.) *Deutsche und Deutschland aus russischer Sicht*. Bd. 2, München: Fink, 480–516.

Belle, Marie-Alice and Brenda M. Hosington. 2017. "Translation, history and print. A model for the study of printed translations in early modern Britain", in: *Translation Studies* 10:1, 2–21.

Buzelin, Hélène. 2018. "Sociological models in translation history", in: D'hulst, Lieven and Gambier, Yves (eds.) *A History of Modern Translation Knowledge*. Amsterdam/Philadelphia: John Benjamins, 337–346.

Crang, Mike and Nigel Thrift (eds). 2000. *Thinking Space*. London/New York: Routledge.

Cross, Anthony Glenn. 1971. *N. M. Karamzin. A Study of His Literary Career (1783–1803)*. London/Amsterdam: Feffer and Simons.

Dünne, Jörg and Stephan Günzel (eds). 2006. *Raumtheorie. Grundlagentexte aus Philosophie und Kulturwissenschaften*. Frankfurt am Main: Suhrkamp.

D'hulst, Lieven. 2015. "Quels défis pour l'histoire de la traduction et de la traductologie?", in: *Meta* 60:2 (60e anniversaire. Les horizons de la traduction : retour vers le futur / 60th Anniversary. Translation's Horizons: Back to the Future / 60mo aniversario. Los horizontes de la traducción: regreso al futuro), 281–298.

D'hulst, Lieven and Heleen Van Gerwen . 2018. "Translation space in nineteenth-century Belgium: rethinking translation and transfer directions", *Perspectives* 26:4, 495–508.

Foucault, Michel. 2005. "'Von anderen Räumen'. Übersetzt von Michael Bischoff," in: *Ders. Schriften in vier Bänden. Bd. IV: 1980–1988*. Herausgegeben von Daniel Defert und François Ewald. Frankfurt am Main: Suhrkamp, 931–942.

Goonewardena, Kanishka, Stefan Kipfer, , Richard Milgrom, and Christian Schmid (eds). 2008. *Space, Difference, Everyday Life. Reading Henri Lefebvre*, London: Routledge.

Grot, Jakov (Hrsg.). 1893. *Briefwechsel zwischen Karamsin und Lavater*, St. Petersburg: Buchdruck der Kaiserlichen Akademie der Wissenschaften.

Guldin, Rainer. 2016 *Translation as Metaphors*. (Translation Theories Explained) New York: Routledge.

Günzel, Stephan (ed.). 2010. *Raum. Ein interdisziplinäres Handbuch*. Stuttgart/Weimar: Metzler.

Hake, Günter. 1985. *Kartographie*. Bd. 1–2, Berlin/New York: De Gruyter.

Hexelschneider, Erhard. 2000. *Kulturelle Begegnungen zwischen Sachsen und Russland 1790–1849*, Köln/Weimar/Wien: Böhlau.

Kafanova, Olga. 1989. "Bibliografiia perevodov N.M. Karamzina v 'Vestnike Evropy' (1802–1803 gg.)", *XVIII vek* 16, 249–283.

Kafanova, Olga. 1991. "Bibliografiia perevodov N.M. Karamzina", *XVIII vek* 17, 319–337.

Karamzin, Nikolai. 1998–2009. *Polnoe sobranie sochinenii v vosemnadcati tomach*. Pod. obshchei red. A. F. Smirnov, Moscow: Terra–Knizhnyi klub.

Kershaw, Angela and Gabriela Saldanha. 2013 "Introduction: Global landscapes of translation". *Translation Studies* 6 (1): 135–149.

Kochetkova, Natalya. 1975. *Nikolay Karamzin*, Boston: Twayne Publishers.

Lefebvre, Henri. 1991. *The Production of Space*. Translated by Donald Nicholson-Smith, Oxford UK/Cambridge USA: Blackwell.

Livingstone, David N. 2010. "Landscapes of Knowledge", in: Ders., Peter Meusberger, Heike Jöns (Hg.) *Geographies of Science*, Heidelberg/London/New York: Springer, 3–22.

Lotman, Jurii. 1997. "Sotvorenie Karamzina", in: Lotman, Jurii, Karamzin. *Sotvorenie Karamzina. Stati i issledovaniia 1957–1990. Zametki i recenzii*. St. Petersburg: Iskusstvo, 10–311.

Lotman, Jurii and Boris Uspenskii . 1975. "Spory o jazyke v nachale XIX v. kak fakt russkoj kultury", *Uchenye zapiski Tartusskogo universiteta, vyp.* 358, 168–322

Lotman, Jurii and Uspenskii, Boris. 1984. "Pisma russkogo puteshestvennika i ich mesto v razvitii russkoi kultury", in: *Karamzin, Nikolai, Pisma russkogo puteshestvennika*. Izdanie podgotovoli Jurii Lotman, Nonna Marchenko and Boris Uspenskii, Leningrad: Nauka–Leningradskoe otdelenie, 525–606.

Löw, Martina. 2016. *The Sociology of Space. Materiality, Social Structures, and Action*. Basingstoke: Palgrave.

Marchenko, Nonna. 1984. "Istorija teksta 'Pisem russkogo putešestvennika'", in: *Karamzin, Nikolai, Pisma russkogo puteshestvennika*. Izdanie podgotovoli Jurij Lotman, Nonna Marchenko and Boris Uspenskij, Leningrad: Nauka–Leningradskoe otdelenie, 607–612.

Mejstrik, Alexander. 2006. "Welchen Raum braucht Geschichte? Vorstellungen von Räumlichkeit in den Geschichts-, Sozial- und Kulturwissenschaften." In *Österreichische Zeitschrift für Geschichtswissenschaften* 17 (1): 9–64.

Offord, Derek. 2010. "Nation-Building and Nationalism in Karamzin's History of the Russian State", *Journal of Modern Russian History and Historiography* 3, 1–50.

Panofsky-Soergel, Gerda. 2010. *Nikolai Mikhailovich Karamzin in Germany: fiction as facts*, Wiesbaden: Harrassowitz.

Pogodin, Michail. 1866. *Nikolai Michailovich Karamzin po ego sochineniiam, pismam i otzyvam sovremennikov: Materialy dlia bibliografii s primech. i obiasneniiami*. T. I-II, Moscow: Tipografiia A. I. Mamontova.

Pym, Anthony. 2000. *Negotiating the Frontier: Translators and Intercultures in Hispanic History*. Manchester: St. Jerome.

Pym, Anthony and Grzegorz Chrupała . 2005. "The quantitative analysis of translation flows in the age of an international language", in: Branchadell, Albert and West, Lovell Margaret (eds). *Less Translated Languages*. (Benjamins Translation Library 58) Amsterdam/Philadelphia: John Benjamins, 27–38.

Robinson, Arthur H., Joel L. Morrison, Phillip C. Muehrcke, A. Jon Kimerling and Stephen C. Guptil 1995. *Elements of Cartography (6th edition)*, New York: Jon Wiley and Sons, Inc.

Schmid, Christian. 2010. *Stadt, Raum und Gesellschaft. Henri Lefebvre und die Theorie der Produktion des Raumes*. Stuttgart: Steiner.

Secord, James A. 2004. "Knowledge in Transit", *Isis* 95(4), 654–672.

Simeoni, Daniel. 2007. "Between sociology and history. Method in context and in practice", in: Wolf, Michaela and Fukari, Alexandra (eds) *Constructing a Sociology of Translation*. Amsterdam/Philadelphia: John Benjamins, 187–204.

Simon, Sherry. 2006. *Translating Montreal. Episodes in the Life of a Divided City*. Montreal and Kingston/London/Ithaca: McGill-Queen's University Press.

Simon, Sherry. 2012. "Introduction", in: Simon, Sherry (ed.) *Cities in Translation. Intersections of Language and Memory*. London/New York: Routledge, 1–20.

Simon, Sherry. 2019 *Translation Sites. A Field Guide*. London: Routledge.

Uspenskii, Boris. 1985. *Iz istorii russkogo literaturnogo jazyka XVIII – nachala XIX veka. Jazykovaia programma Karamzina i ee istoricheskie korni*. Moscow: Izdatelstvo Moskovskogo Universiteta.

Venuti, Lawrence. 2005. "Local Contingencies: Translation and National Identities", in: Bermann, Sandra and Wood, Michael (eds) *Nation, Language, and the Ethics of Translation*. (Translation/Transnation) Princeton/Oxford: Princeton University Press, 177–202.

Zhivov, Victor. 2009. *Language and Culture in Eighteenth-Century Russia*. Translated by Marcus Levitt, Boston: Academic Studies Press (Zhivov, Viktor (1996) Jazyk i kultura v Rossii XVIII veka, Moscow: Jazyk russkoi kultury.)

CHAPTER 3

# A transatlantic flow of Spanish and Catalan *romans-à-clef*
## Translators, publishers, and censors from Argentina to Franco's Spain

Sofía Monzón Rodríguez
Utah State University

This chapter explores the editions of *romans-à-clef* written by Henry Miller, Anaïs Nin, and Lawrence Durrell, those that traveled from South America to the Iberian Peninsula in the 1960s, and the Spanish and Catalan translations carried out domestically in Spain. It aims to identify the network of agents that facilitated the translations by examining archival material on the circulation and reception of the works included in my case studies: Miller's *Tropic of Cancer* and *Black Spring,* Nin's *A Spy in the House of Love* and *Ladders to Fire*, and Durrell's *Justine* and *Balthazar,* which arrived in Franco's Spain (sometimes smuggled editions, often censored versions and even "non-translations"). With this documentary material, I illustrate how the translators, publishers and censors involved in this translation flow between North America, Argentina and Francoist Spain interacted to shape the reception of these novels for the Spanish and Catalan readership.

**Keywords:** translation flows, imported translations, author-translator, censorship, *romans-à-clef*

In analyzing an array of literary translations in circulation during Franco's dictatorship (1939–1975), I observed an overlooked translation phenomenon that connects two translation markets across the globe: In the 1960s a substantial flow of Argentinian-made translations was scrutinized by the Francoist censorship board officially located in Spain. Since many of those translations were deemed pernicious according to the censors' moral and religious values, and oftentimes denied for publication, the Spanish and Catalan publishers with a taste for world literature sought to take their chances by trying to get their own editions published.[1] Nonetheless, as all works were reviewed prior to publication up until 1966, when a new Press Law was enforced – subsequently modifying the previous censorship regulations established in 1938 to one of a preemptive kind – local translations were also affected and shaped by the agents appointed by the regime. This, as a whole, made the act of translation arduous for both foreign and domestic literature, and the translation processes long and tedious for translators and publishers who had to deal with the regime's censorship apparatus in a more direct manner (Gómez 2006; Rabadán 2010).

In order to investigate the flow of translations and the network of agents who facilitated or resisted it, I have chosen a corpus of texts that will allow me to explore the matter further. It encompasses several editions of *romans-à-clef* written by Henry Miller (1891–1980), Anaïs Nin (1903–1977) and Lawrence Durrell (1912–1990) that traveled from South America to the Iberian Peninsula, in contrast to the translations carried out by the Spanish publishers in Catalan and Spanish. Simply put, the French term *roman-á-clef* means "novel with a key" and refers to "a novel that has the extraliterary interest of portraying well-known real people more or less thinly disguised as fictional characters" ("Roman-à-clef"). However, a more complete definition can be drawn from Sean Latham's *The Art of Scandal: Modernism, Libel Law, and the* Roman à Clef (2009). For Latham,

> the roman à clef is a reviled and disruptive literary form, thriving as it does on duplicity and an appetite for scandal. Almost always published and marketed as works of pure fiction, such narratives actually encode salacious gossip about a particular clique or coterie. To unlock these delicious secrets, a key is required, one that matches the names of characters to the real-life figures upon whom they are based … [T]he roman à clef profoundly troubles any easy attempt at categorization since it must be defined, in part, by its duplicity. (7–9)

Apart from the literary and personal characteristics that the three authors share, they have been chosen more specifically based on the information found in the censorship files at the Archivo General de la Administración in Spain.[2] For example, the censors' reports on one of these authors would often include mentions of the other two. Additionally, while the publishers would request to publish them

---

1. During Francoism the Catalan territories were politically suppressed by the regime. The censorship system was centralized in Madrid, under the Ministry of Tourism and Information. Censorship laws thus applied to publications in both Spanish and Catalan, as well as to all literary imports regardless of language.
2. General Archive of the Administration (AGA henceforth) is the Spanish national archive building located in Alcalá de Henares, Madrid.

individually, in some instances they were put in the same collections.³ The subject matter of their works – from erotic and sexually explicit content to their characteristic semi-autobiographical, disruptive narrative, hence *roman-à-clef* – and the authors' personal relationships altogether make them an ideal group to be studied under the theme "translation flows."

Even though there is no shortage of scholarship on the translation scene during Francoism,[4] scholars have neglected a thorough study of who the censors, translators and other intermediaries were – the "social actors" in Anthony Pym's words – and "what social networks (extending in many cases beyond the national system of texts) brought the two sides to the metaphorical negotiations table" (Pym 2009: 29). Jeremy Munday also notices a similar phenomenon and declares that it "is inevitably limited if they [scholars] do not seek to combine analysis of the translated product with an investigation of the translation process" (Munday 2013: 132). Overall, the literature on the topic contains case studies that examine certain authors and works censored under Francoism, which, although very detailed and well informed, fall into the category of reception analysis, in which case – and to agree with Pym and Munday – the question of the network of agents remains neglected, as well as the matter of how and why certain Latin American translations travelled and circulated in Franco's Spain. Hence, it is my goal to define the transnational connections between the agents involved in the circulation of the various editions of my case studies that, legally or smuggled, circulated under Francoism in Spanish and Catalan. For this reason, the theoretical framework that I will use takes into account the sociological and cultural impact that translation fosters by stressing the historical and material conditions of the agents involved in the translation processes,[5] with the archive being at the heart of my methodology.

The primary sources retrieved for this study range from censorship and import files taken from the Culture section of Archivo General de la Administración in Alcalá de Henares (Spain) (AGA henceforth) to letters between the publishers and the censorship board, notes between the network of translators and editors, as well as correspondence that some translators shared with the authors kept in their personal archives. Additionally, I shall go beyond the active

---

3. An example of this is Aymà's "Col·lecció Tròpics" containing Miller's *Black Spring* [*Primavera Negra*], Nin's *Ladders to Fire* [*Escales cap al foc*], and Durrell's *The Alexandria Quartet* [*Quarteto de Alejandría*] into Catalan.

4. See Abellán (1980); Neuschäfter (1991); Cisquella (2002); Ruiz Bautista (2008); Lázaro (2004), to name a few.

5. For an in-depth description of this Bordieuan sociological approach see the works of Francesca Billiani (2007).

agents to include the way that the consumers, namely the readers, perceived the products that resulted from this transatlantic exchange of translations. To do this, I showcase interviews, editorial articles and literary reviews that circulated in the press on the translations and reception of Miller, Nin, and Durrell. With this corpus, I aim to shed light on the processes, power dynamics and the networks of actors involved in the translation flow of *romans-à-clef* that took place between North America, Argentina, and Franco's Spain in mid-twentieth century.

## A transatlantic flow of translations in Franco's Spain

One of the many questions in approaching the nature and consequences of such a transatlantic flow of novels revolves around the notion of how much the censorship system of the receiving country could have affected the imported translations from Argentina and whether they were held to a different censorial standard than the translations produced in Spain. However, in order to understand the repercussions of said translational circulation, one has to first think of the historical context of Francoism, its cultural relationship with Argentina, and the translation industries within the two nations. I will not provide an extensive historical account of the editorial market and the literary and translation fields in Francoist Spain, as the topic has been discussed at length in the seminal works of Abellán (1980), Neuschäfter (1991), Cisquella (2002), Ruiz Bautista (2008), etc.; I will instead offer a brief description of the main characteristics that shaped the cultural and literary scene of that time.

Franco's dictatorship began after the *coup d'état* at the onset of the Spanish civil war, with Francisco Franco being proclaimed "Head of the Spanish Government and the Highest General of the Spanish Armed Forces" (Rioja 2010: 2) on 29 September 1936 and would endure until his death on 20 November 1975. The ideological basis of Franco's system of government, founded as it was on strong anticommunist and anti-liberal policies, national Catholicism, traditionalism and militarism (Rioja, 2010: 3), made it an ideal breeding ground for institutional censorship. The basis for the censorship system had already been instituted before the end of the Civil War that brought Franco to power, but was formalized with the Press Law of 22 April 1938 which consolidated censorship policies (Lázaro 2004: 22–24). The norms applied by the censors were not set in stone but, according to the censorship files issued in the first decades of the dictatorship, the bureaucrats were asked to answer a set of questions when assessing every publication: "–Does [the work] attack Catholic dogma? – Morals? – The Church and its Ministers? – The Regime and its Institutions? – The persons who have collaborated with it? – Do the censurable passages designate the whole content of the book?" (Lázaro, 2004: 27 [my translation]). After the Press Law of 1966, these questions still appeared in the reports, though they were hardly ever answered by the censors. Instead, they would write a commentary on the book and, finally, they would recommend it either for publication or rejection. Eventually, a final decision was reached by the board after considering the censors' reports, and the publisher was notified of the decision by mail.

In order to illustrate the encounters the novels in my case study corpus had with the censorship board, the following tables show each time the books were submitted for importation or publication, whether they were accepted or rejected, and the metadata regarding the editions as follows: title, translator, publisher, language, number and years of requests submitted to import or publish the book, whether it was an importation, whether it was accepted and, lastly, the year of publication, if any.

Table 1. *Justine* – Lawrence Durrell (1957), New York: E.P. Dutto and Co. Inc.

| Title | Translator | Publisher | Lang. | Requests | Imp. | Accepted | Publication |
|---|---|---|---|---|---|---|---|
| Justine (1960) | Aurora Bernárdez | Sudameric. | SPA (Arg) | 25 (1962–1975) | Yes | No | – |
| Justine (1961) | n/a* | Pocket Books | EN | 1 (1961) | Yes | No | – |
| – | (no translation) | Aymà | CAT | 1 (1965) | No | w/ changes | – |
| – | (no translation) | Plaza y Janés | SPA | 1 (1965) | No | w/ changes | – |
| Justine (1969) | Manuel de Pedrolo | Aymà | CAT | 1 (1969) | No | w/ changes | "Silencio"** 1969 |
| Justine (1960) | Aurora Bernárdez | Edhasa | SPA (Arg) | 4 (1970–1977) | –*** | w/ changes | "Silencio" 1970 1977 |

* No translator for it is Durrell's original, edited by Pocket Books in 1961.
** The terminology for this legal action was "silencio administrativo" [administrative silence], by which the censorship board would terminate the legal process for a book to be published (Linder 2004: 159), leaving the publication of the book up to the discretion of the publisher.
*** A comparison between the two Spanish versions shows that Edhasa indeed utilized Aurora Bernárdez's translation (Buenos Aires, 1960).

Most of the petitions to circulate Lawrence Durrell's works in Spain sought to import translations commissioned by the publisher Sudamericana (Buenos Aires) during the 1960s. The most recurrent importers on the Spanish end were

Table 2. *Balthazar* – Lawrence Durrell (1958), New York: E.P. Dutto and Co. Inc.

| Title | Translator | Publisher | Lang. | Requests | Imp. | Accepted | Publication |
|---|---|---|---|---|---|---|---|
| *Balthazar* (1961) | Aurora Bernárdez | Sudameric. | SPA (Arg) | 32 (1962) | Yes | No | – |
| *Baltasar* | (no translation) | Aymà | CAT | 1 (1965) | No | w/ changes | – |
| *Balthazar* | Aurora Bernárdez | Edhasa | SPA (Arg) | 5 (1961–1978) | – | w/ changes | 1970 |
| *Baltasar* | (no translation) | Plaza y Janés | SPA | 1 (1965) | – | w/ changes | – |
| *Balthazar* (1983) | M. de Pedrolo | Aymà | CAT | – | – | – | 1983 |

Atheneum, Nuevas Estructuras, Aguilar, Logos, Edaf and Hispar.[6] From 1962, when the first Spanish edition of the novels appeared in Argentina, up to 1976 these publishers repeatedly applied for permission to import Durrell's collection *The Alexandria Quartet* (1957–1960). Aurora Bernárdez's translation of *Justine* (1960) was requested for importation a total of 25 times,[7] whereas there are 32 import files that pertain to Bernárdez's translation of *Balthazar* (1961). Both translations were unsuccessful in passing the censorship filter for importation of books; as one of the censors wrote about *Justine*: "The novel takes place in Alexandria, in the midst of oriental sensuality. A writer and his two lovers are the protagonists of a work full of immoral scenes, some of which are certainly aberrations. Prostitution. Descriptions of sexual acts. It must be suspended" (File 2183–61, catalogue 21/13275).[8]

Another interesting remark is publisher Aymà and Plaza y Janés asking for permission to publish Durrell's *Justine* and *Balthazar* prior to submitting the translated texts. I sense that, since this seems to be a recurrent trend, it might

---

6. In the import files, "[c]ensors would often write their rating on the same page – either a "yes" or a "no" for authorised or denied, along with a brief justification of the decision next to the rejected titles, and, in the case of previously denied imports, the date of the prior review … Once a title was cleared for import, it was assigned a registration number. The administration would then proceed to notify the publisher of which works, translated or otherwise, were authorized and which were banned and would therefore have to be returned to their countries of origin" (Lobejón et al. 2021:106–107).

7. For a textual analysis of Aurora Bernárdez's translations of *Justine* (1960), see Gómez (2009:142–145).

8. All the quotations from the censorship files are my own translations unless otherwise stated.

have been a way for publishers to avoid the cost of the translation, on top of the printing of the galley proofs, before legally having the approval granted from the board.[9] In the two cases, the censors requested the submission of the respective translations in 1965: "Submit the translated text, to which amendments will apply, if necessary" (File 402–65, catalogue 21/15826). With regard to *Justine*, neither the Catalan translation by de Pedrolo nor the Spanish one by Bernárdez were officially authorized for publication.

As briefly explained in Table 1, "silencio administrativo" [administrative silence] was a category given by the censors to a book when they "did not agree with the publishing of the text, neither did they explicitly oppose it" (Gómez 2009: 134). By employing this verdict the censorship board would outright terminate the legal process for a book to be published, as if the petition had never taken place. The two translations of *Justine* submitted for publication by Aymà and Edhasa in Catalan (translated by Manuel de Pedrolo) and Spanish (Argentinian translation by Aurora Bernárdez), respectively, were labelled "silencio administrativo," by the board. Hence, they were not officially authorized to circulate until after the end of the dictatorship. Conversely, Bernárdez's translation of *Balthazar* was approved in 1970 and, together with *Mountolive* and *Clea*, these novels of Durrell's collection that could legally circulate in Franco's Spain.

With the exception of the Catalan translations of Durrell's works by Manuel de Pedrolo, the only Spanish translations available in Spain were those of Aurora Bernárdez that were edited by Sudamericana and distributed by Edhasa. Plaza y Janés' attempt to carry out domestic translations of *Justine* and *Balthazar* was futile, as they never sent the new translations to the board. The reasons for this – although not stated in the censorship files –, might be due to the fact that Edhasa,[10] the publisher that ended up editing Bernárdez's translations in Spain, was in fact a publishing house founded by the Catalan editor Antonio López in Argentina in 1946. López built up the firm while he was in exile, after having participated in the establishing and managing of Editorial Sudamericana ("La editorial"). Thus, the two publishers were extremely connected, as was the prominence of Edhasa in Spain, especially during the last stages of the regime. The Catalan version of *Balthazar* was available in 1983, years after the regime's downfall and the dismantling of the censorship system. His translator, Manuel de Pedrolo,

---

9. In a recent publication, Lobejón et al. (2021) also point out this very idea, in their words: "to limit potential financial losses, publishers would sometimes submit the source text to gauge the viability of a prospective translation into Spanish. In such cases, censors could authorize the production of a translation, which would then undergo another review" (2021: 96).

10. Editorial y Distribuidora Hispano Americana S. A. [Hispanic-American Publisher and Distributor].

translated many of Lawrence Durrell's titles into Catalan: *Justine* (Aymà, 1969), *Tunc* (Edicions 62, 1970), *Mountolive* (Edicions Proa, 1984) and *Numquam* (Edicions 62, 1985).

**Table 3.** *Tropic of Cancer* – Henry Miller (1934) Paris: Obelisk Press

| Title | Translator | Publisher | Lang. | Requests | Imp. | Accepted | Publication |
|---|---|---|---|---|---|---|---|
| *Trópico de Cáncer* (1962) | Mario G. Iglesias | Ediciones S. Rueda | SPA (Arg) | 56 (1962–1976) | Yes | Yes (1963) | – |
| *Trópico de Cáncer* (1962) | Mario G. Iglesias | Aymà | SPA (Arg) | 1 (1967) | Yes | No (1967) | – |
| *Tròpico de Càncer* (1967) | Jordi Arbonès | Aymà | CAT | 1 (1975) | Yes/No* | No | Denied 1977 |
| *Trópico de Cáncer* (1962)** | Mario G. Iglesias | Aymà | SPA | 1 (1976) | Yes | No | Denied 1976 |
| *Trópico de Cáncer* (1977) | Carlos Manzano | Alfaguara/ Bruguera | SPA | 8 (1977–1982) | No | Yes | 1977 |

\* Although Aymà was a publishing house located in Barcelona, the translator into Catalan of Henry Miller's works, Jordi Arbonès (1929–2001), was a Catalan-born writer who actively translated from Buenos Aires, where he lived most of his life. Therefore his translations were in fact sent to Spain from South America.
\*\* In this case, Iglesias's *Trópico de Cáncer* was included in the collection *Novela erótica*, edited by Edaf in 1976.

Miller's *Tropic of Cancer* (1934) was the most imported novel in Franco's Spain in comparison to the other two authors under analysis in this article. From 1962 to 1976 the Argentinian-made translation of Mario Guillermo Iglesias, *Trópico de Cáncer* (Santiago Rueda, Buenos Aires 1962), was requested to be imported a total of 56 times; an average of four times a year in 14 years. Many of these requests were approved by the censorship board, with the importing publishers' (so-called distributors) more recurrent requests from: Atheneum, Aguilar, Hispar, H. Argentina, Nuevas Estructuras, and Edhasa. In contrast, *Black Spring* (1936) – in Patricio Canto's translation, *Primavera negra* (Santiago Rueda, Buenos Aires 1964) – was requested to be imported 35 times from 1964 onwards, but it was not once accepted for importation until 1976. *Tropic of Capricorn* (1937), Miller's last novel of the collection, was requested for importation 44 times, some-

Table 4. *Black Spring* – Henry Miller (1936) Paris: Obelisk Press

| Title | Translator(s) | Publisher | Lang. | Requests | Import. | Accepted | Publication |
|---|---|---|---|---|---|---|---|
| *Primavera negra* (1964) | Patricio Canto | Ediciones S. Rueda | SPA (Arg) | 35 (1964–1975) | Yes | No | – |
| – | (no translation) | Aymà | CAT | 1 (1967) | No | No | – |
| *Primavera negra* (1968) | Jordi Arbonès | Aymà | CAT | 2 (1969–1970) | Yes/No | w/ changes | 1970 |
| *Primavera negra* (1970) | Carlos Bauer y Julián Marcos | Edhasa | SPA | 1 (1970) | No | w/ changes | "Silencio" 1970 |
| *Primavera negra* (1970) | Carlos Bauer y Julián Marcos | Alfaguara-Bruguera | SPA | 1 (1978) | No | w/ changes | 1978 |

times successfully. Most of the petitions to import Miller's novels, even those not included in the collection *The Tropics*, such as *The Roxi Crucifixion, Sunday after War, Max and the White Phagocytes,* had been imported from publisher Santiago Rueda (Buenos Aires). Other translations made in Buenos Aires were also sent to the Peninsula, with editions from publishers Sur,[11] Siglo XX editors[12] and Losada.[13]

Interestingly enough, Iglesias's translation of *Tropic of Cancer* contains Anaïs Nin's preface to the book that appeared in the Grove Press English edition of 1961. The same translation was repeatedly accepted for importation from 1963 to 1976. Additionally, in 1967 the Catalan publisher Aymà applied for permission to edit and circulate Iglesias's translation. This time the outcome was negative, with an unfavorable report written by the censors, who condemned Miller's novel: "This book is the monologue of a degenerate ... It is full of violence and constant sensuality ... a very descriptive, true pornographic lecture that triggers revulsion in the reader" (File 2791–61, catalogue 21/18052). The next application regarding Iglesias's translation of *Tropic of Cancer* was in 1976. In this case, the novel was part of a special edition edited by publisher Aymà: the collection *Novela erótica contemporánea* (1976). It contained Iglesia's translations of *Tropic of Cancer* and

---

11. *El mundo del sexo, La sabiduría del corazón*, and *El tiempo de los asesinos*.
12. *El ojo cosmológico, Pesadilla de aire acondicionado*, and *El Puente de Brooklyn*.
13. *Recordar para recordar*.

*Tropic of Capricorn* together with D. H. Lawrence's *Lady Chatterley's Lover* translated as *Primera Lady Chatterley* by Federico López Cruz, and Miller's *Nexus* (translated by Lis G. de Echevarria); all of these were Argentinian editions compiled by Edaf in a special collection. It was not accepted for publication. On the contrary, the final censor's report goes further and denounces the book: "The publication of this book will trigger social scandal, even complaints and *lawsuits*. Henceforth, I find it appropriate to find against it, appealing to legal authority to identify the possible existence of a *crime*" (File 5179–76, catalogue 73/05474, emphasis added). In spite of the negative resolution, the publisher, bearing in mind that the dictatorship had officially ended, registered the title in 1976.

Contrary to *Trópico de Cáncer,* the Argentinian-made translation of *Black Spring* translated by Patricio Canto (1964) was not approved for importation, even though the petitions were submitted by different publishers for more than a decade and the two versions were published by Santiago Rueda. See the censors' notes on *Black Spring:* "obscene, impious, blasphemous, dirty novel, the author completes here what he did not narrate in *The Tropics*" (File 956–64, catalogue 66/6456); "Rabelaisian" (File 1170–64, catalogue 66/6457); "autobiography with pornographic allusions. Denied" (File 498–65, catalogue 66/6461); "it reads like a book written by a madman" (File 1201–74, catalogue 66/6563). Despite how hard peninsular publishers tried to get Miller's novels published in Franco's Spain, the domestic edition of *Black Spring* in Spanish – translated by Carlos Bauer and Julián Marcos in 1970 – shared the same fate and was not published until the end of Francoism in 1978 by publisher Alfaguara-Bruguera. Nevertheless, Jordi Arbonès's Catalan translation, *Primavera negra* (Aymà 1968) was approved for publication in 1970, after publisher and translator managed to submit a "clean" version of the novel, i.e. harshly by the publisher, as this censor highlights: "This novel, already authorized in Catalan, which is a *carefully-done* translation unlike this Spanish one under review … " (File 11036–70, catalogue 66/06214, emphasis added).[14]

With regard to Anaïs Nin's novels, only three of her works were requested for importation from 1969 to 1978: *Under a Glass Bell* (P. Owen London, 1968); *The Diaries of Anaïs Nin (1931–1934)* ed. Brace and World. NY (1966); and *A Spy in the House of Love* ed. Penguin Books (1973). What is noteworthy is that all three English editions were approved for importation on a number of occasions and, what is more, none of the reports contained any negative comments about the books. This is in strong contrast to earlier comments in the censorship files when the publishers attempted to carry out Spanish and Catalan translations domestically. For example, in 1965, Aymà applied for permission to translate the whole collec-

---

14. For a textual study of these translations, see Monzón (2020: 210–214).

**Table 5.** *Ladders to Fire* – Anaïs Nin (1946; 1959) Gunther Stuhlmann NY

| Title | Translator(s) | Publish. | Lang. | Requests | Imp. | Accepted | Publication |
|---|---|---|---|---|---|---|---|
| – | (no translation) | Aymà | SPA | 1 (1965) | No | w/ changes | – |
| – | (no translation) | Aymà | CAT | 1 (1965) | No | w/ changes | – |
| *Escalas hacia el fuego* | David Casanueva | Aymà | SPA | 1 (1971) | No | – | 1971 |
| *Escales cap al foc* (1976) | Jordi Arbonès | Aymà | CAT | – | – | – | 1976 |

**Table 6.** *A Spy in the House of Love* – Anaïs Nin (1959) Gunther Stuhlmann NY

| Title | Translator(s) | Publisher | Lang. | Requests | Imp. | Accepted | Publication |
|---|---|---|---|---|---|---|---|
| – | (no translation) | Aymà | SPA | 2 (1965) | No | w/ changes | – |
| – | (no translation) | Aymà | CAT | 2 (1965) | No | w/ changes | – |
| *Una espia a la casa de l'amor* (1968) | Manuel Carbonell | Edicions Proa[*] | CAT | 2 (1968–1969) | – | – | "Silencio" 1968, 1969 |
| *Una espía en la casa del amor* (1968) | Carmen Alcalde y Mª Rosa Prats | Aymà | SPA | 2 (1968–1969) | – | – | "Silencio" 1968, 1969 |
| *A Spy in the House of Love* (1954) | n/a[**] | Penguin Books | EN | 4 (1973–1978) | Yes | Yes | – |

[*] In 1962 Aymà acquired the funds of several publishers, Edicions Proa among them, and continued to edit their publications ("Societat Anònima").
[**] No translator for it is indicated in Nin's original, edited by Penguin Books in 1954.

tion *Cities of the Interior* into Spanish and Catalan. The censors' comments on the novel are as follows: "Slow, short narrations, full of psychoanalysis and erotism, with a tendency towards lesbian passion. The book is dangerous due to its profound and morbid erotism, save the last story … ["Solar Barque"] it reminds one of Marcel Proust's and James Joyce's works. It can't be authorized" (File 9212–65, catalogue 21/16873). However, a second censor believed otherwise: "Sensual content ... but there is nothing decisive enough for the book not to be authorized" (ibid.).[15] Hence, the censorship board requested the submission of the translations onto which the necessary amendments could apply.

Nevertheless, only a few months later, Aymà requested permission to separately translate *A Spy in the House of Love* and *Ladders to the Fire* and, unlike the previous application to translate the entire collection, both get rejected: "This North American writer is comparable to the kind of erotic and obscure literature written by Henry Miller – with whom she has worked – and Lawrence," and goes on when reviewing *A Spy in the House of Love*: "'There is, in Sabina, many Sabinas who also want to live and love.' Once and again the author exposes such a destructive worldview of modern love" (File 7088–65, catalogue 21/16626). Consequently, both *A Spy* and *Ladders* are rejected. After this, Aymà appeals the decision, making the following assertions about Nin: "Born in Barcelona, she is the daughter of the remarkable Spanish musician Joaquín Nin. She is a colleague of Henry Miller, Lawrence Durrell, and other great writers; her novels are well received by the critics and have already been translated into French and Italian" (File 7088–65, catalogue 21/16626).

This information indicates how unique and multifaceted the case of Anaïs Nin's was. On the one hand, in trying to get the approval to translate and circulate her works in translation, the local publishers attempted to appeal to the national sentiment (affective load with nationalist connotations) of the censors (gatekeepers of the regime's cultural politics) by highlighting Nin's blood connections with Spain. On the other hand, the fact that no Spanish translations of Nin's novels were yet circulating in the Latin American market made it possible for the Spanish and Catalan publishers to own the translation rights before the South American publishers. Hence, Aymà also used this as a counter-argument to influence the boards' verdict:

> Considering that Anaïs Nin is extremely pleased with our support to publish some of her works in her *natural languages* – Castilian and Catalan – it would be regrettable if, due to the rejection hereby appealed, the author were inclined to accept her publishers requests to pass the publication rights of her novels in Spanish to a South American publisher.
> 
> (File 7088–65, catalogue 21/16626, emphasis added)

---

15. A book was normally reviewed by at least two censors (called 'readers' at that stage). The files found at the archive contain the various censors' reports and the ultimate decision of the board.

In spite of Aymàs's arguments, the censors' reports show a decisive dismissal of Nin's works, even more so than the reluctance they demonstrated when reviewing Durrell's *Justine* in particular. In Nin's novels, female sexuality is paramount and passages containing sexual encounters, this time from a feminine perspective, abound. In the years leading up to the Press Law of 1966, the predominance of the Catholic Church had a great deal of influence on censorial decisions. Hence, topics considered immoral or pernicious (blasphemy, sexuality, liberal feminism) were harshly condemned and censored (Andrés 2012: 13). Therefore none of Spanish and Catalan translations of *A Spy in the House of Love*, though made locally, were officially authorized during Francoism, but branded administrative silence. The only translation that successfully passed the censorship filter – other than the originals accepted for importation – was that of David Casanueva (Aymà 1971), which suggests that, as occurred with Arbonès' translation of Miller's novels into Catalan, it could have been subject to the publishers' self-censorship.[16]

**The editorial market under Francoism: A need for translations**

The order for presenting the above-mentioned data does not correspond chronologically with the date of publication of the originals: *The Tropics* (1934–1937), *Cities of the Interior* (1946–1959), *The Alexandria Quartet* (1957–1960). Instead, they appear either according to the date the publishers asked for permission to import the English originals or/and the Argentinian-made translations, where they existed, or according to the requests submitted for the translations to circulate after being edited and published domestically. In this respect, Durrell's novels in *The Alexandria Quartet* were the first to be scrutinized by the censors (1961–1976), followed by Miller's *The Tropics* (1962–1977) and Nin's *Cities of the Interior* (1965–1978). The reasons behind this, far from being accidental, can be explained by the role that the Argentinian translation market played in Francoist Spain.

In the case of Henry Miller's and Lawrence Durrell's collections, the Argentinian publishing houses Ediciones Rueda and Editorial Sudamericana, both based in Buenos Aires, held the copyright for the Spanish translations of *Tropic of Cancer* (translated by Mario Guillermo Iglesias, 1962), *Black Spring* (trad. Patricio Canto, 1964), *Justine* (translated by Aurora Bernárdez 1960), and *Balthazar* (translated by Aurora Bernárdez 1961). Gómez has observed that the importation

---

**16.** With the new Press Law of 1966, it became the norm that "publishers were compelled to self-censor their publications to limit the economic impact of an adverse decision, a sequestered book or a lawsuit" (Lobejón et al. 2021: 65).

of Argentinian-made translations was "a practice that had become frequent in post-war Spain due to the economic difficulties the country was experiencing" (Gómez 2009: 128). The Latin American translation market in the 1950s and 1960s was flourishing, with Argentina holding the publishing hegemony within the Spanish-speaking world: "It all started with the bloody Spanish Civil War (1936–1939) that plunged the peninsular book market into such a crisis that it could no longer provide for the Latin American market" (Petersen 2019, my translation). Consequently, Spain's weak position in the literary and cultural scene worldwide after almost two decades of Francoism allowed the Latin American publishing houses to fill this significant void: "With this opportunity, not only did the old publishing houses adapt part of their activity to cope with the external market, but also new firms were established, which, in some cases, turned into the most dynamic and innovative publishers that Argentina ever had" (ibid.). Publishers such as Santiago Rueda, Emecé, Losada and Sudamericana are examples of this.

Moreover, Gómez asserts that in part because of the emigration of Spanish nationals fleeing the conditions of post-war Spain, a number of publishing houses emerged in places such as Argentina and Mexico (Gómez 2009: 132). One such publisher, Edhasa (Hispanic-American Publisher and Distributor), was established in Argentina by Antonio López, a Catalan exile who had worked closely with Editorial Sudamericana ("La editorial"). This explains why, in the case of Durrell's *The Alexandria Quartet,* the local publishers tried to import the translations already done in Argentina and, after being approved for circulation, no other Spanish translation was carried out in the Peninsula. Gómez argues that the practice of reprinting and circulating South American editions in Franco's Spain meant that they "could be relatively cheaply imported" (2009: 132), instead of commissioning a new translation made locally. After studying the censorship and import files on three authors, it can be argued, however, that the question of cost is merely a contributing factor, as this issue can also be boiled down to a copyright issue, i.e. the Argentinian publishing houses held the rights for the translation; hence, it was easier and more cost-efficient to use their translation or, perhaps, this was their only choice in the midst of a copyright struggle.

Furthermore, regarding the inconsistency in importing the Argentine translations of both Henry Miller's and Lawrence Durrell's works – *The Tropics* and *The Alexandria Quartet,* respectively – into Spain, the censors' reports and final verdicts showcase the arbitrariness with which the board allowed certain novels into the country. For instance, the Argentinian-made translations of Miller's *Tropic of Cancer* and *Tropic of Capricorn* were imported on several occasions, whereas the translation of *Black Spring* was denied consistently. Similarly, the Argentine translation of Durrell's *Balthazar,* published by Sudamericana (translated by Aurora

Bernárdez), was denied importation throughout the 60s. Nevertheless, in 1970, the distributor Edhasa was granted the publication rights of Bernárdez's very same translation, except it was an edited version for the Peninsula. Sudamericana did not just import and circulate a foreign translation, but changed material aspects of the book, such as covers, art, and pagination.

On the other hand, the fact that Anaïs Nin's works submitted for publication in Spain during this period were exclusively domestic translations rather than imported ones from Argentina – unlike Miller's and Durrell's novels in their Spanish versions – can be explained by Spanish publishers fighting to hold exclusive translation rights for Nin's works. Publisher Aymà stated as much in their letter to the censorship board in 1965 after the censorship board rejected the circulation of *A Spy in the House of Love* in Spanish and Catalan. In 1975, Aymà sends another letter with reference to Miller's *Tropic of Cancer* arguing a similar circumstance: "We wish to declare that the reason why we ask to publish a Catalan edition is due to the fact that we cannot publish the novel in Spanish, because the translation rights of Henry Miller's works in Spanish were granted to South American publishers some time ago" (File 4979–75, catalogue 73/04812). These two instances demonstrate that the need of Spanish publishers to import translations was also a question of copyright, or lack thereof. Moreover, knowing that some of Nin's books were not officially authorized for publication but given administrative silence, in spite of being translated domestically in Spain, reinforces the point that all translations, no matter their origin, had to undergo a process in which both form and matter had to be meticulously scrutinized by the censors. That is to say, all translations were, *a priori,* held to the same censorial standards. Nevertheless, for the Spanish readership the outcome could vary depending on whether there was a Spanish translation somewhere in South America: this meant, at least, that the book could still be smuggled into the country, as Jordi Cornellà-Detrell points out (2016: 41).

Cornellà-Detrell also claims that the Spanish and Catalan translation fields were consistently impacted by the Francoist regime and by the socio-economic changes that the country went through during these decades. Contrary to what scholars such as Hans-Jörg Neuschäfter have stated, Cornellà-Detrell asserts that "there were not numerous originals awaiting publication, and this explains why the cultural awakening relied heavily on imported texts ... The paradox, typical of cultures in crisis or in the process of establishing themselves, is that this could only be achieved by adapting massive amounts of foreign works" (2013: 132).[17]

---

[17] Cornellà-Detrell's position can as well be endorsed by Itamar Even-Zohar's polysystem theory in an attempt to understand the evolution of the translation scene during the Francoist dictatorship, by "stressing the importance of the historical context and advancing thinking

Cornellà-Detrell's theory is proven to be right as soon as one analyzes the enormous number of applications to import and distribute foreign literature during the 1960s and 1970s, notwithstanding the rigid control imposed by the regime through its censorship machinations.

## Negotiating the translation flow: Recurrent publishers and translators

In the late 60s the Francoist regime began cautiously to embrace more liberal principles and attempted to project a modernized image of the nation in terms of policy, the economy, and culture. This ultimate need for flexibility was reflected within the censorship system through the establishment of a new law, *Ley de prensa e imprenta*, passed on 18 March 1966 by the new minister of Information and Tourism, Manuel Fraga Iribarne. In this stage, a more liberal section of the censorship board led by the General Director of Information, Carlos Robles Piquer, clashed with the reactionary and religious factions who saw themselves as the true preservers of the "legitimate, true moral and ideological order of the regime" (Jané-Lligé 2016: 84, my translation).

Furthermore, from the 1960s onwards books were no longer banned simply based on language (i.e. literature written in Catalan), which explains the numerous applications I found at the AGA on the Catalan translations of Miller, Nin and Durrell. Overall, in Borja de Riquer's words, "this period saw the most accelerated, deep-seated social, economic and cultural transformation in Spanish history – in stark contrast to the arthritic grip of the Francoist regime" (1995: 259). An example of this cultural transformation during the last stages of the dictatorship was the actions of the Catalan publisher Aymà. After transferring ownership in 1962 to Joan Baptista Cendrós i Carbonell, today considered a Catalan "mecenes i activista cultural" ("Joan Baptista"), he and Joan Oliver – Aymà's literary editor-in-chief – took advantage of the opportunity to publish in Catalan and attempted to translate and circulate those foreign *romans-à-clef* that were available only in Spanish and whose Spanish translation rights belonged exclusively to South American publishers such as Sudamericana, Santiago Rueda, Losada, or Siglo XX Editores.

At the AGA I found letters to the censorship board showing how Aymà's editors sought to distribute the works of Miller, Nin and Durrell in Catalan from 1965 onwards. In order to persuade them to reconsider their adverse verdicts on these publications, Joan Oliver would fight the case and list a number of reasons for the

---

about the ways in which texts travel across borders and are received in new cultural contexts" (Bassnett 2011: 69).

censors to allow the books for publication in the name of culture and world literature. For instance, Aymà's letter to the censors pertaining to the publication of *Tropic of Cancer* in Catalan (Arbonès's translation) claims that "critics and scholars view Henry Miller as one of the most important, surprising, and revolutionary authors of this century, whose works mark an epoch and a moral attitude towards life … " (File 4979–75, catalogue 73/04812). In a different letter, Ricardo Domenech, writing on behalf of Aymà, tries to make the same case for Miller's *Black Spring* to be distributed in Spain:

> *Black Spring* can't be considered pornographic at all. Miller's narrative is vitalism, he writes with a sincere prose that fits in the current times. It's therefore a paradox that, while films can portray highly sexualized content with the condition of being labeled as 'Cine de Arte y Ensayo,' books with similar characteristics are still treated with the same rigor as before. I assure you … that some of the current films played at our cinemas have been banned in other European countries. Could not this kind of humanly valuable literature that does not align with old sexual and moral prejudices be studied under the same light and permitted to circulate?. (File 5279–69, catalogue 66/03099)

As the censorship files reveal, Aymà sent letters of this nature on many occasions with the aim of appealing the censors' verdicts against the translations of the works of Miller, Nin and Durrell during the late 60s to the mid-70s. Most of the time the censors remained firm on their decisions; nonetheless, there were times when they marked the pages with the passages that needed to be erased in order for the novel to be authorized. Jordi Arbonès's translation of *Black Spring* is one of the texts that, after having been subject to self-censorship by the publisher and translator, was permitted to circulate in 1970.[18]

Overall, allowing Catalan publishers back into the market led to a boom in their book industry – Aymà being one of the publishers that experienced a notable growth in the 1960s and 1970s; in words of Jordi Jané-Lligé: "Edicions 63, the resumption of Aymà/Proa and the 'A tot vent' collection, the creation of new Catalan collections in existing publishing houses … are some of the indisputable signs of this transformation" (2016: 75, my translation). This, together with the "freedom" in disguise promoted by the 1966 Press Law with regard to Catalan publications, has to do with the fact that Catalan was a minority language, and so there were fewer readers who could in fact consume these publications. This often made censors more willing to consider Catalan translations for publication, whilst they rejected them outright in Spanish, as in the case of Jordi Arbonès's Catalan translation of Miller's *Black Spring*.

---

**18.** For a study of the censored passages, see Monzón (2020: 210–214).

As far as the translators behind Aymàs's editions of Miller, Nin, and Durrell that circulated – or attempted to circulate – during Francoism are concerned, Jordi Arbonès (1929–2001) and Manuel de Pedrolo (1918–1990) were two professionals who translated an array of *romans-à-clef* into Catalan:

> Between 1967 and 2001 [Arbonès] translated 11 books by Henry Miller (of which 9 have been published); before that, only 1 of Henry Miller's novels had ever appeared in Catalan (*Devil in Paradise*, translated in 1966 by Arbonès's friend, the Catalan writer Manuel de Pedrolo ... Then, 3 others books have been translated; which means that out of a total of 13 different translations of Henry Miller that are available today in Catalan, 9 (70%) are Jordi Arbonès's work.
>
> (Alsina 2005: 379)

In July 1967, Arbonès wrote his first letter to Henry Miller from Argentina, where he was based most of his life. He recounts that he is writing the prologue to his translation of *Black Spring* and how much he admires Miller's *oeuvre*: "A few years ago I discovered some of your books (*Tropics, Black Spring, Obscenity and the Law of Reflection* ...). Up to the finding out of your books [sic], I had been living covered by a blanket of shadows in my own country, a little nation subdued by the Spanish States: Catalonia" (Arbonès 1967).[19] Later he claims:

> This situation has been going on for the last 30 years, but now it has changed a little ... Lately they have authorized the publishing of some foreign authors that were up-to the present time in the 'black lists:' Sartre, Kafka, Hemingway, Malraux ... I am translating *Black Spring* into Catalan, and I thought you would be glad to know that your books will be read by a slavered people [sic] in an old language ... I would like very much to pursue this correspondence [sic].
>
> (Arbonès 1967)

In his next letter to Miller, he outlines how Aymà is having problems publishing his translation: "[the publishers] were rather too optimistic thinking they could publish *Black Spring*, because of the obscurantism I talked about in my letter has not vanished quiet [sic]. As Aymà's editor Joan Oliver told me in a last letter, your *Spring* is of a kind that will delay blooming in our country" (Arbonès 1968). However, because of Aymàs' efforts, *Primavera negra* was approved in 1970, becoming the only domestic Catalan translation of the works studied in this article that could legally circulate in Franco's Spain before the end of the dictatorship.

---

**19.** The correspondence between Jordi Arbonès and Henry Miller was written in English. Therefore, the quotations of Arbonès' letters presented herein do include some grammatical mistakes and typos.

From the late 1960s, Aymà commissioned an array of Catalan translations from De Pedrolo and Arbonès, both great connoisseurs and admirers of the novels of Miller, Nin, and Durrell. Taking advantage of the incipient opening up of both Spanish and Catalan culture during the last years of Francoism, Aymà led the translation market in the Peninsula, introducing numerous foreign works intro the country until 1983, when it ceased its publishing activity ("Societat Anònima"). Aymàs' network of editors and translators gives us a clear insight into not only how the translation market operated in Franco's Spain, but also on a broader scale: their efforts to compete with the Latin American publishers is also indicative of an urge to penetrate through the dark veil of censorship. This urge is exemplified even in their repeated failures to push translations through the censorship apparatus – unless self-censored by them (see Monzón 2020: 210–214). Yet they were not dissuaded from trying to make these works accessible to the public in as "faithful" a translation of the original as they could get away with. Following the fall of the dictatorship and the end of the censorship system, they would succeed in publishing the works that had been suppressed through the final years of the regime.

## First readers, second readers

In providing a definition for the term "structural censorship," Pierre Bourdieu determines that the internalization of the cultural *habitus* and dominant discourse takes effect by means of formal rules and laws embodied in the form of censorship (cited in Merkle 2002:15). André Lefevere also recognizes this phenomenon and defines it as "institutional censorship" (Lefevere 1992: vii). In a context such as Francoist Spain, the agents in charge of enforcing the norms that governed the cultural and literary fields were the bureaucrats appointed by the regime who acted as gatekeepers of this institutional censorship. Under Francoism, censors were the first readers of books; sometimes they were "renowned writers ... sometimes intellectual scholars ... some well-known ecclesiastical censors ... or civil servants who were often members of FET-JONS" (Andrés 2012: 18, my translation).[20] All publications were scrutinized by these first readers, whose reports affected a book's viability, whether at home or abroad, determining what the general public were allowed to consume.

---

**20.** FET-JONS is short for Traditionalist Spanish Phalanx and of the Councils of the National Syndicalist Offensive [*Falange Española Tradicionalista y de las Juntas de Ofensiva Nacional Sindicalista*]. Created by Francisco Franco during the Civil War in 1937, it was the only legal political group during the dictatorship.

Therefore, translations that passed through the system successfully were always reflections of structural censorship, as I have shown with the censors' comments on the novels of Miller, Nin, and Durrell reviewed by the board. For that reason, and to quote Lefevere, a translation can be perceived "to no small extent [as] indicative of the ideology dominant at a certain time in a certain society" (1992: 41). Thanks to the reports submitted by these first readers and the letters they shared with the publishers and editors, the archive becomes a major instrument to investigate structural censorship, giving "a clear insight into the way in which discourses are produced and circulated, thereby placing the study of translation in its cultural and national context" (Billiani 2007: 6). Using Bourdieu's and Lefevere's theories, scholars can study the "narratives encapsulated in the correspondence between different cultural agents, we can understand how a community negotiates its own identity and textuality as well as its cultural aesthetic paradigms, which, in the specific case of translations, can act as either subversive or conservative forces" (5).

Be that as it may, more than merely textual and translational conclusions can be drawn when foregrounding what I call "second readers," namely the consumers of the publications vying for circulation. The censorship files hint at another interesting factor that, on occasion, made possible the circulation of a novel: the nature of the publication submitted to the censorship board, i.e. including the paratext. In an attempt to avoid the banning of a novel, some publishers restricted their print runs – which increased the cost of their publications – by targeting more affluent readers with a superior edition of the book with hard covers and elegant designs finished with golden motifs, etc. This has been observed mainly in Henry Miller's and Anaïs Nin's files. For example, in 1975 Aymà asserted that *Tropic of Cancer* "cannot be prohibited in our country, *this edition in particular*, for it is a book whose print run and price would entail a restricted circulation that would make it practically unaffordable by a readership very little prepared to consume this kind of literature" (File 4979–75, catalogue 73/04812, emphasis added).

Sometimes the publishers also argued that the book should pass for "high literature," by addressing a selected, very educated readership. This occurred when Aymà attempted to publish Lawrence Durrell's works: "Durrell's novels – clearly high literature – belong to the genre of 'difficult novels,' and do not target mass consumption: only a limited public of selected readers, greatly educated, who can grasp Durrell's elaborate and complex style" (File 3823–70, catalogue 66/05561). Correspondingly, with regard to Anaïs Nin the publishers claimed that her prose was "singular, beautiful, with aesthetic and human values that are only appreciated by a very restricted group of readers made up of educated people; a fact that would greatly limit the moral danger of its influence" (File 7088–65, catalogue 21/16626).

Despite the publishers' attempts to import and translate the works of Miller, Nin and Durrell in Franco's Spain, the reality of censorship meant that, in the end, the Spanish "second readers" often had access only to smuggled editions that were published in Latin America. In the words of a famous Spanish literary critic and writer, Francisco Umbral, in 1977:

> In Spain, Miller was much more than a mere literary experience: he was, in the prosperous years of Francoism, a breath of freedom ... I used to stay in bed, with nothing to do, reading Miller in those *disgusting* South American editions that were like stolen somewhere and passed around all the public toilets in Madrid".
> (Umbral, my translation, emphasis added)

More recently, in "Una versión española del canon," Juan Bonilla also recounts his experience of enjoying Miller's *The Tropics* in Iglesias's Spanish translation: "It was the 80s in Spain, although I was reading a translation done in Chile in the late 50s" (Bonilla, my translation). Much like Umbral, Bonilla reflects on the Spanish editions that he had access to and points out how the most influential books he read as a teenager

> were translated in America by Americans. Now I look back and think to myself: how awful. Because I have not reread many of those books but I have the feeling that, if I were to read them again, I would not find half the magic my memory remembers. What I would find is the young guy I was, someone grateful to reach those lands of happiness, unease and mystery thanks to translators on the other side (who were often plagiarized here using the 'professional criteria' of changing a word here, four expressions there). (ibid.)

The translations that both Francisco Umbral and Juan Bonilla remember reading up until the 1980s were indeed those of Mario Guillermo Iglesias, published in Buenos Aires in the 1960s by the publisher Santiago Rueda.

## Coda

Above all else, this article has sought to illustrate not only the ordeals faced by publishing houses seeking to publish controversial literature in Francoist Spain, but also the networks and transatlantic connections that were created as a result of navigating the environment of literary censorship. The works of Henry Miller, Lawrence Durrell, and Anaïs Nin offer only a glimpse into the myriad files in the Spanish government's censorship archive, but the provocative nature of the works – from their sexualized, suggestive and often explicit content to the surrealist, disturbing, subversive and at times bizarre writing – made these works particular targets of the censors' ire, thus making them ideal candidates for showing just what type of content was to be prohibited outright, smuggled or manipulated, should the translation be publishable.

The fact that only some imported novels could pass through the censorship filter indicates not only the arbitrariness of the censorship operations in judging a book, but also how obtaining permission to import a novel did not always mean that the book would be published or distributed widely. A distributing publisher based in Spain would import a translation, or an original, normally with the purpose of producing their own version of the work. In such cases, the new edition also had to be presented to the censorship board prior to publication. That is to say, importing a book could be a mere formality; that was precisely the case with the Argentine translations of Miller's *Tropic of Cancer* and *Tropic of Capricorn* that were sometimes accepted for importation. The copies to be imported were normally very low in number (either one or a few copies of each work in most cases). As Lobejón et al. (2021) have noticed, "[publishers/distributors] could not import in batches, but had to submit one request per book … From 1965 onwards, the system was streamlined considerably, resulting in companies being able to import up to 25 titles at a time" (106). Hence, importing a foreign literary work did not imply that the general public could get it for their own consumption, but it was done for the publisher's own use, generally with the intention of adapting it to the target readership, or for inclusion in the publisher's catalogue. This explains the high number of applications to import Miller's and Durrell's works by different publishing houses throughout the years. Nonetheless, the imported translations and others like them *did* circulate, as the "second readers" Umbral and Bonilla claim; those shabbily worn copies passed around dingy underground Madrid networks were most likely editions illegally brought in from Argentina.

It has also been observed that, in the event of a translation made in Latin America (e.g. Durrell's *Justine* and *Balthazar*), a distributing company linked to the publisher in question would often publish the same translation in a new edition for Spain, instead of a Spanish publishing house producing a brand-new translation in Spanish. An example of this is Aurora Bernárdez's translations of Durrell's novels into Spanish that were distributed by Edhasa in Spain, after being published in Argentina in the early 60s. Nevertheless, the competitiveness within the Spanish-speaking international book market was to change yet again. Whilst in 1940s and 1950s Argentina experienced a boom in their publishing industry, the "opening" that Spain was slowly heading towards in the 1970s meant that the Iberian publishers sought to re-position themselves in the global market, especially by translating literary works into Catalan. Hence, as seen in the case of Anaïs Nin's reception in Spain, publishers such as Aymà were at the forefront of translating world literature into Spanish and Catalan. Furthermore, the correspondence between the publishing agents and the censorship board regarding the works of Henry Miller, Anaïs Nin, and Lawrence Durrell reinforced the importance for the domestic publishing houses of obtaining translation rights before their Latin American competitors did.

All in, despite the Francoist censorship apparatus' best efforts to impede the flow of novels that arrived in the country, this article has shown that some editions did manage to find their way through. In the end, a transatlantic flow of translations was indeed possible. No matter how hard some of the agents involved in the translation and distribution processes worked to suppress it, in particular the censors or "first readers," the desire of the Spanish readership base for access to works of this kind could not be suppressed. Whether from domestic translations subject to censorship, works imported from Latin America, or raw and gritty smuggled editions, Spain's appetite for literature of this nature shows a nation that, after enduring the suppression of their domestic and exogenous cultural production for over 30 years, yearned for thought-provoking and cathartic *romans-à-clef* from abroad. This flow of translations from the Americas and its impact on the Spanish and Catalan readership during Francoism is indicative of a larger sociopolitical trend that would culminate in the 1980s with the eventual reopening of Spain to the world at large.

## References

Abellán, Manuel Luis. 1980. *Censura y creación literaria en España (1939–1976)*. Barcelona: Península.

Alsina, Victòria. 2005. "Jordi Arbonès i Montull: Translating in difficult times." In *Less Translated Languages*, ed. by A. Branchadell and L. Margaret. Amsterdam: John Benjamins Publishing Company, 375–389.

Andrés, Gabriel. 2012. *La batalla del libro en el primer franquismo: política del libro, censura y traducciones italianas*. Madrid: Huerga and Fierro.

Arbonès, Jordi. 1967. "Carta a Henry Miller." Accessed November 20, 2021. https://www.omnia.ie/index.php?navigation_function=2&navigation_item=%2F164%2F49299&repid=1 no pag.

Arbonès, Jordi. 1968. "Carta a Henry Miller." Accessed November 20, 2021. https://www.omnia.ie/index.php?navigation_function=2&navigation_item=%2F164%2F49300&repid=1 no pag.

Bassnett, Susan. 2011. "From Cultural Turn to Translational Turn: A Translational Journey." *Literature, Geography, Translation*, Newcastle Upon Tyne: Cambridge Scholars Publishing, 67–80.

Billiani, Francesca. 2007. *Modes of Censorship and Translation: National Contexts and Diverse Media*. Manchester: St. Jerome Publisher.

Billiani, Francesca. 2007. "Renewing a Literary Culture through Translation: Poetry in Post-War Italy." In *Translation as Intervention*, ed. Jeremy Munday. Continuum, 138–60.

Bonilla, Juan. 2007. "Una versión española del canon." *Club de traductores literarios de Buenos Aires*. Accessed November 30, 2021. https://clubdetraductoresliterariosdebaires.blogspot.com/2017/11/una-version-espanola-del-canon-4.html https://clubdetraductoresliterariosdebaires.blogspot.com/2017/11/una-version-espanola-del-canon-4.html No pag.

Cisquella, Georgina et al., 2002. *La represión cultural en el franquismo: diez años de censura de libros durante la Ley de Prensa (1966–1976)*. Barcelona: Anagrama.

Cornellà-Detrell, Jordi. 2016. "Barcelona, la Ciutat dels llibres prohibits. Importació, venda i consum de llibre il.legals durant el franquisme." *L'avenç* 419: 40–48.

Cornellà-Detrell, Jordi. 2013. "The Afterlife of Francoist Cultural Policies: Censorship and Translation in the Catalan and Spanish Literary Market." *Hispanic Research Journal* 14 (2): 129–143.

Gómez, Cristina. 2006. "¿Traduzione Tradizione? El polisistema literario español durante la dictadura franquista: la censura." *RiLUnE* 4: 37–49.

Gómez, Cristina. 2009. "Censorship in Francoist Spain and the Importation of Translations from South America: The Case of Lawrence Durrell's *Justine*." In *Translation and Censorship: Patterns of Communication and Interference*, ed. by E. Chuilleanáin, C. Cuilleanáin, and D. Parris, 132–146. Dublin: Four Courts Press.

Jané-Lligé, Jordi. 2016. "La traducción de narrativa dels anys 60 i la censura." In *Traducció i censura en el franquisme*, ed. by L. Vilardell, 75–96. Barcelona: Publicacions de l'Abadia de Montserrat.

"Joan Baptista Cendrós i Carbonell." *Gran enciclopèdia catalana*. Accessed November 30, 2021. https://www.enciclopedia.cat/ec-gec-0016854.xml No pag.

"La editorial." *Edhasa*. Accessed November 30, 2021. https://www.edhasa.es/quienes_somos. No pag.

Latham, Sean. 2009. *The Art of Scandal: Modernism, Libel Law, and the Roman à Clef*. Oxford: Oxford UP.

Lázaro, Alberto. 2004. *H. G. Wells en España, estudio de los expedientes de censura (1939–1978)*. Madrid: Editorial Verbum.

Lefevere, André. 1992. *Translation, Rewriting and the Manipulation of Literary Fame*. London: Routledge.

Linder, Daniel. 2004. "The censorship of sex: a study of Raymond Chandler's *The Big Sleep* in Franco's Spain." *Traduction, Terminologie, Rédaction* 17 (1): 155–182.

Lobejón, Sergio, Cristina Gómez Castro, and Camino Gutiérrez Lanza. 2021. "Archival research in translation and censorship: Digging into the 'true museum of Francoism.'" *Meta. Journal des traducteurs* 66 (1): 92–114.

Merkle, Denise. 2002. "Presentation." *Censorship and Translation in the Western World. TTR*. 15 (2): 9–18.

Monzón, Sofía. 2020. "The struggles of translating Henry Miller in Franco's Spain (1939–1975): the different versions of *Black Spring* (1936)." *Transletters. International Journal of Translation and Interpreting* 4: 203–219.

Munday, Jeremy. 2013. "The Role of Archival and Manuscript Research in the Investigation of Translator Decision-Making." *Target* 25 (1): 125–139.

Neuschäfter, Hans-Jörg. 1991. *Macht und Ohnmacht der Zensur: Literatur, Theater und Film in Spanien (1933–1976)*. Stuttgart: Metzler.

Petersen, Lucas. 2019. "Santiago Rueda un editor insólito." *Noticias. Cultura.* Accessed November 30, 2021. https://noticias.perfil.com/noticias/cultura/2019-08-13-santiago-rueda-un-editor-insolito.phtml. No pag.

Pym, Anthony. 2009. "Humanizing Translation History." *Hermes* 42: 23–48.

Rabadán, Rosa (ed). 2010. *Traducción y censura inglés-español: 1939–1985*. León: Universidad de León.

Rioja, Marta. 2010. "English-Spanish Translations and Censorship in Spain 1962–1969." *InTRAlinea* 12: 1–8.

Riquer, Borja de. 1995. "Social and Economic Change in a Climate of Political Immobilism." In *Spanish Cultural Studies, an Introduction: The Struggle for Modernity*, ed. by J. Graham, and J. Labanyi. Oxford, New York: Oxford University Press.

"Roman-à-clef." 2021. Britannica. Accessed November 30, 2021. https://www.britannica.com/art/roman-a-clef/additional-info No pag.

Ruiz Bautista, Eduardo. 2008. *Tiempo de censura: la represión editorial durante el franquismo.* city: TREA.

"Societat Anònima Editora Aymà." *Gran enciclopèdia catalana.* Accessed November 30, 2021. https://www.enciclopedia.cat/ec-gec-0006357.xml. No pag.

Umbral, Francisco. 1977. "Tribuna: Diario de un snob: Henry Miller." Accessed November 30, 2021. https://elpais.com/diario/1977/12/28/sociedad/252111610_850215.html. No pag.

CHAPTER 4

# Recognition versus redistribution?
Translation flows and the role of politically committed publishers in Spain

Fruela Fernández
University of the Balearic Islands

The study of book translation flows has become a crucial tool in understanding cultural dynamics during a period of globalization. This chapter applies a thematic analysis of such flows to the understanding of debates in the Spanish left since the beginning of the 2008 economic crisis. Utilizing a conceptual opposition formulated by Nancy Fraser and Axel Honneth, the study tests to what extent struggles over identity and difference ("recognition") might obscure or hinder the importance of the struggle for the improvement of material conditions ("redistribution") of a majority of people. To this end, the chapter conducts a range of analyses and classifications of the translation choices made by a group of politically committed publishers.

**Keywords:** book translation flows, book publishing, translation and politics, Spanish politics, activism and translation

## Introduction and research context

Since the turn of the 21st century, the study of book translation flows – that is, the number of books translated into or from a certain language, the ratio of translations within the publishing sector of a given country, and other relevant characteristics of such exchanges – has undoubtedly become an important tool in understanding cultural dynamics across the world.

A key strand within these works has entailed the study of what Johan Heilbron (1999) called "a cultural world-system" of book translations. Expanding on de Swaan's claim (1993) that globalization has enabled the emergence of a global system of languages, Heilbron argued that book translations exist within a specific world-structure with its own internal dynamics and tensions. Arranged around central, semi-peripheral and peripheral languages, this system is strongly hierarchical. In a nutshell, this implies that countries and/or areas with central languages tend to translate less than those with (semi-)peripheral ones, while books written in central languages are more frequently translated than those produced in languages of lesser importance within the hierarchy.

Following this line of analysis, scholars have studied the particularities of languages located in different sectors of this system. For example, Brisset and Aye (2007) have shown that English enjoys a "hypercentral" position, as it was the source language for 55 per cent of the books translated across the world during the period 1979–2007. At the opposite side of the system, Linn (2006) analyzed translational trends for a specific peripheral language (Dutch), while Loogus and Van Doorslaer (2021) have discussed how translation policies contribute to the promotion of another (Estonian).

Although translation flows are highly dependent on this global structure, Heilbron and Sapiro (2016: 383–397) have emphasized that they cannot be understood without a clear analysis of the specific characteristics of each national field (Bourdieu 1989), as power dynamics, economic issues, cultural struggles and other internal factors have a decisive influence upon translational choices. In this sense, Abramitzky and Sin (2014), focusing on the Eastern bloc before and after the fall of the USSR, have shown how political factors can decisively condition the degree and directionality of exchanges between languages, a claim reinforced by Brissett and Colón (2020: 242–245). Also working on the former Communist bloc, Popa (2010) has revealed the multiple political nuances and gradations that conditioned the translation and reception of Eastern European texts in France over several decades. Similarly, Sorá (2003) focused on the political and cultural factors that influenced the translation and reception of Brazilian literature in Argentina during the 20th century, leading to a striking paradox: although the number of translations published was important, they did not receive any substantial attention from critics and writers.

In this chapter, my approach is closer to this second strand of study, which privileges internal factors in the understanding of translation flows. Employing a thematic analysis, I harness the study of book translations as a tool to assess the evolution and relevance of debates within the Spanish intellectual and political field since the 2008 economic crisis. Utilizing the concepts formulated by Nancy Fraser and Axel Honneth (2003) in a now classic debate, I test the following political question: can struggles over identity and difference ("recognition") obscure or hinder the importance of the struggle for the improvement of material conditions ("redistribution") of a majority of people? This debate has plagued the global left since the decline of the Fordist model (Laclau and Mouffe 1985) and, as explained in the following section, has taken on a very specific form in recent Spanish politics, contributing to harsh critiques and tense exchanges within the various families of the left.

To shed further light on this matter, I place it within a specific cultural field, with my analysis focusing on the translation choices made by a series of politically committed publishers. This type of Spanish imprint bears similarities to the British "radical publishers" or the French "édition indépendante critique" (Noël 2012) and is defined by a logic of political engagement. As I have shown elsewhere (Fernández 2020, 2021), these publishers accord paramount importance to translation, have strong links with social movements and left-wing parties, and have played a central role in the renewal of the cultural and political landscape of present-day Spain. In the central part of this chapter, I study the translation output of a select group of these publishers over the years 2008–2021 and systematize it according to the opposition between "recognition" and "redistribution" in order to draw relevant insights for a more nuanced understanding of the debate.

## Spain after the 15M: Political tensions and reconfigurations

One of the most notable responses to the consequences of the 2008 economic crisis was the "movement of the squares" (Della Porta 2015; Gerbaudo 2017), which started in 2011 with various popular uprisings in Arab countries (Tunisia, Egypt, Libya or Syria, among others) before spreading to the global North. Its first "cluster" (Gerbaudo 2017: 31) among Western countries began in Spain in 2011, where a series of protests and occupations known as the 15M or "indignados" expanded across cities and towns (Razquin 2017: 71–72), galvanizing the country over several months through their experiments with popular participation and direct democracy (Sitrin and Azzellini 2014: 121–150; Della Porta 2015: 157–210). The Spanish protests would eventually inspire other events, such as later actions in Portugal (Baumgarten 2013, 466), Greece (Douzinas 2013: 12) and the USA (Romanos 2018).

In its initial phases, the 15M's stance against corruption, politicians' privileges and other shortcomings in Spanish democracy drew notable support from a wide variety of citizens (Urquizu 2016: 22–25). As a result, the movement created a major crisis in Spanish politics (Antentas 2017) and opened a new "political cycle" (Rodríguez 2016: 15–18) that gave a major boost to multiple grassroots initiatives – such as the anti-eviction movement (Flesher Fominaya 2015) – and facilitated the emergence of various political projects (Delclós 2015, Chapter 5), including the political party Podemos, founded in 2014 (Rivero 2015).

Despite the decisive impact of the 15M upon Spanish society, its political legacy is disputed and controversial. The first years of the new "cycle" seemed notably successful, as a series of grassroots platforms managed to win important local elections (such as in Madrid and Barcelona) in 2015, while Podemos and its allies became the third largest political group in parliament later in the same year. However, both fronts rapidly lost popular support and, in 2019, local platforms were defeated in the majority of elections, while the Podemos alliance foundered and lost half of its parliamentary MPs (from 69 to 35). Despite this major drop, Podemos managed to become the junior coalition partner in the Spanish government in January 2020, a move that has been described as "the final assimilation" of the 15M by the establishment and therefore signaling its demise as a political alternative (Rodríguez 2020).

It is in this context that the "recognition" versus "redistribution" debate must be placed. The electoral stagnation of the post-15M left has coincided with two opposing tendencies: on the one hand, the emergence of other protests beyond the 15M umbrella, most notably the feminist movement and its highly successful "feminist strike" in 2018 (Fernández 2021: 69–89); on the other hand, the surge of the far-right party VOX (third biggest party in parliament since 2020), mirroring the recent growth of right-wing platforms across the world (e.g. Trump's term as US president and the sustained results of far-right parties in Germany, France and Italy). In response to this conjunction of events, a number of left-wing political agents, journalists and writers have come to the fore in recent years to criticize the strategy of the Spanish left in terms that strongly replicate the recognition/redistribution opposition. Some of them had been previously associated with post-15M projects (such as former Podemos senator Óscar Guardingo or journalist Víctor Lenore), while others have stronger ties with the Communist Party, such as journalist Daniel Bernabé.

Through the political magazine *El viejo topo*, the online journals *El Confidencial* and *Vozpópuli*, and an intense usage of social media and online platforms (Twitter, YouTube), these critics argue that the Spanish left is giving excessive importance to identity issues – in particular gender, race and sexuality – at the expense of economic matters, which they place as the major duty of the left. In this vein, Bernabé's highly successful book *La trampa de la diversidad* [*The diversity trap*] (Bernabé 2018), a harsh critique of identity politics that has sold over 15,000 copies at the time of writing, claims that many causes associated with struggles for recognition (such as gay marriage or gender-awareness) have been appropriated and co-opted by neoliberalism in order to distract voters from more necessary campaigns in the fields of the economy and labor. Along similar lines, Guardingo has accused the post-15M left of losing touch with their traditional working-class voters, dismissively describing its message as: "Feminism, LGBTQI+, *Welcome refugees*, and a little labourism" (Guardingo 2021; italics in the original). Meanwhile, Esteban Hernández, opinion editor for *El Confidencial*, has praised the emergence of new nationalistic currents within the Spanish left that do not shy away from adopting certain proposals from the far-right on migration or security, since they imply "a return to material matters [*lo material*], through a defence of labour" (Hernández 2018a).

Another important fact for this research is how various authors within this political strand characterize identity issues and civil rights as an "imported" debate. In this sense, for instance, Bernabé has claimed that interest on matters such as queer theory has been copied from the American left, which he describes as "politically useless" and "toxic" (Bernabé interviewed in Batalla 2018). Similarly, Juan Soto Ivars (2020) has criticized Spanish demonstrations in support of Black Lives Matter as a "psychological distortion" created by globalization, arguing they paid greater importance to an American conflict than to a national crisis (the coronavirus pandemic).

As briefly mentioned earlier, debates between diverse approaches and conceptions is not new for the global left. In the early 1980s, the tension between the emergent social movements and the traditional working class, which was declining at the time as a leading subject for the left, was emphasized by Ernesto Laclau and Chantal Mouffe in their highly influential *Hegemony and Socialist Strategy* (1985: 1–3). Similarly, in the exchange that provides the key concepts for this chapter, Fraser and Honneth (2003: 1–2) highlighted the break between the Fordist era – during which redistribution concerns were pushed to the margins, as social justice was understood exclusively on "distributive terms" – and our post-industrial world, in which "the question of recognition" has become "impossible to ignore". In their view, this profound break between two different conceptions of the world of labor implies that "redistribution" and "recognition" have been "often dissociated from one another" (2003: 8) in political action, leading to strong "polarization" between supporters of one approach and the other. In this way, beyond its specific characteristics, the Spanish debate provides us with a case study for a recurring rift that requires closer inspection.

## Politically committed publishers in Spain and a thematic analysis of book flows

Political debates are often based on intuition, affects and partisan readings (Holmes 2015; Joint Research Centre 2019), as neither individuals nor collectives have access to the full perspective of data and information on a given political terrain. Therefore, in order to test the validity and relevance of an argument, it is necessary to focus on a particular area, with its specific laws and dynamics. In this section, in the light of the aim of shedding light on the redistribution versus recognition debate, I study the choice of book translations published by a series of politically committed publishers from 2008–2021.

As I have shown elsewhere in greater detail (Fernández 2020, 2021), this type of publisher, whose importance and visibility grew notably after the 2008 crisis, relies heavily on translations, which made up over 50% of their catalogues from 2011–2019 (Fernández 2021: 41–43). Beyond the relevance of these figures, the centrality of translation in their editorial projects responds to a desire to transform and reinvigorate political debate within Spanish society. After a lengthy period (1980s to the early 2000s) that privileged apolitical and disengaged products (Echevarría 2012), the damaged reputation of the cultural establishment after the beginning of the 2008 economic crisis and the emergence of the 15M protests generated a pressing need among many citizens to search for alternative models and points of reference (Fernández 2021: 36–39). In this way, translation has contributed to filling the "vacuums" (Even-Zohar 1990: 47) left by this absence of politicized texts and, therefore, acquired a paramount role during this period, as it "participates actively in shaping" (1990: 46) the center of this emerging new culture.

Importantly, these publishers have also established a dual relationship with the political and activist fields, as their publications are influenced by current events and influence them in turn: they respond to ongoing debates in the field, yet also contribute to them through their publications (see Fernández 2020 for examples). Furthermore, they have established a productive engagement with politicians and activists, who often become authors of paratexts for their translations (see Fernández 2021: 43–45 for examples).

Therefore, politically committed publishers can offer a good indicator of the issues that concern the post-15M Spanish left, since they combine an awareness of these problems with a role of intellectual leadership. At the same time, their intensive use of translation is relevant to test one of the criticisms raised by supporters of redistribution, namely that interest in struggles for recognition are part of an "imported" debate.

For the present analysis, I have chosen six publishers – Akal, Capitán Swing, Errata Naturae, Traficantes de Sueños, Pepitas de Calabaza, and Virus – that were already active at the beginning of the global economic crisis (2008) and continue to be active at the time of writing (2021). This timeframe enables us to trace the evolution of book translations from the pre-15M context through its development and aftermath, reaching well into the current phase of political debates. The series used for data extraction are those focusing on political non-fiction within these publishers' catalogues: Akal's *Cuestiones de Antagonismo* ("Matters of Antagonism"; Akal 2021a) and *Pensamiento Crítico* ("Critical Theory"; Akal 2021b); Capitán Swing's (2021) *Ensayo* ("Essay"); Errata Naturae's *La chica de dos cabezas* ("The two-headed girl"; 2021a) and *Libros Salvajes* ("Wild Books": 2021b); Traficantes de Sueños's (2021) *Historia* ("History"), *Mapas* ("Maps"), and *Prácticas Constituyentes* ("Constituent Practices"); Pepitas de Calabaza's (2021) *Ensayo*; and Virus's (2021) *Ensayo* and *Folletos* ("Pamphlets").

After systematizing their translation output using the Spanish ISBN database and professional websites, the data confirm that, in line with previous findings, these publishers have a strong reliance on translation, as shown in Table 1. Books originally written in Spanish are always secondary and, in some cases (Capitán Swing and Errata Naturae) border on marginality. This does not only confirm the centrality of translation within their publishing projects, but also shows to what extent translation enjoys a "primary" position (Even-Zohar 1990: 46) within this cultural sector.

Table 1. Books originally written in Spanish and translations published (2008–2021) by a selection of politically committed publishers. (Data for 2021 reflect only publications until the end of June.)

| Publisher | Original Spanish | Translated books | % of translations |
|---|---|---|---|
| Akal | 44 | 86 | 66.5 |
| Capitán Swing | 15 | 167 | 91.76 |
| Errata Naturae | 2 | 72 | 97.28 |
| Pepitas de Calabaza | 31 | 58 | 65.17 |
| Traficantes de Sueños | 17 | 70 | 80.46 |
| Virus | 14 | 42 | 75 |

Building upon these data, I have classified book translations within five main areas across the redistribution/recognition debate. Firstly, a section of topics strictly associated with the Redistribution pole: "Political strategy" (e.g. political proposals and theories, manifestos, etc.) and "Labor issues" (e.g. unemployment, salaries). Secondly, "Racial Issues" and "Feminism/Sexuality", which form the core of the Recognition pole. Finally, the fifth indicator, "Ecology/Climate Change", does not strictly belong to either pole, although preoccupation with climate change has been criticized as a smokescreen by some Spanish supporters of redistribution (e.g. Bernabé on ecologism as the "green fever"; Domínguez 2019).

Using the results from this classification, I test an initial hypothesis: If redistribution supporters are correct, numbers should reflect a strong surge of book translations focusing on recognition issues in recent years, accompanied by decreasing numbers of translated books dealing with redistribution issues. Within this hypothesis, I distinguish between two potential sub-approaches: the "pure recognition" one (growing numbers of translations on racial and gender/sexual issues) and the "extended recognition" (increase of translation on racial and sexual identities plus ecology).

Initial analysis of the overall figures for the period (see Table 2) does not seem to validate these claims, at least not fully. Translations focusing on redistribution issues constitute a clear majority of the output for the publishers studied (58.58%), while those dealing with recognition issues are relatively marginal (22.03%). However, when combined with translations on ecology, this fraction grows notably (up to 41.42%), giving some potential support to the "extended recognition" reading.

Table 2. Translations published (2008–2021) by a selection of politically-committed publishers according to thematic axes. (*Data for 2021 reflect only publications until the end of June.)

| Year | Racial issues | Feminism / sexuality | Ecology/ climate | Labor issues | Political strategy |
|---|---|---|---|---|---|
| 2021* | 8 | 5 | 6 | 8 | 5 |
| 2020 | 10 | 5 | 19 | 12 | 12 |
| 2019 | 7 | 9 | 14 | 8 | 16 |
| 2018 | 5 | 8 | 15 | 13 | 10 |
| 2017 | 4 | 6 | 13 | 8 | 21 |
| 2016 | 5 | 6 | 12 | 16 | 14 |
| 2015 | 4 | 2 | 5 | 12 | 10 |
| 2014 | 5 | 1 | 2 | 19 | 14 |
| 2013 | 1 | 1 | 4 | 7 | 11 |
| 2012 | 0 | 1 | 2 | 9 | 12 |
| 2011 | 5 | 1 | 1 | 4 | 14 |
| 2010 | 1 | 3 | 0 | 5 | 7 |
| 2009 | 1 | 2 | 2 | 4 | 8 |
| 2008 | 1 | 2 | 1 | 5 | 6 |
| Total | 57 | 52 | 96 | 130 | 160 |

Nevertheless, a closer inspection of this data shows that the number of redistribution translations changes around 2014–2016, leading to an increased presence in publishers' catalogues. At a global level, these years were characterized by the emergence of some of the political tensions evoked above, which have led supporters of redistribution to their criticisms of other currents of the post-15M left. On the one hand, this period saw the emergence of important movements for recognition, such as Black Lives Matter (Lebron 2017), which campaigns against systemic racism and violence towards black people in the USA, and the global feminist movement *Ni Una Menos* ("Not even one [woman] less"), which started in Argentina in 2015 to protest against femicide and violence against women (Gago and Cavallero 2017). On the other hand, it was also a decisive moment of growing support for the nationalistic right-wing, with cases such as the Brexit referendum and Donald Trump's election in 2016. Therefore, it would be safe to hypothesize that this political scenario might have had an impact on later translation choices. In order to analyze this potential drive, Table 3 shows translational output only for 2015–2021, which represents exactly half of the period studied.

Table 3. Translations published (2015–2021) by a selection of politically committed publishers according to thematic axes. (*Data for 2021 reflect only publications until the end of June.)

| Year | Racial issues | Feminism / sexuality | Ecology/ climate | Labor issues | Political strategy |
|---|---|---|---|---|---|
| 2021* | 8 | 5 | 6 | 8 | 5 |
| 2020 | 10 | 5 | 19 | 12 | 12 |
| 2019 | 7 | 9 | 14 | 8 | 16 |
| 2018 | 5 | 8 | 15 | 13 | 10 |
| 2017 | 4 | 6 | 13 | 8 | 21 |
| 2016 | 5 | 6 | 12 | 16 | 14 |
| 2015 | 4 | 2 | 5 | 12 | 10 |
| Total | 43 | 41 | 84 | 77 | 88 |

This detailed snapshot of a shorter, and more recent, period provides a more nuanced understanding of publishing trends. Firstly, the difference in weighting between the redistribution and "pure recognition" categories has been reduced, although it remains substantial: 49.56% of the translations (redistribution) versus 25.12% (recognition). However, the trend is rather different when the "extended recognition" approach is taken into account, as the ecology category has a notable share of the total. By adding this category, the balance between blocs is reshaped: 49.56% (redistribution) versus 50.34% (extended recognition).

Finally, in order to further refine the analysis, Table 4 shows the specific thematic output for each publisher for the whole period. Although politically committed publishers share important characteristics and engagements, a publishing field is not simply an aggregation of companies, but a space in which different publishers have different editorial projects and follow different strategies

(Bourdieu 1989). Therefore, there is always a tension between the perceived "autonomy" of each publisher and the "constraints" of each field (Bourdieu 1999, 4). In fact, editorial policies play a key role in translation choices (Sapiro 2012, 2016), as publishers search for a balance between the dominating trends of their period and the necessity to differentiate themselves from other publishing houses.

Table 4. Translations published (2008–2021) by specific politically-committed publishers according to thematic axes

| Publisher | Racial issues | Feminism / sexuality | Ecology/ Climate | Labor issues | Political strategy |
| --- | --- | --- | --- | --- | --- |
| Akal | 12 | 3 | 1 | 37 | 33 |
| Capitán Swing | 28 | 29 | 29 | 42 | 39 |
| Errata Naturae | 0 | 1 | 42 | 4 | 25 |
| Pepitas de Calabaza | 2 | 0 | 12 | 14 | 30 |
| Traficantes de Sueños | 11 | 18 | 2 | 22 | 17 |
| Virus | 4 | 1 | 10 | 11 | 16 |
| Total | 57 | 52 | 96 | 130 | 160 |

Breaking down these data confirms some previous readings, yet also fine-tunes them. Firstly, with the exception of Errata Naturae, we see that the redistribution bloc is dominant for every publisher, ranging from 81.4% of translations published by Akal down to 48.5% in the catalogue of Capitán Swing. Secondly, only two publishers have devoted important attention to recognition issues: Traficantes de Sueños (41.43%) and Capitán Swing (34.13%), which is arguably the publisher with the most balanced distribution of topics across its listing. Finally, three publishers present noteworthy combinations between the ecological and the redistribution strands, a fact that casts doubt upon the validity of the "extended recognition" hypothesis: Errata Naturae (58.33% for ecology, 40.28% for redistribution), Pepitas de Calabaza (75.86% redistribution, 20.69% ecology), and Virus (64.29% redistribution, 23.81% ecology).

As suggested earlier, these choices must be understood in relation to the editorial policies and political engagements of each publishing house. Akal, the imprint with the highest ratio of redistribution translations, has also published key names within the group of critics of recognition, such as Víctor Lenore (2018), Esteban Hernández (2018b), and particularly Daniel Bernabé, whose *La trampa de la diversidad* (2018) was, as already noted, a key driving force behind the debate. In fact, upon the publication of Bernabé's second book (2020), he was presented as one of Akal's flagship authors by their editorial team (Akal 2020). Therefore, a certain homogeneity can be perceived between support for national and translated authors within the redistribution approach.

At the opposite end, Traficantes de Sueños, the publisher with the highest percentage of recognition translations, has repeatedly backed protest movements within this strand, such as the feminist strike – publicly supported by the publishing collective on several occasions (Traficantes de Sueños 2018a, 2019) – or Black Lives Matter. In 2017, Traficantes translated a history of the latter movement (Taylor 2017), which led to an extended series of book launches and talks with author Keeanga-Yamahtta Taylor in 2018 (Traficantes de Sueños 2018b). Similarly, in 2020 it released a collective book, written by Spanish activists, aimed at "learning from Black Lives Matter" (Rodríguez, Alabao and Pérez 2020). In a similar vein, Capitán Swing has devoted substantial attention to race issues and feminism since the beginning of its editorial activity (see Capitán Swing 2021b, 2021c for detailed listings).

Finally, the focus on ecology and climate change is strongly connected to the intellectual foundations of all three publishers involved, even though different readings are derived from these engagements. In Errata Naturae's case, its commitment to this area of political action finds its roots in an identification between nature, ecological awareness, and personal freedom, best symbolized through its prolonged attention to Henry David Thoreau's work. Errata Naturae's engagement with Thoreau – defined by the publishers as "a natural-born dissident" (Errata Naturae 2021c) – began in 2013 with a translation of his classic *Walden* (Thoreau 2013) and is manifested in six further translations, including a biography (Richardson 2017) and a commemorative edition of *Walden* with artworks (Thoreau 2017) on the bicentenary of Thoreau's birth. Meanwhile, in the case of Pepitas de Calabaza and Virus, their interest in political ecology is linked to an espousal of alternative modes of collective action that defy mainstream ideologies. While Pepitas has devoted greater attention to the relationship between ecology and a critique of modern industrial and technological civilization, particularly through authors such as Lewis Mumford (2013, 2017) and William Morris (2013), Virus has emphasized the relationship between cooperation, communal governance and ecology, in figures such as anarchist thinkers Murray Bookchin (2012, 2019) and Janet Biehl (2017, 2018).

Ultimately, this analysis of data for book translations across different axes leads us to reappraise the hypothesis that was being tested on the negative impact of a focus on recognition issues upon redistribution studies. Although the importance attributed to redistribution in publishing catalogues diminished slightly in the final stretch of the 2008–2021 period, it is still an area of clear and evident relevance for the majority of politically committed publishers studied. Furthermore, this change does not seem to be connected to a major surge in interest in "pure" recognition matters, such as feminism and racial/sexual identities, which remain relatively secondary despite their increasing presence after 2014–2016 (highlighted in Table 3). In fact, as Table 4 shows, this growth is driven mostly by two specific publishers (Traficantes de Sueños and Capitán Swing) and is not necessarily a shared trait within the field. Finally, the key reason for the slightly reduced visibility of redistribution issues lies in the tremendous growth of interest in ecology and climate change, particularly from 2015 onwards (84 of 96 translations under this label appeared during this later period). However, this should not necessarily be interpreted as a supporting argument for an opposition between ecology and redistribution, as data show that these categories can be combined for political purposes by certain publishers (such as Errata Naturae, Pepitas de Calabaza and Virus).

## Conclusions and future paths

In this chapter I have used a thematic analysis of book translation flows to shed light on the accuracy and pertinence of the argument put forward by those political actors who posited that the post-15M left in Spain devoted excessive attention to recognition matters (sexual and racial identities) to the detriment of advancing redistribution causes (labor and political strategies), traditionally espoused by the left. The underlying assumption of this analysis was the porosity between the cultural and the political fields after the 15M, particularly considering the dual role of politically committed publishers in this new context: since their catalogues are influenced by political events, and at the same time influence these events, they should bear traces of any relevant evolution within the political field.

In the light of data gathered in this research, this hypothesis does not seem to be fully accurate, at least in its current form and within the field studied. The idea that "the Spanish left" – a very broad and loose category – is embracing a given set of political preoccupations seems to be a generalization that is not widely supported. While it is true that recognition matters increased in importance in publishers' catalogues during the second half of the period studied, this drive has not indicated a major shift in the importance attributed to redistribution issues, which continue to dominate the choice of translations for most publishers, even in the case of those who attribute growing importance to recognition matters.

In fact, the reconfiguration of these blocs seems to support an argument posited by Fraser and Honneth (2003: 2–5), who defend the extent to which redistribution and recognition are enmeshed within the political arena and therefore highlight the difficulty of separating one from the other. In this sense, instead of viewing the rebalancing of these preoccupations within the intellectual field as a threat for the left, it could be argued – as Fraser and Honneth did (2003: 2) – that "an adequate understanding of justice" should encompass *both* "sets of concerns". Hence, growing attention to recognition within the publishing field could be interpreted to a certain extent as a perceived necessity by some publishers to devote more space and consideration to this side of social justice.

At the same time, as Slavoj Žižek has cleverly argued (2012), "every perception of a lack or a surplus ('not enough of this', 'too much of that')" in ideological discourses always requires a particular configuration of the symbolic universe that allows these lacks or surpluses to be seen and described as such. In other words, when Spanish critics of recognition claim that the post-15M left is paying "too much" attention to issues of racism, feminism or LGBT rights, there is no specific measure of assessment that allows them to make these claims, even if it is presented as self-evident from their ideological viewpoint. Therefore, a political analysis needs to go beyond this symbolic configuration and focus on concrete data in order to reveal to what extent these kinds of claims are correct or not.

In this sense, the impression that data analysis creates regarding critiques of recognition is one of exaggeration, a discursive technique that is often connected to parody – a feature that is obvious in some of the statements quoted earlier, such as Soto Ivars's and Guardingo's. As Judith Butler (1998: 33–34) has argued, a "parody of an intellectual position" requires "a prior affiliation with what one parodies", as parody is based on "a certain ability to identify, approximate, and draw near". Furthermore, Butler claims that "to enter into parody is to enter into a relationship of both desire and ambivalence", as "the one who performs the parody aspires, quite literally, to occupy the place of the one parodied". This argument sounds reasonably close to a description of the position of the redistribution supporters that were described earlier: a former proximity to the post-15M left combined with a determination to correct it and replace it with other political alternatives, which ultimately leads – as we have seen – to criticisms based upon exaggeration and parody of existing trends and strategies.

Finally, the emergence of ecology as a relevant partner for redistribution issues – as seen in the case of certain imprints within the chosen set – suggests that political struggles are constantly being redrawn in the light of evolving situations and challenges. Advocating an unaltered approach to political action over time, as Spanish supporters of redistribution seem to do, fails to take into account changes in the external conditions. In fact, the alliance between workers and ecologist movements had already been defended as necessary in the 1980s by one of the leading figures of Spanish Marxism, Manuel Sacristán (2005: 115–155) – a precedent that redistribution backers, closer in their positions to the Communist left, cannot possibly ignore.

Despite these important findings, however, it is evident that further lines of enquiry could be followed from here. While politically committed publishers have a central role to play in left-wing debates, they represent only a specific sector within the intellectual field. In order to further test this hypothesis, it would be potentially relevant to compare these data, for instance, with those from large corporate publishers, which are less sensitive to post-15M debates, but reach a wider circle of readers. Alternatively, a second route could be taken, comparing data for more established publishers within the political field – such as the ones studied in this chapter – with publishers that have emerged in recent years in order to check and compare potential disparities and different trajectories.

Finally, from the perspective of the study of translation flows, this chapter has confirmed the complexity of factors that influence the production and reception of book translations, as argued by Heilbron and Sapiro (2016: 383–397), among others. As demonstrated, global and national events, such as the emergence of strong movements for recognition in recent years, have an impact on the thematic choices of Spanish publishers: for instance, the number of book translations on recognition issues have generally grown in accordance with external events that condition political debates. At the same time, however, it has been proved that each publishing house follows a specific path, based upon its editorial policies (Sapiro 2012, 2016) and its own political engagements, which makes translation trends far less predictable than could be initially hypothesized: each publisher devotes varying degrees of attention to existing topics and combines them in particular ways. In this sense, this specific case study has also shown how translation flows can help to understand the different shapes that a political debate can assume within a cultural field, providing a quantitative basis that grounds and locates qualitative analysis within a specific context.

## References

 Abramitzky, Ran and Isabelle Sin. 2014. "Book Translations as Idea Flows: The Effects of the Collapse of Communism on the Diffusion of Knowledge." *Journal of the European Economic Association* 12(6): 1453–1520.

Akal. 2020. "La distancia del presente." Accessed October 11, 2021. https://www.akal.com/libro/la-distancia-del-presente_50882/.

Akal. 2021a. "Cuestiones de antagonismo." Accessed October 11, 2021. https://www.akal.com/coleccion/cuestiones-de-antagonismo/.

Akal. 2021b. "Pensamiento crítico." Accessed October 11, 2021. https://www.akal.com/coleccion/pensamiento-critico/.

Antentas, Josep Maria. 2017. "Spain: from the Indignados Rebellion to Regime Crisis (2011–2016)." *Labor History* 58 (1): 2–26.

Batalla, Pablo. 2018. "Entrevista a Daniel Bernabé". *El Cuaderno Digital*, September. https://elcuadernodigital.com/2018/09/10/entrevista-a-daniel-bernabe/

Baumgarten, Britta. 2013. "Geração à Rasca and beyond: Mobilizations in Portugal after 12 March 2011." *Current Sociology* 61 (4): 457–473.

Bernabé, Daniel. 2018. *La trampa de la diversidad*. Madrid: Akal.

Bernabé, Daniel. 2019. "Daniel Bernabé: 'Toda esta fiebre verde valdrá para que los trabajadores paguen los platos rotos'." *La Marea*, 25 September, 2019. https://www.lamarea.com/2019/09/25/daniel-bernabe-toda-esta-fiebre-verde-valdra-para-que-los-trabajadores-paguen-los-platos-rotos/

Bernabé, Daniel. 2020. *La distancia del presente. Auge y crisis de la democracia española (2010–2020)*. Madrid: Akal.

Biehl, Janet. 2017. *Ecología o catástrofe. La vida de Murray Bookchin*. Translated by Paula Martín Ponz. Barcelona: Virus.

Biehl, Janet. 2018. *Las políticas de la ecología social*. Translated by Colectividad Los Arenalejos. Barcelona: Virus.

Bookchin, Murray. 2012. *Anarquismo social o anarquismo personal*. Translated by Roser Bosch. Barcelona: Virus.

Bookchin, Murray. 2019. *La próxima revolución*. Translated by Paula Martín Ponz. Barcelona: Virus.

Bourdieu, Pierre. 1989. "Les conditions sociales de la circulation internationale des idées." In *L'espace intellectuel en Europe*, ed. Gisèle Sapiro [2009], 27–39. Paris: La Découverte.

Bourdieu, Pierre. 1999. "Une révolution conservatrice dans l'édition." *Actes de la Recherche en Sciences Sociales* 126–127: 3–28.

Brisset, Annie, and Bertrand Aye. 2007. *Translation and Cultural Diversity: Report on World Translation Flows*. Paris: UNESCO.

Brisset, Annie, and Raúl Colón. 2020. "World Translation Flows: Preferred Languages and Subjects." In *The Routledge Handbook of Translation and Globalization*, eds. Esperança Bielsa and Dionysios Kapsaskis, 230–250. London: Routledge.

Butler, Judith. 1998. "Merely Cultural." *New Left Review* 227: 33–44.

Capitán Swing. 2021a. "Ensayo." Accessed October 11, 2021. https://capitanswing.com/ensayo/.

Capitán Swing. 2021b. "Black Power." Accessed October 11, 2021. https://capitanswing.com/tematicas/black-power/.

Capitán Swing. 2021c. "Feminismo." Accessed October 11, 2021. https://capitanswing.com/tematicas/feminismo/.

De Swaan, Abram. 1993. "The Emergent World Language System: An Introduction." *International Political Science Review* 14(3): 219–226.

Delclós, Carlos. 2015. *Hope is a Promise. From the Indignados to the Rise of Podemos in Spain*. Ebook. London: Zed Books.

Della Porta, Donatella. 2015. *Social Movements in Times of Austerity*. Cambridge: Polity Press.

Douzinas, Costas. 2013. *Philosophy and Resistance in the Crisis*. Cambridge: Polity Press.

Echevarría, Ignacio. 2012. "La CT: un cambio de paradigma." In *CT o la Cultura de la Transición. Crítica a 35 años de cultura Española*, ed. by Guillem Martínez, 25–36. Barcelona: Mondadori.

Errata Naturae. 2021a. "La muchacha de dos cabezas." Accessed October 11, 2021. https://erratanaturae.com/product-category/la-muchacha-de-dos-cabezas/.

Errata Naturae. 2021b. "Libros salvajes." Accessed October 11, 2021. https://erratanaturae.com/product-category/libros-salvajes/.

Errata Naturae. 2021c. "Henry David Thoreau." Accessed October 11, 2021. https://erratanaturae.com/autores/henry-david-thoreau/.

Even-Zohar, Itamar. 1990. "The Position of Translated Literature within the Literary Polysystem." *Poetics Today* 11 (1): 45–51.

Fernández, Fruela. 2020. "Tool-box, Tradition, and Capital: Political Uses of Translation in Contemporary Spanish Politics." *Translation Studies* 13 (3): 352–368.

Fernández, Fruela. 2021. *Translating the Crisis. Politics and Culture in Spain after the 15M*. Abingdon: Routledge.

Flesher Fominaya, Cristina. 2015. "Redefining the Crisis/Redefining Democracy: Mobilizing for the Right to Housing in Spain's PAH Movement." *South European Society and Politics* 20 (4): 465–485.

Fraser, Nancy and Axel Honneth. 2003. *Redistribution or Recognition? A Political-philosophical Exchange*. Translated by Joel Golb, James Ingram, and Christiane Wilke. London: Verso Books.

Gago, Verónica and Luci Cavallero. 2017. "Argentina's Life-or-Death Women's Movement." *Jacobin*, 7 March, 2017. https://www.jacobinmag.com/2017/03/argentina-ni-una-menos-femicides-women-strike/.

Gerbaudo, Paolo. 2017. *The Mask and the Flag. Populism, Citizenism and Global Protest*. London: Hurst.

Guardingo, Óscar. 2021. "La izquierda menguante contra Daniel Bernabé y Ana Iris Simón." *Vozpópuli*, 12 September. https://www.vozpopuli.com/altavoz/cultura/izquierda-daniel-bernabe-ana-iris-simon.html

Heilbron, Johan. 1999. "Towards a Sociology of Translation: Book Translations as a Cultural World-System." *European Journal of Social Theory* 2(4): 429–444.

Heilbron, Johan and Gisèle Sapiro. 2016. "Translation: Economic and Sociological Perspectives." In *The Palgrave Handbook of Economics and Language*, ed. By Victor Ginsburgh and Shlomo Weber, 373–402. London: Palgrave.

Hernández, Esteban. 2018a. "El Vox de la izquierda (y el regreso de los viejos partidos)." *El Confidencial*, September 14, 2018. https://blogs.elconfidencial.com/espana/postpolitica/2018-09-14/vox-izquierda-monereo-anguita-partidos-viejos_1615706/

Hernández, Esteban. 2018b. *El tiempo pervertido. Derecha e izquierda en el siglo XXI*. Madrid: Akal.

Holmes, Marcus. 2015. "Believing This and Alieving That: Theorizing Affect and Intuitions in International Politics." *International Studies Quarterly* 59 (4): 706–20.

Joint Research Centre. 2019. *Understanding Our Political Nature. How To Put Knowledge and Reason at the Heart of Political Decision-Making*. Luxembourg: Publications Office of the European Union.

Laclau, Ernesto and Chantal Mouffe. 1985. *Hegemony and Socialist Strategy*. London: Verso Books.

Lebron, Christopher. 2017. *The Making of Black Lives Matter: A Brief History of an Idea*. Oxford: Oxford University Press.

Lenore, Víctor. 2018. *Espectros de la movida. Por qué odiar los años 80*. Madrid: Akal.

Linn, Stella. 2006. "Trends in the Translation of a Minority Language: The Case of Dutch." In *Sociocultural Aspects of Translating and Interpreting*, ed. by Anthony Pym, Miriam Shlesinger, and Zuzana Jettmarová, 27–39. Amsterdam: John Benjamins.

Loogus, Terje and Luc Van Doorslaer. 2021. 'Assisting Translations in Border Crossing: An Analysis of the Traducta Translation Grants in Estonia'. *Translation Spaces* (online preprint).

Morris, William. 2013. *Cómo vivimos y cómo podríamos vivir*. Translated by Federico Corriente. Logroño: Pepitas de Calabaza.

Mumford, Lewis. 2013. *Historia de las utopías*. Translated by Diego Luis Sanromán. Logroño: Pepitas de Calabaza.

Mumford, Lewis. 2017. *El mito de la máquina. Técnica y evolución humana*. Translated by Arcadio Rigodón. Logroño: Pepitas de Calabaza.

Noël, Sophie. 2012. *L'édition indépendante critique: engagements politiques et intellectuels*. Lyon: Presses de l'Enssib.

Pepitas de Calabaza. 2021. "Ensayo." Accessed October 11, 2021. https://www.pepitas.net/catalogo/ensayo.

Popa, Ioana. 2010. *Traduire sous contraintes. Littérature et communisme*. Paris: CNRS Éditions.

Razquin, Adriana. 2017. *Didáctica ciudadana: la vida política en las plazas. Etnografía del movimiento 15M*. Granada: Universidad de Granada.

Richardson, Robert. 2017. *Thoreau. Biografía de un pensador salvaje*. Translated by Esther Cruz. Madrid: Errata Naturae.

Rivero, Jacobo. 2015. *Podemos. Objetivo: asaltar los cielos*. Barcelona: Planeta.

Rodríguez, Emmanuel. 2020. "La fase de absorción o el gobierno progresista." *Ctxt*, February 10, 2020. https://ctxt.es/es/20200203/Firmas/30955/gobierno-de-coalicion-15M-podemos-emmanuel-rodriguez.htm

Rodríguez, Fernanda, Nuria Alabao, and Marisa Pérez. 2020. "Lo que aprendemos de Black Lives Matter." *Traficantes de Sueños*, August 2, 2020. https://www.traficantes.net/resena/lo-que-aprendemos-de-black-lives-matter

Romanos, Eduardo. 2018. "Immigrants as Brokers: Dialogical Diffusion From Spanish Indignados to Occupy Wall Street." *Social Movements Studies* 15 (3): 247–262.

Sacristán, Manuel. 2005. *Seis conferencias. Sobre la tradición marxista y los nuevos problemas*. Barcelona: El Viejo Topo.

Sapiro, Gisèle. 2012. "*Editorial Policy* and Translation." In *Handbook of Translation Studies*, ed. by Yves Gambier and Luc van Doorslaer, 32–38. Amsterdam: John Benjamins.

Sitrin, Marina and Dario Azzellini. 2014. *They can't represent us! Reinventing democracy from Greece to Occupy*. London: Verso Books.

Sorá, Gustavo. 2003. *Traducir el Brasil. Una antropología de la circulación internacional de las ideas*. Buenos Aires: Libros del Zorzal.

Soto Ivars, Juan. 2020. "Minneápolis, provincia de Barcelona". *El Periódico*, June 8th. https://www.elperiodico.com/es/opinion/20200608/minneapolis-provincia-de-barcelona-por-juan-soto-ivars-7991274

Taylor, Keeanga-Yamahtta. 2017. *Un destello de libertad. De #blacklivesmatter a la liberación negra*. Translated by Ezequiel Gatto. Madrid: Traficantes de Sueños.

Thoreau, Henry David. 2013. *Walden*. Translated by Marcos Nava. Madrid: Errata Naturae.

Thoreau, Henry David. 2017. *Walden. Edición ilustrada*. Translated by Marcos Nava. Madrid: Errata Naturae.

Traficantes de Sueños. 2018a. "*Y después del 8M, ¿qué? Propuestas para un programa económico feminista*." Accessed October 11, 2021. https://www.traficantes.net/nociones-comunes/y-despu%C3%A9s-del-8m-%C2%BFqu%C3%A9.

Traficantes de Sueños. 2018b. "*Keeanga-Yamahtta Taylor: Un destello de libertad. Del #BlackLivesMatter a la liberación negra*". Accessed October 11, 2021. https://traficantes.net/actividad/keeanga-yamahtta-taylor-%C2%ABun-destello-de-libertad-del-blacklivesmatter-la-liberaci%C3%B3n-negra%C2%BB.

Traficantes de Sueños. 2019. "8M 2019 Huelga feminista." Accessed October 11, 2021. https://www.traficantes.net/node/198938.

Traficantes de Sueños. 2021. "Catálogo." Accessed October 11, 2021. https://www.traficantes.net/editorial.

Urquizu, Ignacio. 2016. *La crisis de representación en España*. Madrid: Libros de la Catarata.

Virus. 2021. "Catálogo." Accessed October 11, 2021. https://www.viruseditorial.net/ca/editorial/catalogo.

Žižek, Slavoj. 2012. "INTRODUCTION The Spectre of Ideology". In *Mapping Ideology*, ed. by Slavoj Žižek. Ebook. London: Verso Books.

CHAPTER 5

# From intersection to interculture
## How the classical Ottoman intercultural scene came to be*

Sare Rabia Öztürk
Boğaziçi University

The present chapter explores some of the pre-Ottoman cultural dynamics in the Middle East that led to the meeting of Turkish, Arabic and Persian as densely intercrossing languages in the formation of the classical Ottoman cultural sphere. It aims to chart the movement of people, knowledge, customs, practices and centers of power across the Middle East in a historical survey that will offer a networked flow of such movements and highlight the place of translation in the process. It roughly covers the period from the 5th century to the 14th century, which is about a hundred years into the start of the Ottoman empire in the region.

The central premise is that the historical flows between the three cultures associated with Arabic, Persian and Turkish led to the classical Ottoman setting of *interculture* (Paker 2002), whereby Ottoman translators engaged with Persian and Arabic as both source languages and language components of an Ottoman epistemic discourse. It highlights the degree to which cultural input can be influenced by intercultural transfers in several domains such as science, literature, bureaucracy, education and religion.

**Keywords:** intersection, Ottoman interculture, transfer map, network, flow

## Introduction

The Ottoman culture was home to a multiplicity of ethnicities and languages. In the classical era of the empire (14th to 17th century) and the centuries that led to it, Turkish, Persian and Arabic were prominent languages (used in varying

---

* A note on transliterations: The transliteration of Turkish and Arabic words is conducted in accordance with the IJMES transliteration system. For proper names (persons or institutions) with self-proclaimed English transliterations, the preferred transliteration is retained.

degrees and regardless of the ethnicities of their users) in certain domains such as religion, science, education, bureaucracy and literature.[1] The present chapter explores some of the cultural dynamics in the Middle East prior to the establishment of the Ottoman state which paved the way for the classical Ottoman setting of *interculture* (Paker 2002) whereby Ottoman translators engaged with Persian and Arabic as both source languages and language components of an Ottoman epistemic discourse. Inspired largely by Anthony Pym's idea of *transfer maps* (2014), it aims to chart the movement of people, knowledge, customs, practices and positions of power across the Middle East in a historical survey that will offer a networked flow of such movements and highlight the place of translation in the process.

## The Ottoman interculture

The notion of *interculture* serves to highlight the dynamics of exchange and hybridity that underlie cultural formations. By briefly presenting the following arguments about the notion, it is intended to arrive at an understanding of interculture that considers both boundary-crossing (transfer) and intercrossing (the formation of hybrid entities). Based on the following discussion, intercultures can be regarded as sites of operation for cultural mediators that, while working toward one culture, engage the other culture(s) in the whole process, making them constituents of the final product.

Anthony Pym (1993, 2000, 2014 [1998]) proposes the notion of interculture as a way of situating actors who are engaged in cultural transfer in a place of overlap between the source and target cultures, rather than being in either one of them. Adopting a systemic,[2] target-oriented view of translation, Gideon Toury responds to the idea of interculture, situating such sites of operation not between the interacting cultures but within the target system, either as a general part of it or one that has been "crystallized into an autonomous (target!) systemic entity" (1995: 28). Saliha Paker argues that such a process of crystallization was evident by the 16th century Ottoman cultural setting, whereby Ottoman Turkish, in the "literary-epistemic domain" (2002: 138) had, on the one hand, absorbed Persian

---

1. For more information see Paker (1998).
2. Toury's systemic view can be traced back to Itamar Even-Zohar's work on culture, in which the latter offers a relational perspective that links cultural products with surrounding factors. From this point of view, translational or transferal phenomena are embedded in systemic entities (source and target systems) that interact to create their products. See Even-Zohar 1990, 2010 for further information.

and Arabic as linguistic components and, on the other, interacted with them as source languages. This, Paker argues, resulted in practices of transfer that did not necessarily fit into modern understandings of translation and originality, bringing source and target together in a process of cultural production that went beyond substitution.

Such hybrid language and practices of transfer, as evidenced in Mahmut Tokaç's (2006) study on medical manuscripts written in, or translated into, Ottoman Turkish was not confined to the literary domain – an issue which invites further investigation into the historical conditions that netted together the three cultures associated with these languages and generated the intercultural condition of classical Ottoman intellectual production. This chapter explores some of the cultural dynamics in the Middle East that set the scene for the "Ottoman interculture" (Paker 2002:137) in which translators of the classical era engaged with Persian and Arabic as both source languages and language components of an Ottoman epistemic discourse. Of course, neither the Ottoman culture nor the cultural settings that preceded it were shaped solely through the interaction of two or three languages, and the language variety far exceeded that number in most of the cases. The three languages in question are addressed in this chapter not as the sole components of the cultural scene, but as the dominant linguistic elements that comprised the syntax of scientific, literary, educational and bureaucratic discourses.

## Translation history and transfer maps

Pym proposes a method for translation history that is based on restoring historical networks of relations through establishing what he refers to as "transfer maps" (2014:92). He notes that

> ... the networks most pertinent to translation seem likely not to be limited to any one culture. They might be expected to relate points in different cultures (cross-cultural links) and to develop in social settings shared by two or more cultures (intercultural groups). (Pym 2014:91)

He suggests that by correlating events, people and transferred goods in a historical setting, it becomes possible to make visible some parts of an underlying network. He also notes the importance of including "nontranslational modes of transfer" (2014:92) in histories of translation for a better understanding of certain undercurrents, noting that by so doing we would be "mapping movements instead of stable boundaries" (ibid.).

He breaks movement (which would be represented as lines in a visual map) down to *object transfers* (the movement of texts) and *subject transfers* (the movement of people who make possible the object transfers). Another component of Pym's map is what he calls *changeover points*. These indicate acts of transfer (translation) which would appear as nodes on a line that traces the movement of an object from source to target culture. Finally, a transfer map is bound to have *terra incognita*, i.e. "blank spaces that ... [indicate] an absence of contemporary knowledge" (2014: 101) about past events. Acknowledging blank spaces is an act of reflexivity which reminds readers of historical accounts that the writing of history is never a finalized process.

Inspired largely by Pym's idea of transfer maps, the present chapter aims to follow the movement of people, knowledge, customs, practices, and positions of power across the Middle East from around the 5th century and moving into the early Ottoman period (13th century), stopping roughly about the 14th century (which marks the beginning of its classical era). To draw a comprehensive map of cultural transfers, but also to avoid closing off the narrative account to other historical possibilities, the following part of the chapter is divided into two sections, which are structured differently. The first section aims to capture certain nodes in the development of such history from around the 5th century (in which the Roman and Persian empires provided the setting for the different cultural flows) until the flourishing of Baghdad as an intellectual center during the 9th century under Abbasid rule. In this section, the emphasis will be on the networked flow of knowledge through the gathering and shifting of groups of specialized people (mostly scholars and physicians) and their translational activities (subject and object transfers).

The second section establishes the *Abbasid context* as an umbrella condition that is comprised of the many Islamic states (including Persian and Turkic political entities) which entered the historical scene while the Abbasid caliphate was still considered to be a central authority in the region. In this section, complex flows of cultural influence and political power that were activated through other groups of specialized people (mostly Persian intelligentsia and Turkic slave warriors) will be discussed in the light of their impact on translational activities and language use in cultural production (another set of subject and object transfers). Certain *changeover points* will also be addressed in which cultural influence and political power switched over from one group to another across time and space. One thing to note is that while Pym is interested in the transfer of "things that are material rather than mental" (2014: 92, footnote), the present chapter also highlights the transfer of knowledge, cultural practices and positions of power.

## Connecting dots, charting flows

From pre-Islamic encounters to the Baghdad School

The Roman-Persian wars that were waged over the first six centuries of the Gregorian calendar inaugurated many of the dynamics that led to the intersection of the three cultures in question. With the emergence of Islam in the sixth century in the Arabian Peninsula and its subsequent spread to the Middle East, North Africa and beyond, the cultural flow gained momentum, geared by complex shifts of power among the many actors in the region.

*Pre-Islamic encounters*

During the 5th and 6th centuries the conflicts between Persian and Roman empires were carried out into the Arabian Peninsula. Arab peoples such as the Jafnids and the Naṣrids began to feature in this context as allies to one or the other of the conflicting parties. They fought in these armies and many converted to Christianity under the influence of the Romans (Fisher and Wood 2016; Fisher 2011). Around that time, Turkic tribes such as the Eftalites featured as part of the same conflict in the Eurasian Steppe, siding with and fighting for/against Persians or Romans. Such context was an early instance of intersection for the four cultures, and an "indirect" (Cihan 2015: 92, my translation) or mediated meeting point between Arabs and Turks. One upshot of this encounter was that Arab poets of the pre-Islamic era would describe in their poetry aspects of Turkish bravery witnessed by Arab soldiers as both took part in regional wars. One aspect of *transculturation*[3] (to borrow from Tymoczko 2014) from this era was that certain martial practices which Turkic people employed, such as tying the swords to the belts, were adopted by the Persians (Cihan 2015).

The region was also home to certain religio-linguistic and socio-political encounters. Christians of the "Syro-Mesopotamian steppe" (Fisher 2011: 34) were called Syriac regardless of their origin, and the Syriac dialect (a branch of Aramaic) was used to distinguish Aramaic Christians from pagans of the same origin (Qazānjī 2010; Çelik 2010). Persians were also familiar with Aramaic. Darius I (r. 522–486 BC) of the Persian Achaemenid Empire facilitated the use of this language, widely spoken at the conquered lands of the ancient Near East, for "effective diplomatic communication among the provinces of the empire" (Bae 2004: 16). Moreover, the region was home to Arab migrants in the 6th century, Christians from southern Arabia and Yemen who were fleeing from pressure by

---

3. The term refers to the process through which units of transfer that are not necessarily verbal are integrated into the receiving culture.

the Jewish Ḥimyarite king, Dhū Nuwās. These migrants helped spread Arabic in the region (Qazānjī 2010).

*From Alexandria to Jundishapur*

The Alexandrian library under Greek patronage was an important destination for knowledge, preserved in Greek translation, from various sources (Montgomery 2000). From Alexandria, a complex transfer map can be drawn all the way to the ancient city of Jundishapur, which would further illuminate the pathways to the intersection of the three cultures under discussion.

Under the Roman rule, a group of Nestorian Christians were clustered in Mesopotamia, far from the Roman capital and from the orthodoxy of the center. These Christians who spoke Syriac were also versed in Greek. The learned among them brought to this region much of the philosophy and science of the Alexandrian corpus by translating them into Syriac. Among the prominent translators of the era was Sergius of Reshaina (d. 536), a Mesopotamian physician who translated into Syriac works by Galen, Aristotle and Hippocrates (Luttikhuizen 2005; Modanlou 2011; Nacmâbâdî 2017). Scott Montgomery notes at this point a shifting of power (what this chapter regards as changeover points) between Greek, Syriac and later Arabic:

> ... translation proved to be the means by which Syriac became a true competitor to Greek as a language of knowledge embodiment and transfer. And it is exactly this maturation, whose total product was a language that retained its Semitic qualities while adopting many Greek elements, that made Syriac the very logical, indeed inevitable, intermediary between Greek and Arabic later on.     (2000:71)

In the 5th century, many members of this community moved out of the Roman territory into Persian lands, settling in the multicultural city of Jundishapur, where they were encouraged under the patronage of the Sassanian kings to practice their scholarship and apply the medical knowledge that they had accumulated beforehand (Montgomery 2000; Miller 2006; Luttikhuizen 2005; Aydınlı 2007; Qazānjī 2010). In the 6th century the city saw another wave of emigration, this time from Athens, by members of the Platonic Academy after it faced Roman "imperial pressure" (Blumenthal 1978:369). Gradually, the intellectual components of the schools of Alexandria and Athens were more or less transferred to this new center, a factor which expanded its intellectual capacity.

The Persian king-patrons of Jundishapur were keen to include in the multicultural community of scholarship the knowledge of Indian culture and medicine through translation. Greco-Syriac and Indian knowledge were translated into Pahlavi, which also saw its golden age in this period. Greek, Pahlavi and Syriac were three main languages through which scholarly and scientific activities were carried out in Jundishapur (Qazānjī 2010; Luttikhuizen 2005; Uslu 1993; Söylemez 2005). By the 6th century, past a stream of subject and object transfers and changeover points, Jundishapur was living its golden age. It had a medical complex consisting of a *bimaristan* (hospital), a medical school, "a pharmacology laboratory, a translation bureau, a library, and an observatory" (Söylemez 2005:1).

*From Jundishapur to Baghdad*

The Sassanid rule came to an end in the 7th century through Islamic conquest. Nevertheless, the Jundishapur academy maintained its importance as a center for teaching medicine and was administered by the Nestorian physician members of the Bakhtishu family.

The Abbasid caliphate ascended to the throne in the 8th century and soon made Baghdad its capital. The Nestorians of the region, near the new capital, facilitated the transfer of Greco-Syriac knowledge into Arabic. In 765, Jirjis ibn Bakhtishu, who was administering the Jundishapur school at the time, was summoned to the court of the Abbasid caliph al-Manṣūr to cure him of an illness. This incident initiated the gradual transfer of the Jundishapur scientific knowledge (and with that, its intellectual power and status) into Baghdad, a process which manifested an intensity of changeover points. The Jundishapur scholars transferred not only their practice, but also their accumulated knowledge of science and philosophy into the new capital through translation. Beside its status as capital of the new caliphate, Baghdad rose as a scholarly center that was modeled after Jundishapur. The intellectual activity in the city gained momentum during the reign of Caliph al-Ma'mūn (r. 813–833) with the acceleration of translational activity (Aydınlı 2007). Greek, Syriac, Pahlavi and Sanskrit provided source-language material to be translated into Arabic. Besides being a powerful language of poetry, Arabic had now become the language of science and would continue to be so even in non-Arabic Muslim regions (in our case the Seljuk and Ottoman lands) (Fazlıoğlu 2003).

Several mediators were active in this era. Around the Nestorian physician and pharmacologist Yūḥannā ibn Māsawayh (l. 777–857) a group of students of science gathered who were also translators. Among them were the Muslim mathematician al-Ḥajjāj ibn Yūsuf ibn Maṭar, the Sabian scholar Thābit ibn Qurrah, the Greek scientist Qusṭā ibn Lūqā, and the Nestorian physician Ḥunayn ibn Isḥaq (l. 809–873), who was placed in charge of translational activity in Baghdad in 830 (Tschanz 2003; Söylemez 2005). Ḥunayn was a prominent mediator whose meticulous work and dedication, along with the strong patronage of the Baghdad aristocracy, would open the door to massive intellectual activity in the region. He travelled to get hold of available Greek sources of knowledge and demonstrated meticulous care in selecting from existing copies of his sources (Ṭāhā 1976; Tschanz 2003; Tanrıverdi 2007). Together with his students, Ḥunayn accomplished the "monumental task of rendering in Arabic and Syriac all of the most important Greek medical texts written over a millennium" (Tschanz 2003: 39). He contributed to the field of medicine with the works he authored himself and he accelerated the further movement of science in the East and the West. The question-and-answer method he used in composing *al-Masāil fī al-Ṭibb li al-Muta'allimīn* (questions on medicine for students) was used in conducting entrance exams for medical students, a tradition that was carried well into the Seljuk era (Sadeghi, Ghaffari and Alizadeh 2018; Terzioğlu 2005).

The scientific and scholarly activities that left their mark on these centuries ushered in what came to be known as the Islamic Golden Age of socio-cultural and intellectual growth. It would last until the siege of Baghdad in 1258 under the Mongol ruler Hulagu Khan (Hemmings 2019).

The Abbasid context

The Abbasid context is used in this section as an umbrella term to cover the many Islamic states (including Persian and Turkic political entities) that emerged while the Abbasid caliphate was still considered to be a more or less central authority in the region, even though such authority was reduced to a symbolic one after the events of 1258.[4] The three cultures in question will be addressed in pairs: with each pair, the third component will be left momentarily in the background as a reminder of the impossibility of a perfect and neat weaving of history in one single account. The discussion does not focus on the Abbasid context to the exclusion of the Islamic period that preceded it. Contextual dynamics that pertain to the Rāshidūn caliphate (r. 632–661) or the Umayyad dynasty (r. 661–1031)[5] also form parts of the transfer map.

*Arabs and Persians*

The Arab conquest expanded to Persian territory during the reign of the Rāshidūn caliphate and with the expansion came the encounter with Persian administrative practices in the newly acquired lands. Some such practices and the lower-ranking officials who applied them were retained, a factor which facilitated the transfer and consequent development of the Persian documentation practice known as

---

4. For more information see Yıldız (1988).
5. The reign of the Abbasids did not erase the Umayyad presence (albeit diminishing its authority considerably in the Middle East) and they continued to coexist until the early 11th century. For more information see Martinez (2008).

*dīwān* into the Arabic and eventually non-Arabic Muslim context as part of an established governmental and administrative system (Yarshater 1998).

During the Umayyad and the early Abbasid eras, the *kuttāb* (secrateries) class of mostly Persian origin were effective in shaping the formative aspect of Muslim Arab civilization, notably in the realm of "caliphal court etiquette and Arabic prose literature" (Yarshater 1998: 57–58). Two of the *kuttābs* who stood out as cultural mediators in the period were 'Abd al-Ḥamīd al-Kātib' (who endowed the emerging administrative language with elements from the Sassanid culture) and 'Abdullah ibn al-Muqaffa' (ibid.), a Persian convert to Islam who had an important role in shaping Arabic literary prose through the language he used when rendering into Arabic the famous Indian fable *Kalīla and Dimna* from its Pahlavi translation (Lunde 2011).

On the other hand, the Arab culture provided Persian members of the Abbasid region with transcultural elements which they in turn integrated into their social profile. The Persian family of *kuttābs* known as al-Barāmika (the Barmakids), who were highly influential in the Abbasid court, adopted characteristics of Arab Bedouin social manners such as *karam* (generosity) and were famous for this (Goiten and Sourdel in Fawzī 2009).

An important issue to note at this point is the Arabization of the *dīwān* corpora that began in 700 CE under the Umayyads, a line of movement and transfer which saw another stream of changeover points. Fārūq 'Umar Fawzī notes that the Arabization of the *dīwān* corpora contributed greatly to the ultimate Arabization of the Islamic region. He considers this step "the first systematic translation movement from regional languages" (2009: 217, my translation)[6] and a step towards the ensuing transfer of ancient Greek knowledge (mainly during the Abbasid era).

Eventually, Arabization led to the decline of Persian, which gradually lost its "clerical status" (al-Durūbī 2017: 41, my translation)[7] and its position as an official language. However, it made a comeback as a literary language with the rise of the Persian Sunni Muslim Samanid dynasty (r. 819–999) in Transoxania and Khurāsān. Literary input in Persian was encouraged under Samanid sponsorship, a feature which was carried out into the Gazhnavid and Seljuk eras (both with Turkic roots). Moreover, works from other fields that were composed in Arabic were transferred into the Persian intellectual system. Among them was Muḥammad ibn Jarīr al-Ṭabarī's famous *Tārīkh al-Rusul wa al-Mulūk* (history of messengers and kings), translated into Persian by the Samanid vizier and intellectual Abū 'Alī al-Bal'amī (ibid.).

---

6. Original statement: "أول حركة ترجمة منظمة من اللغات الإقليمية".
7. Original statement: "وفقدت مركزها الكتابي".

Such lines of transfer as the ones illustrated above chart not only the changing over of certain cultural items or elements (texts; administrative, social and linguistic customs), but also the transfers of cultural influence and political power along the intricate routes taken in the transfer of numerous subjects and objects.

*Arabs and Turks*

With the expansion of Muslim territory under Arab rule into Iran and Khurāsān in the 7th century, an important instance of subject transfer in the military realm took place, namely the integration of Turkic slave warriors into the Arab army. During the late 7th-century Umayyad era, the governor of Khurāsān Sa'īd ibn 'Uthman incorporated Turkic captive soldiers from Samarqand into his army. His predecessor 'Ubaydullah ibn Ziyād had settled in Basra a group of 2,000 Turkic archers who were captured in Bukhara (Akyürek 2013; Cihan 2015; Aksu 2008). The Turkish presence in the Muslim Arab army grew in the Abbasid era into a systematically organized military faction that came to be known as the *mamlūk* [slave] soldiers. These soldiers went on to acquire high military and political status and eventually built their own province, the Mamluk sultanate, in the 13th century in a vast territory that extended from Egypt to southern Anatolia (Kızıltoprak 2004).

Before that, however, two other Turkish powers from a *mamlūk* background ruled over parts of Arab-Muslim lands, namely the Ṭūlūnid (r. 868–905) and the Ikhshidid/Akşit (r. 935–969) dynasties. The first was established by Tolunoğlu Ahmet (Aḥmad ibn Tūlūn), a *mamlūk* commander who was appointed by the Abbasid court as governor of Egypt and succeeded in turning it into an independent state that was ruled for forty years by members of the Tolun/Ṭūlūn family. Ibn Tūlūn ushered in a cultural revival in Egypt and was interested in medical development (Durant 1988; Çapan 2019). Though the ruling class was of Turkic origin in this instance, they constituted a minority and Arabic was the official language (Alican, 2016). The second dynasty was established by another *mamlūk* commander, Muhammed bin Tuğç (Muḥammad ibn Tughch), who was appointed governor of Egypt and, like Ibn Tūlūn, turned it into an independent state. The Ikhsidids were also interested in cultural and scientific progress and contributed to the development of medical facilities and practices (Ağırakça 2000; 'Awaḍ 2009).

Turkish began to gain importance with the rise of the Mamluk sultanate, which came to power after the Ayyubid dynasty (ca. 1171–1260), the latter having branched out from the Zengid *atabegs*[8] of the Seljuk sultanate and replaced the Fatimid dynasty in Arab lands. The Ayyubids had brought south Kipchak and

---

8. An official title for provincial governance.

Caucasian Turks who would become, in accordance with the geo-political norms of the region, *mamlūk* soldiers. In time, political power switched over to these soldiers who would rule over Egypt, Syria and the Hijaz region of Arabia (Yiğit 2004). Moreover, it was through one of the Mamluk sultans, al-Ẓāhir Baybars, that the Abbasid caliphate was restored after the 1258 calamity, an act which would endow Baybars as a Muslim ruler with power and legitimacy in the region (Yıldız 1988).

The ruling class mostly spoke Turkish among themselves, but they were keen to acquaint young *mamlūks* with Arabic (al-Durūbī 2017). On the other hand, learning Turkish was facilitated for the Arabic-speaking populace through the grammar books and dictionaries that constituted part of the cross-cultural production of the time (Eckmann 1963). Moreover, the government chancery used translation actively and the officials learned to speak Turkish for diplomatic purposes. At the chancery, letters would arrive and be sent in both Turkish and Arabic. Moreover, some historical, religious and literary works were translated by order of the Mamluk sultans from Arabic into Turkish (al-Durūbī 2017). Persian was also a source language that contributed to the imported literature of the era. The Mamluk intellectual repertoire also saw contributions in Turkish as well as the acquisition of copies from the literature of other Turkic lands (Eckmann 1963).

Interest in the language of *mamlūks* had begun before the sultanate was established. In the 11th century, the Turkic lexicographer Karşgarlı Mahmud (Maḥmūd al-Kasgharī) presented a bilingual (Turkish-Arabic) dictionary to the Abbasid caliph al-Muqtadī bi Amrillah. Other dictionaries followed, including one that was compiled by the famous Arab grammarian Abū Ḥayyān al-Andalusī (al-Durūbī 2017). Though Turkish was gaining importance, it would not be accurate to call this a changeover point in terms of linguistic power, for the scholarly custom was still to write in Arabic in most of the Islamic world. That is why many scholars of Turkic origin like Abū Naṣr al-Fārābī composed their works in Arabic (Bozkurt 2018).

*Turks and Persians*

Racial discrimination in the Umayyad era was a factor which accelerated its demise. The Abbasid call against the Umayyad rule used that feature to mobilize the non-Arab Muslims (called *mawālī*) of Khurāsān for its advantage. These included Turks and Persians (Aksu 2008).

After that, Turks and Persians continued to be part of the multicultural scene in the Abbasid context. In fact, the extensive incorporation of Turkic slave warriors into the Abbasid military system took place in part as a response to the rising influence and power of Persian entities in the Arab caliphate (Yıldız 1988).

When the Samanid dynasty rose as a Persian Sunni power in the region, they also integrated into their army and political structure Turkic slave warriors. Of these, the commander Alp Tegin took the foundational steps towards establishing the Ghaznavid empire (r. 977–1186) when he settled with his Turkic soldiers in the city of Gazne (Ghazna, eastern Afghanistan). With Sebük Tegin, the establishment took on the identity of a semi-independent, Perso-Turkic Muslim dynasty. Persian was the official language of the Ghaznavids, besides featuring heavily in the literature of the era. The famous epic *Shahnameh* by the Persian poet Firdawsī was the product of these dynamics (Merçil 1996; al-Durūbī 2017). Other Turkic states that emerged were:

- The Karakhanid (Karahanlı) dynasty (r. 840–1212), which overlapped with the Abbasid context through intersecting with the Samanids and Ghaznavids in Transoxania and eastern Turkistan and embraced Islam. Al-Kasgharī, the lexicographer mentioned above, belonged to this culture;
(Özaydın 2001; Akün 2022)
- The Khwārezm-Shāh (Harezmşah) dynasty (r. 1097–1231) which branched out from the Seljuks and was put to an end by the Mongol expansion after having ruled in Khwārezm and Iran. (Taneri 1997)

This region, around the time span of such Perso-Turkic dynasties, was home to major scholars of medicine such as al-Rāzī, al-Fārābī, al-Bīrūnī and Ibn Sīna (Altıntaş 2007). The Karakhanid and Khwārezm tongues were precursors to the Caghatay (Çağatay) Turkish which generated a considerable literature that flourished in the Timurid era (r. 1405–1506) (Özkan 2002).

*The Seljuk sultanate.* Several references have been made in the discussion so far to the Seljuk sultanate (r. 1040–1308), the predecessor of the Ottoman State. The remainder of this section will address this strongest thread (the Seljuks) in the weave of pre-Ottoman dynamics that led eventually to the intercultural setting of its classical era.

The Seljuk presence in the region began when Selçuk Beg of Oghuz Turks settled with his tribe in the ancient city of Jend (Cend) near the Syr Darya (or Jaxartes) River, where they engaged with the Samanids and Karakhanids and accepted Islam. The Seljuk territory went on to expand into Khurāsān and Anatolia. They answered the Abbasid call for help to fight the Buyid (Muslim Shia) dynasty (r. 945–1055), which ended in 1055 under the Seljuk sultan Tughrul Beg (Sümer 2009; Karadeniz 2019; Özaydın 1993). Within a few years Tughrul Beg was recognized by the Abbasid caliph al-Qā'im bi Amrillah as *Qāsīm Amīr al-Mu'minīn* (partner of the prince of believers, indicating joint sovereignty). This was an important moment in the history of the politics of the Muslim Middle East, as it finalized the ongoing changeover of political power from Arabs to Turks

(Çay 2009).⁹ Seljuk rulers were not *mamlūks* and, unlike the Mamluk sultans, they were not a foreign minority ruling over an Arabic-speaking populace.

That said, the Perso-Arabic dynamics that prevailed at the foundation of the sultanate had affected its language. While Arabic was used as the language of education at *madrasas* (institutes of learning), Persian became increasingly dominant in the bureaucracy and in literature. The situation started to change in favor of Turkish with the Anatolian *beyliks* (principalities along the western Anatolian borders) when they became more independent (from the sultanate) by the late 13th century (Kartal 2008; Özkan 2002; Emecen 2012; İnalcık 2006). The beys encouraged translation into Turkish (a practice which found support in the Ottoman setting as well), which ultimately led to increased input in Turkish until it became the language of literature and scholarship: "From the 14th century on, literature, medicine, history, astronomy, Islamic religious and philosophical studies began to be written in Turkish" (Tokaç 2006: 165).

Of course, the Turkish now being referred to, Ottoman Turkish, was a combination of several languages, with Arabic and Persian providing ample sources for its vocabulary and alphabet. It was still an autonomous language which would draw on Persian and Arabic as source languages, a factor which placed the Ottoman translators of the classical era in their unique place within the *Ottoman interculture* (Paker 2002), in the target culture/language but also overrunning it.

## Conclusion

The present chapter surveyed some of the pre-Ottoman Middle Eastern cultural dynamics that led to the intercrossing of Turkish, Arabic and Persian in classical Ottoman cultural input and practices of translation. Inspired largely by Pym's idea of transfer maps, which posited that a mapping of translations is essentially a mapping of movement; it charted the flow of people, ideas, cultural norms and political power across the region and highlighted the role of translation in the process.

The discussion revealed layers of interaction between the three cultures – which would not have been possible without interaction with other cultures and ethnic, religious and linguistic groups (mainly the Greco-Syriac culture) at the same time. Such interactions involved instances of subject and object transfer, constituting lines of movement on the transfer map. Through translations of written material and the processes of importation, aspects of one culture were integrated into another (most notably the *dīwān* practices and the acquisition of *mamlūk* soldiers).

---

9. The argument is put forward by Çay, but he does not use the concept of changeover.

Schools of thought were transmitted through translational activity from Athens and Alexandria to Christian Mesopotamia to Arabic Baghdad, all the way to Mamluk Egypt, Sāmānid Transoxania, Anatolia of the beyliks and Ottoman Istanbul across a stream of changeover points. Persian kings, various Muslim rulers (caliphs, sultans, governors), clergy and most importantly translators of different ethnic, linguistic and religious backgrounds played a key mediatory role in the realization of linguistic and cultural flows. Their movement across time and space formed lines of transfer on the map which this chapter undertook to briefly draw.

Many of the changeover points also marked the transfer of cultural influence and political power from one group to another across time and space; the shifting, through translation, of linguistic dominion in cultural input from Greek to Syriac to Persian, Arabic and Turkish; and the shifting of political authority among the groups that used these languages. The chapter illustrated how intercultural transfers shaped cultural input in several domains such as scholarship, literature, bureaucracy and religion.

Different contexts saw different flows of movement, two of which were emphasized in particular in the chapter: the networked flow of knowledge through the gathering and shifting of groups of specialized people (mostly scholars and physicians) from the 5th into the 9th century, and the flows of cultural influence and political power that were activated in the Abbasid context through other groups of specialized people (mostly Persian intelligentsia and Turkic slave warriors).

The intercrossing lines of transfer over the three cultures associated with Arabic, Persian and Turkish ultimately led to the classical Ottoman setting of an interculture in which Persian and Arabic were both source languages and language components of works composed in Ottoman Turkish.

## References

Al-Durūbī, Samīr. 2017. "Ḥarakat al-Tarjama wa al-Taʿrīb fī Dīwān al-Inshāʾ al-Mamlūkī: Al-Bawāʿith wa al-Lughāt wa al-Mutarjamāt." *Majallat Majma al-Lugha al-Arabiyya al-Urdunī* 62, 1–62.

Ağırakça, Ahmet. 2000. "İhşîdîler." *Türkiye Diyanet Vakfı İslam Ansiklopedisi*, https://islamansiklopedisi.org.tr/ihsidiler.

Alican, Musatafa. 2016. "Türklerin kurduğu ilk İslam devleti: Tolunoğulları." *Beyaz Tarih*, October 19, https://www.beyaztarih.com/turk-tarihi/turklerin-kurdugu-ilk-islam-devleti-tolunogullari.

Aksu, Ali. 2008. "İmam İbrahim'in Ebû Müslim'e Gönderdiği Mektup Bağlamında Abbâsî İhtilal Hareketinde Etnik Grupların Rolü." *İSTEM* 6(12), 53–70.

Akün, Ömer Faruk. 2022. "Kâşgarlı Mahmud." *Türkiye Diyanet Vakfı İslam Ansiklopedisi*, 2022. https://islamansiklopedisi.org.tr/kasgarli-mahmud.

Akyürek, Yunus. 2013. "Emevîler Dönemi Fetih Politikası ve Mâverâünnehir'in Fethi." *T.C Uludağ Üniversitesi İlahiyat Fakültesi Dergisi* 22(1), 85–115.

Altıntaş, Ayten. 2007. "Selçuklu Tıbbı." In *Tıp tarihi ve tıp etiği ders kitabı*, 83–86. Istanbul: İstanbul Üniversitesi Matbaası.

'Awaḍ, Ibrāhīm al-Sayyid Shaḥāta. 2009. "Al-Ḥayāt al-fikriyya fī Miṣr fī 'ahd al-Dawla al-Ikshīdiyya", Phd thesis (Cairo University, 2009).

Aydınlı, Osman. 2007. "Süryani Bilginlerin Çeviri Faaliyeti ve Mu'tezilî Düşünceye Etkisi." *Hitit Üniversitesi İlahiyat Fakültesi Dergisi* 6(11), 7–33.

Bae, Chul-hyun. 2004. "Aramaic as a Lingua Franca During the Persian Empire (538–333 B.C.E.)." *Journal of Universal Language* 5, 1–20.

Blumenthal, H. J. 1978. "529 and its sequel: What happened to the Academy?" *Byzantium* 48(2), 369–385.

Bozkurt, Fuat. 2018. *Türklerin Dini*. Konya: Salon Yayınları.

Cihan, Cihad. 2015. "Türk-Sasani Askerî İttifakları ve Sasani Ordusunda Türkler." *Mustafa Kemal Üniversitesi Sosyal Bilimler Enstitüsü Dergisi* 12(32), 89–107.

Çapan, Fatma. 2019. "İslam Dünyası'nda bimaristanlar ve gelişme süreçleri." *Gaziantep University Journal of Social Sciences* 18(3), 1205–1219.

Çay, Abdülhaluk Mehmet. 2009. *Tarih: Türkiye Tarihi (Selçuklu Devri)*. Ankara: Türkiye Kültür ve Turizm Bakanlığı.

Çelik, Mehmet. 2010. "Süryânîler." *Türkiye Diyanet Vakfı İslam Ansiklopedisi*, 2010. https://islamansiklopedisi.org.tr/suryaniler.

Durant, Will. 1988. Qiṣṣat al-Ḥaḍāra, translated by Zakī Najīb Maḥmūd et al. Beirut, Lebonan: Dār al-Jīl.

Eckmann, János. 1963. "The Mamluk-Kipchak Literature." *Central Asiatic Journal* 8(4), 304–319.

Emecen, Feridun. 2012. "Uç Beyi." *Türkiye Diyanet Vakfı İslam Ansiklopedisi*, 2012. https://islamansiklopedisi.org.tr/uc-beyi.

Even-Zohar, Itamar. 1990. "Polysystem Theory." *Poetics Today* 11(1), 9–26.

Even-Zohar, Itamar. 2010. *Papers in Culture Research*. Tel Aviv: Unit of Culture Research, Tel Aviv University.

Fazlıoğlu, İhsan. 2003. "Osmanlı Döneminde 'Bilim' Alanındaki Türkçe Telif ve Tercüme Eserlerin Türkçe Oluş Nedenleri ve Bu Eserlerin Dil Bilincinin Oluşmasındaki Yeri ve Önemi." *Kutadgubilig Felsefe-Bilim Araştırmaları* 3, 151–184.

Fawzī, Fārūq 'Umar. 2009. Tārīkh al-Nuẓum al-Islāmiyya: Dirāsa li Ṭaṭawwur al-Mu' assasāt al-Markaziyya fī al-Dawla fī al-Qurūn al-Islamiyya al-'Ūlā. Amman: Dār al-Shurūq.

Fisher, Greg and Philip Wood. 2016. "Writing the History of the 'Persian Arabs': The Pre-Islamic Perspective on the 'Nasṛids' of al-Ḥīrah." *Iranian Studies* 49(2), 247–290.

Fisher, Greg. 2011. *Between Empires: Arabs, Romans, and Sasanians in Late Antiquity*. Oxford: Oxford University Press.

Hemmings, Jay. 2019. "The sack of Baghdad in 1258 – one of the bloodiest days in human history." *War History Online*, 15 February, 2019. https://www.warhistoryonline.com/medieval/the-sack-of-baghdad-in-1258.html.

İnalcık, Halil. 2006. "Klasik Edebiyat Menşei: İranî Gelenek, Saray İşret Meclisleri ve Musâhib Şairler". *Türk edebiyatı Tarihi*, vol. 1, edited by Talât Sait Halman et al., 221–282. Istanbul: T.C. Kültür ve Turizm Bakanlığı.

Karadeniz, Yılmaz. 2019. "Siyasi Güç ve Dini Meşruiyet Açısından Büyük Selçuklu-Abbasi Halifeliği İlişkileri." *Manas Sosyal Araştırmalar Dergisi* 8(2), 2060–2081.

Kartal, Ahmet. 2008. "Anadolu Selçuklu Devleti Döneminde Dil ve Edebiyat." *Divan Edebiyatı Araştırmaları Dergisi* 1, 95–168.

Kızıltoprak, Süleyman. 2004. "Memlük." *Türkiye Diyanet Vakfı İslam Ansiklopedisi*, 2004. https://islamansiklopedisi.org.tr/memluk.

Lunde, Paul. 2011. "Kalila wa-Dimna." *Muslim Heritage*, 30 January 2011. https://muslimheritage.com/kalila-wa-dimna/.

Luttikhuizen, Frances. 2005. "The Nestorians: A Forgotten Link in the Transfer of Greek Science to the West." Paper presented at the Mediterranean Studies Conference, Messina, 25–28 May, 2005.

Martinez, Gabriel. 2008. "The Fall of the Umayyads of Cordova: The End of the Arab Caliphate." *Mediterranean Historical Review* 5(2), 117–149.

Merçil, Erdoğan. 1996. "Gazneliler." *Türkiye Diyanet Vakfı İslam Ansiklopedisi*, 1996. https://islamansiklopedisi.org.tr/gazneliler.

Miller, Andrew C. 2006. "Jundi-Shapur, Bimaristans, and the Rise of Academic Medical Centres." *Journal of the Royal Society of Medicine* 99, 615–617.

Modanlou, H. D. 2011. "Historical Evidence for the Origin of Teaching Hospital, Medical School and The Rise of Academic Medicine." *Journal of Perinatology* 31(4), 236–239.

Montgomery, Scott L. 2000. *Science in Translation: Movements of Knowledge Through Culture and Time*. Chicago: University of Chicago Press.

Nacmâbâdî, Mahmood. 2017. "Sasaniler dönemi tıbbı," translated by Ahmet Altıngök and Cemal Bilici. *Oğuz-Türkmen Araştırmaları Dergisi*, 1(1), 190–266.

Özaydın, Abdülkerim. 2001. "Karahanlılar." *Türkiye Diyanet Vakfı İslam Ansiklopedisi*, 2001. https://islamansiklopedisi.org.tr/karahanlilar.

Özaydın, Abdülkerim. 1993. "Cend." *Türkiye Diyanet Vakfı İslam Ansiklopedisi*, 1993. https://islamansiklopedisi.org.tr/cend.

Özkan, Mustafa. 2002. "Selçuklular ve Beylikler Devrinde Türk Dili." *Genel Türk Tarihi, vol. 4, Orta Çağ*, edited by Hasan Celâl Güzel and Ali Birinci, 486–510. Ankara: Yeni Türkiye Yayınları.

Paker, Saliha. 1998. "Turkish Tradition." In *Routledge Encyclopedia of Translation Studies*, edited by Mona Baker, 571–582. London: Routledge.

Paker, Saliha. 2002. "Translation as *Terceme* and *Nazire*: Culture-Bound Concepts and Their Implications for a Conceptual Framework for Research on Ottoman Translation History." In *Crosscultural Transgressions: Research Models in Translation II – Historical and Ideological Issues*, edited by Theo Hermans, 120–143. Manchester: St. Jerome Publishing.

Pym, Anthony. 1993. "Why Translation Conventions Should be Intercultural Rather than Culture-Specific: An Alternative Link Model." *Parallèles* 15, 60–68.

Pym, Anthony. 2014 [1998]. *Method in Translation History*. New York: Routledge.

Pym, Anthony. 2000. *Negotiating the Frontier: Translators and Intercultures in Hispanic History*. New York: Routledge.

Qazānjī, Fu'ād Yūsuf. 2010. Uṣūl al-Thaqāfa al-Siryāniyya fī Bilād mā Bayn al-Nahrayn. Amman and Baghdad: Dār Dijla.

Sadeghi, Sajjad, Farzaneh Ghaffari, and Mehdi Alizadeh. 2018. "Al-Masā'il fī al-Ṭibb: Ḥunain ibn Isḥāq's Historic Medical Text with a Distinctive Style of Islamic Medical Education." *Journal of Medical Biography* 29(1), 1–5.

Söylemez, Mehmet Mahfuz. 2005. "The Jundishapur School: Its History, Structure, and Functions." *The American Journal of Islamic Social Sciences* 22(2), 1–27.

Sümer, Faruk. "Selçuklular." *Türkiye Diyanet Vakfı İslam Ansiklopedisi*, 2009. https://islamansiklopedisi.org.tr/selcuklular.

Ṭāhā, Salīm. 1976. "Al-Ta'rīb wa Kibār al-Mu'arribīn fī al-Islām". *Sūmar* 32(1–2), 339–389.

Taneri, Aydın. Hârizmşahlar. *Türkiye Diyanet Vakfı İslam Ansiklopedisi*, 1997. https://islamansiklopedisi.org.tr/harizmsahlar.

Tanrıverdi, Eyyüp. 2007. "Arap Kültüründe Çeviri Çalışmaları ve Huneyn bin İshak Ekolü." *Dîvân Disiplinlerarası Çalışmalar Dergisi* 12(23), 93–150.

Terzioğlu, Arslan. 2005. "Yerli Ve Yabancı Kaynaklar Işığında Selçuklu Hastaneleri ve Tabebetin Avrupa'ya Tesirleri". In *Türkler, vol. 5, Orta Çağ*, edited by Hasan Celal Güzel, Kemal Çiçek, and Salim Koca, 1386–1411. Ankara: Yeni Türkiye Yayınları.

Tokaç, Mahmut. 2006. "Osmanlı Dönemi Türkçe Tıp Yazmaları." In *Osmanlılarda Sağlık*, edited by Coşkun Yılmaz and Necdet Yılmaz, 165–186. İstanbul: Biofarma.

Toury, G. 1995. *Descriptive Translation Studies and Beyond*. Amsterdam, Netherlands: John Benjamins Publishing.

Tschanz, David W. 2003. "Hunayn bin Ishaq: The Great Translator." JISHIM 1, 39–40.

Tymoczko, Maria. 2014. "Reconceptualizing Translation Theory: Integrating Non-Western Thought About Translation". In *Translating Others*, vol. 1, edited by Theo Harmans, 13–32. New York: Routledge.

Yarshater, Ehsan. 1998. "The Persian presence in the Islamic World." In *The Persian Presence in the Islamic World*, edited by Richard G. Hovannisian and Geroges Sabagh, 4–125. Cambridge: Cambridge University Press.

Yıldız, Hakkı Dursun. 1998. "Abbâsîler." *Türkiye Diyanet Vakfı İslam Ansiklopedisi*, 1988. https://islamansiklopedisi.org.tr/abbasiler.

Yiğit, İsmail. 2004. "Memlükler." *Türkiye Diyanet Vakfı İslam Ansiklopedisi*, 2004. https://islamansiklopedisi.org.tr/memlukler.

PART 2

# Current flows

CHAPTER 6

# Recirculated, recontextualized, reworked
Community-driven video game fan translation practices in Turkey[*]

Selahattin Karagöz
Ege University

This chapter explores non-commercial translation practices in video games with an expired shelf life in Turkey. Pursuant to the paratextual analysis of fan material that contextualizes the game or localization process, this chapter concludes that the non-professional translators translate, circulate and recontextualize the games regardless of their commercial value and that it is their gaming capital that drives this specific form of circulation.

**Keywords:** game localization, fan paratexts, gaming capital, virtual communities, fan productivity, translation sociology

## Introduction

Video games have already surpassed any other entertainment product globally. Because any video game is sold, consumed and promoted worldwide, the global success of the game industry is partly a result of localization (Mangiron 2012: 122). The video game is a commercial product, and "the game sector is a high stakes competitive business which needs to operate internationally, making translation an essential support function" (O'Hagan and Chandler 2016: 309). As Dietz (2007: 3) argues: "the market competition is fierce, and the average 'shelf life' of a game is extremely brief" in the gaming industry. Therefore, the games should be translated before or very soon after their release in the profit-driven official game localization cycle. Localization of a game years after its release date is uncommon;

---

[*] This chapter is adapted from the Ph.D. thesis. Karagöz, Selahattin. 2019. "Amateurs, Experts, Explorers: Video Game Localization Practices in Turkey" Ph.D Thesis. Yıldız Technical University. This thesis was supported by TUBITAK (The Scientific and Technological Research Council of Turkey) within scope of 2214-A - International Research Fellowship Programme for PhD Students (2015/2).

the game's shelf life would have already expired at that point, and the localization would fail to meet commercial requirements.

Simultaneous or rapid localization is an essential factor in the distribution of games as commodities. Game publishers even apply "a simultaneous international release, often abbreviated as 'simship', in an absolute minimum of five languages (English, French, Italian, German and Spanish, referred to in industry circles by the acronym E-FIGS) to capitalize on their marketing campaigns and to minimize the effects of piracy" (Bernal-Merino 2015: 9).

Non-professionals translate games for the gaming community in the absence of profit-driven or commercial localization, which often originates from "fans' attention to linguistic and cultural barriers pertaining to their objects of interest which led to fan-initiated translation activities" (O'Hagan 2017: 184). Organized in virtual communities or acting as self-assigned translators, the translators translate the games which have not been accompanied by the official localization as "the computer-based nature of computer games continues to encourage intervention with both software and hardware" (Dovey and Kennedy 2006: 14). Non-professionals with a command of a language and a set of skills can create a patch from the original game; the games are patched, and the language patches are distributed via dedicated websites or community pages.

Non-commercial localization practices are pretty common in the Turkish gaming community or sphere. Turkey has a massive market for the video game industry with over 36,000,000 game consumers and a 450,000,000 USD market size (Gaming in Turkey 2020: 52). Still, the English proficiency of the general population is relatively low. Turkey ranks 70th out of 112 countries worldwide and 34th out of 35 in the Eurozone (EF EPI Turkey), implying that localization into Turkish is critical for game content accessibility. As a result, the Turkish localization sphere is characterized by numerous virtual communities devoted to non-commercial translation activities into Turkish to meet demands not met by commercial localization.

As this chapter suggests, the context of non-commercial localization activities in Turkey is characterized by belated translation. A high number of "previously" popular video games have been translated by non-professionals regardless of their release date for and within the Turkish gaming community. For instance, "The Clive Barker's Undying", once labelled as garnished with "superb graphics, truly impressive sound effects, and fast-paced, enjoyable action sequences" (Kasavin 2001), was released in 2001, while the language patch was released in 2019. The relationship between the joy a video game offers and technological development may not always be interwoven, but the developments in game technology critically influence game design and graphics. According to Newman (2004: 31), "the development of gaming systems has had a profound impact on the form and structure of videogames ... videogames have been transformed as new audio-visual, processing, storage and interface capabilities have arisen and designers have been offered new opportunities." The graphics in "Clive Barker's Undying" may not seem that "superb" or the gameplay mechanics may not be regarded as "fancy" after 18 years. Such belated localization is exemplified by other projects as well. "Knight Rider: The Game II," which was released in 2004, was patched in 2019. "Colin McRae DIRT 2," which was released on 8 September 2009 was patched in 2019. "Prince of Persia: Warrior Within," which was released on 30 November 2004 was patched in 2019. "Postal I," which was released in 2003, was patched in 2019. "Formula I 2011," which was released in 2010 was translated in 2019. "The Tomb Raider I" released in 1996, "The Tomb Raider" released in 1997 and "The Tomb Raider III: Adventures of Lara Croft," released in 1998 were all patched in 2019. Even "Crisis," which was released in 2007 with native Turkish language support was patched on 18 April 2020. By the given dates, the games above had already lost their commercial value and would not be translated in a profit-driven cycle. However, non-professional translators construct an alternative path of circulation through which the games are translated regardless of their commercial value or release date. This case reveals the need for further investigation into the mechanism behind the belated release of the language patches in Turkey.

This chapter adopts a sociological lens to describe the path of alternative circulation of the games' "belated" selection, translation and patch release process, as well as to locate the position of non-professional translators within this production cycle. It discusses how individuals launch, design and contextualize their non-commercial localization practices.

The chapter discusses findings from fan paratext analysis of the 29 selected documents by the belated translation projects' non-professional translators. The material was published on the web pages of Oyunceviri, a virtual umbrella community of amateur translation practices and a personal blog about the localization process in STAR WARS – Knights of the Old Republic in search of gaming capital (Consalvo 2007: 4), the reworking of cultural capital referring to "being knowledgeable about the games".

As described in the following pages, Oyunceviri presents an ideal virtual space for analysing non-professional localization practices. The community's principles of free participation, collective production and flexible workflow enable translators to start their own projects, join ongoing projects, and contextualize projects in fan paratexts. In terms of this chapter's focus, translators' fan paratexts have a two-fold function. On the one hand, they are mediums of gaming capital materialization. On the other hand, they illustrate how the localization process is shaped. Therefore this chapter also generates fresh insights into the perception of paratextual research.

Documenting "personal" histories of design and contextualization processes may play a vital role in the perception of "unofficial circulation systems", and this paper constructs a local sociology of production driven by the interplay between personal memories, tastes, participation and community structures/principles. This is the first longitudinal study to analyse individuals' making of non-professional localization practices. As discussed in this chapter, the communities attracted overwhelming academic interest. This chapter argues that the focus should instead be on translators who initiate the projects, and future research should investigate the members of the communities as well. For this purpose, this chapter offers a two-fold mechanism of exploration. On the discursive level, it critically introduces the notion of gaming capital and discusses how it can be employed in the research on the fan localization sphere and non-commercial translation practices. On the practical level, this chapter argues that fans' gaming knowledge and experience powerfully shapes non-professional localization practices in Turkey. In exploring member-driven non-commercial projects the chapter starts with a brief discussion of previous research. Then it critically introduces and discusses gaming capital. This is followed by a brief description of the non-commercial localization sphere in Turkey, turning specifically to the Oyunceviri community and the cycle of "community structure and gaming capital". In conclusion, it discusses the findings of the paratextual analysis and illustrates how the non-professional translators contextualize the belated localization process.

## Theorizing non-professional localization practices

Patch circulation systems in the Turkish context are shaped by various motivations, acts and affordances of individuals or groups (Karagöz 2019). Theorizing on how and why individuals or groups translate for their peers for free in the context of Turkey can also offer telling examples of the position of non-professional translators who "offer their work for free or for very poor payment, primarily and en masse facilitate translation crowdsourcing and/or online collaborative translation and thus a part of main translation scene" (Zwischenberger 2021: 14). Previous studies on non-commercial translation practices in media circulation focus almost exclusively on fansubbing. Research illuminates the role of fan translation in the circulation of media texts (Wongseree et al. 2019); its role in the expansion of anime fandom (Pérez González 2007); the intervention of fansubbers in the circulated material in censored environments (Khoshsaligheh et al. 2018; Guo and Evans 2020) and the role of fansubbers in commercialized platform and settings (Dwyer 2012). Few studies critically examine other forms of volunteer work in multimedia settings, as exemplified in the study on "the fan-based translation in the transcultural flow and consumption of online wuxia literature" (Li 2021).

There have also been numerous studies to investigate the localization practices in games by non-professionals and their direct or indirect empowerment. For instance, Sanchez (2009) documents the technical details and process of ROM hacking. Mia Consalvo (2016:136) critically describes how previous members of communities later "created the licensed versions of smaller games that are created by people much like themselves and release those via digital distribution to a growing audience". Minako O'Hagan (2017:189) discusses the effect of user empowerment on the game localization process and the positions of "fan communities as users, critics and in some cases (co-)creators, of localised games." In a similar vein, Norris (2014) illustrates "how the fans are concerned with Yakuza game and how it should be translated into the Western market" along with the works on the role of fan translation in "unintended", the non-industry-driven flow of video games (Consalvo 2012, 2013; Muñoz Sánchez 2009). The review of the previous research also indicates that the vast majority of existing studies in the broader literature have examined the amateur translation practices in the Japanese-Western market pair, but the research on the other market pairs is rather limited, but includes a recent work on the Arabic world context by Al-Batineh and Alawneh (2021) on the localization practices by the community "Games in Arabic (GIA)".

On the other hand, most previous studies on the Turkish localization sphere were limited to translational choices in localization (Öncü Yilmaz and Canbaz 2019; Önen 2018; Zan 2018). The broader context of the previous literature failed to precisely address the fan production, community-driven or non-professional localization practices. Seminal contributions to the non-professional translations research in Turkish localization communities have been made by Karagöz (2019) and Sarıgül and Ross (2020). Sarıgül and Ross (2020) briefly compare community translation practices in volunteer and professional video game localization environments, while Karagöz (2019) describes fan affordances in detail. In his work, he examines virtual communities of practice, including their structure, workflow-participation principles and evaluation processes and the grift relationship between the fan communities and localization industry. The relatively small body of literature concerned with non-professional translation in the Turkish context fails to address the non-professional translator-driven (initiated) non-commercial translation practices. Karagöz and Sarıgül-Ross focus on the communities, their structure and translation processes; however, as illustrated in the following pages, the non-commercial localization practices are characteristically projects launched by individuals. The non-commercial localization sphere is not a monolith of community-driven projects. Instead, it is shaped by personal gaming histories, personal ventures or fandom-driven practices.

The research in this chapter does not fit well with the research trends described above. Instead, this chapter draws attention to the non-commercial translation activities in the alternative flow of once-commercial but currently emotion-nostalgia packed products in the Western-Turkey market pair. As far as this work is concerned, these games circulated in Turkey without official localization. They are patched by non-professionals, years after their release date, unlike officially unreleased Japanese games in the Western context.

No study to date has examined the member-driven community practices through focusing on the non-professionals who launch and design the localization process in the Turkish context. This chapter adopts such a focus. McDonough Dolmaya (2011: 77) argues that "the relatively recent tendency in translation studies to focus on the agents involved in the translation process rather than just on the texts themselves can be described as sociological in nature". In a similar vein, this chapter also explores sociological implications. It suggests that non-professional localization practices occur within the space shaped by community structure (of free participation, collective production, flexible workflow) and non-professional translators' gaming knowledge. This interplay between community and non-professional translators produces belated localization practices that can best be described in terms of a local sociology of production. A currency should be adopted to construct a sociology of non-profit driven production. This chapter posits that gaming capital may be a key to discuss the non-professional driven non-commercial localization in Turkish context; what follows is a brief discussion of gaming capital.

## Gaming capital: Paratextualizing the making of non-professional translation practice

The communities are often "an assemblage of many smaller subcommunities, each with their own goals and interests" (Zimmermann 2019: 897). Smaller subcommunities are an assemblage of individuals with personal interests, goals, and tastes as well. This is evident in localization communities in Turkey; the members have diverse interests, expertise, and leisure time to allocate to the projects. The decentralized production chains – which do not adopt a top-down production model; instead translators launch their own projects – allow numerous concurrent projects with no strict deadlines, which any member with proper skillset can join (Karagöz 2019: 372). Non-professional translators can participate in projects that interest them, and they can "contextualize" their own "content." This chapter proposes that non-professional translators' tastes, choices and preferences shape non-commercial translation practices in the communities and their gaming capital governs participation, production, and contextualization and argues that this form of capital is materialized in fan paratexts.

The concept of gaming capital, a "reworking of Pierre Bourdieu's 'cultural capital', was introduced by game researcher Mia Consalvo (2007: 4). According to her definition (2007: 18), gaming capital entails "being knowledgeable about game releases and secrets and passing that information on to others". She holds the view that gaming capital is associated with the paratextual industries of gaming. According to Consalvo (2007: 184), "players can accumulate various forms of gaming capital not only from playing games but also from the paratextual industries that support them."

Paratextual industries cover any material surrounding gameplay itself. The industries shape the gaming experience; they contextualize the game and gameplay. Consalvo critically examines the accumulation, circulation and commodification of gaming capital in her seminal work. She (2007: 31) argues that "a part of the value of having gaming capital is being able to display it." The gaming capital is displayed on forums, communities and convention spaces of the game users and "with Internet, players began to individually create their own sites and spaces for circulating knowledge as well as creating their own forms of gaming capital" (2007: 184) and the display of gaming capital may contextualize the content created by the gamer.

In the present study gaming capital refers to such exchange and display value. According to Walsh and Apparley (2009), "gaming capital establishes a local sociology of the media ecology of videogames as it plays a key role in the development of communities of practice". This chapter examines the non-commercial localization projects and it posits that non-professional translators are empowered to display *their gaming capital*. The members of the communities select the games to translate; they design the localization process, and finally, the language patch is released on the web pages accompanied by a fan paratext.

The translators can tell the story of the localization process, provide technical details on the language patch, publish patch manuals, or simply declare their experiences/impressions on the game on the web pages. In terms of this chapter's focus, this contextualization practice is defined as a form of gaming capital showcase.

This type of documentation includes patch technical details, setup manuals, game visuals, frequently asked questions, and a list of project contributors. In some cases, the pages are densely packed with personal notes. The translators can tell the story of the language patch, their own gaming experiences, childhood memories or gaming history. As a result, contextualization is not limited to game patches; translators can recontextualize a once-commercial product based on their own gaming capital. This type of documentation is referred to as fan paratext in this chapter.

As illustrated in the Introduction, this chapter suggests that the gaming capital is materialized in fan paratexts and the paratextual analysis may help the researcher to trace the roots of belated localization practices.

Paratext, a term offered by Gérard Genette, refers to any text surrounding, presenting and contextualizing a text (Genette 1997). This concept has also been reworked by Consalvo (2007: 9) to further refer to "the peripheral industries surrounding games". In her perception, paratexts shape the gameplay experience and "instruct the player in how to play, what to play, and what is cool (and not) in the game world." (2007: 22); paratextual material contextualizes and helps the player to focus better on the gameplay (2007: 44).

Consalvo focuses on accumulation of gaming capital and the interwoven relationship between the paratext and the gameplay. According to her (2007: 38), gaming capital can be accumulated through consumption of paratexts, the gaming capital is gained through reading, watching or listening to the material provided by the gaming magazines, walkthroughs, forums, and content published by the communities.

Consalvo primarily adopted the paratext concept to illustrate how the out-of-game material shapes gameplay; however, the fan paratext in web pages does not function in this way. The paratexts in pages often contextualize the localization process, not the game. Therefore, the user would not accumulate "gaming capital" on gameplay or the game itself; instead, the paratexts essentially describe how the patch works. Thus, this chapter extends the gaming capital concept to the "out-of-game-related material".

In terms of this chapter's focus, gaming capital refers to the currency which shapes non-professional localization process. The commercial value in the localization industry can be attributed to the videogame's shelf life or life span. However, the member-driven projects do not originate from "commercial value"; they may often be traced back to their gaming capital including their personal choices, preferences, gaming histories or nostalgia. As discussed in the following pages, gaming capital has two functions: it drives the localization process for the games whose shelf life has expired, and it is materialized as a form of empowerment.

In reworking the concept of paratext, on a discursive level, the chapter illustrates that paratexts are showcases of gaming capital. Their function is no longer limited to players' accumulation of gaming capital. On the practical level, their analysis offers valuable insights into how a localization project is launched and how the game is perceived by a non-professional translator. The findings of paratextual analysis may illuminate the translational history of game patches, translators' profiles, translational choices and their preferences. The findings may provide a vivid picture of an alternative circulation of games with an expired shelf life as the paratext contextualizes the games as well. Unlike their commercially contextualized version, the games of belated localization are contextualized by the translators. Conceptual discussion of game recontextualization practices goes beyond the boundaries of translational research; the findings from paratextual research play an important role in addressing the issue of circulation of patches and the interaction between gaming capital, empowerment and the free participation principle, which is discussed in detail in the following pages.

Having argued that fan paratexts in web pages may be labelled the showcases of gaming capital, the following section briefly illustrates how gaming capital is materialized in the fan paratexts and how the belated translations may be contextualized. The patches contextualized in the gaming capital of the "non-professional translators" in the Oyunceviri context is a good illustration of such display.

## Oyunceviri community: Empowerment, gaming capital and paratextual production

According to Fernández Costales (2013: 89) "the impact the web has had on the promotion of fan culture seems quite clear due to the number of devoted sites that have appeared on the web." This can be briefly illustrated by a growing number of non-professional localization communities in Turkey. Numerous independent or interrelated communities organize on a virtual space, translate video games for their peers and they distribute the patches through websites. The non-commercial localization sphere in Turkey is characterized by communities with diverse profit models (subscription-based communities exemplified by the Animus Project community, a community dedicated to famous Assassins Creed series), diverse platforms (Donanımhaber Community originating from a technology-oriented forum, Steam Translation Server, a Steam based community, or the Oyunceviri community (with a dedicated website) or structure (as exemplified by the Turkceoyunmerkezi community, which previously provided links to the pirated content on their official website) (Karagöz 2019: 372).

Moving on now to discuss the interaction between gaming capital and community structure, this chapter focuses its attention on Oyunceviri. Branded "a volunteer community to help Turkish gamers play in their native language" (Oyunceviri 2017), the community has published over 130 patches and completed 15 official localization projects. An official localization project refers to collaboration practices between community members and game developers. In such projects, the language patches are prepared by the community members and they are released in the game by the developer.

Oyunceviri is a typical virtual community "with named contributors joining and gaining status within the enterprise, participating in decision-making and agenda-setting as internal project promoters and as active co-constructors of enterprise management" (Haythornthwaite 2009: 1).

Piroth and Baker (2020: 2) argue that "translators, whether professionally trained or otherwise, volunteer their time and skills in many contexts." This is confirmed by the Oyunceviri community. Unpaid volunteers translate for others or their peers; they initiate and design non-profit translation projects that can be classified as non-commercial production.

The practices exemplified so far fit well into the category of "unsolicited and often legally illicit user-based translation activities" (O'Hagan 2009: 21) in organizational structure and workflow. In the unsolicited model "self-organized collectives of users undertake specific translation tasks. These translations are later distributed to potential users through the WWW" (Jiménez-Crespo 2017: 21), which perfectly illustrates the non-commercial localization in Oyunceviri.

The non-commercial translation practices are often associated with fan translation as well. Fan translation "or the adaptation of multimedia products by amateur translators" (Fernández Costalez 2013: n.p.) originates "from the fans and with no expectation of financial gain" (Mangiron 2018: 131). As O'Hagan (2009: 10) argues: "fan translation fits well in the category of prosumers where potential consumers of translations double as translation producers." A prosumer is often "a type of participatory user that both uses and creates the content he/she enjoys online" (Jiménez-Crespo 2017: 19) in translation context.

Fan translations, driven by prosumers "a consumer who takes part in the production or distribution process, without being paid for it in wages" (Olivier Frayssé and Mathieu O'Neil 2015: 4) in the prosumption process which involves "both production and consumption rather than focusing on either one (production) or the other (consumption)" (Ritzer and Jurgenson 2010: 13) may be identified as "an alternative mechanism to official professional translation for reproducing and often recontextualizing media texts for global circulation" (Wongseree, O'Hagan and Sasamoto 2019: 1). Accordingly, non-professionals' video game localization is a practice where the boundaries between producers and consumers blur. The translators act as prosumers as "in the emerging prosumption paradigm, a person can seamlessly shift from consumer to contributor and creator" (Don and Williams 2006: 143).

As illustrated in previous research, "the terms crowdsourced / user-generated / fan-generated / prosumer / activist / non-professional / amateur / volunteer / community translation [were] used to describe more or less the same phenomenon" (Saadat 2017: 350). The terminological discussion of the non-professional translation practices is beyond the scope of this paper; however, it is obvious that given "the lack of availability of official translation, user-translators step in and showcase their domain-specific knowledge and technical skills" (O'Hagan 2009: 21) as exemplified in the Turkish context of volunteer localization.

The non-commercial translation practices in the Oyunceviri context may be labelled fan translation, the unpaid volunteer translators may obviously be referred to as prosumers, the production process may be classified as prosumption, and the whole production network may be defined as an unsolicited user-based translation activity. Prosumption accounts for the flexible production process in the localization communities, but it fails to illuminate the currency exchanged in non-commercial localization process. This chapter argues that the production process in the game localization communities is based on the evaluation and showcase practices of how knowledgeable the member is about the games. This can briefly be illustrated by admission to the community tests. Success in a test of the potential translators' expertise in specific game genres is a requirement for community membership. Having proved their expertise, the translators are empowered to launch their own projects. Belated localization of the games is a good illustration of this as well. The games listed in the introduction had lost their commercial value by the time the patches were released. As illustrated above, the listed games were not the preferences even of the non-profit driven community; however, they were translated through the translator-initiated projects. As far as the non-commercial localization practices and non-professional translator-driven projects are concerned, the chapter suggests that gaming capital is at the heart of the non-commercial production process, and it shapes the practice.

Broadly understood, the content production in the Oyunceviri community is based on the principles of free and skills-based participation, collective production and flexible workflow.

1. Free and skills-based participation. As noted by the community administration, "anyone can apply and anyone with a proper skillset can join the community" (Eliaçık 2013a). The participation in the community is on a voluntary basis and the content production is "for free" and is dependent on "free labour" (Terranova 2000). After filling out a form with personal information and the amount of free time the candidate has available for community service, they are given three test translation templates. The first template is from the adventure game "The Rise of the Tomb Raider," the second is from the story-driven puzzle game "The Talos Principle," and the third is from the independent story game "Goodbye Deponia." It is evident that the partici-

pation is free, but it is merit-based; the sample tests ask for the candidate's linguistic skills and knowledge of several video game genres which can be defined as "gaming capital".
2. Collective production. The projects are started by self-selected amateur translators, as opposed to the typical production paradigm where a commissioner does it. Due to limited time, the community declines requests from non-members in favour of presenting games that have just been released and have accessible language files (Sıkça Sorulan Sorular 2017). Therefore, translators with gaming capital and language skills can participate in decision-making and agenda-setting. Members are also empowered to initiate any project that has not been polled by the community, and approved patches are published on the website. The patches production is not centralized or centrally controlled; the members can join any project they wish. Consequently, the labour force at hand cannot be directed to a single project and the labour is shared among the ongoing projects.
3. Flexible workflow. According to the community, they are unable to provide specific release dates (Akdoğan 2014). The lack of strict deadlines may be attributed to the reliance on free or leisure labour. The members may not contribute to the project as they may experience personal issues, problems in personal affairs, or they just feel unmotivated. (Eliaçık 2013b)

The Oyunceviri community is a telling example of how gaming capital works in the virtual communities. Non-professional translators can join the community, participate in ongoing projects, or start their own projects using their gaming capital. In a broader sense, the translators do not accumulate their gaming capital in the Oyunceviri. However, gaming capital is inextricably linked to community membership and collective production practices. The projects are prompted by the translators' gaming capital.

On the other hand, fan paratexts have a community-wide display function for gaming capital. Translators are empowered to display their gaming capital in the fan paratexts. Now that the construction of how gaming capital operates has been described, the following section discusses paratextual production and gaming capital on a practical level.

## Reframing paratexts: Documenting histories of production

The detailed analysis of fan paratexts demonstrates that the content of a typical fan paratext can be classified into three categories: (1) community-oriented content, (2) technical content, and (3) contextual content.

The project information tags in the community-oriented content show the project title, project completion level, and the percentage of contribution by any member. This type of content includes an index function and encodes useful content information for peer users.

The set-up manuals, how-to content and frequently asked questions are labelled technical content with an assistance function. Because language files are not embedded in the game, users must patch the game with the content via a grift process, which necessitates a set of technical skills, and this type of content assists the user in technical issues. Technical content can partially display translators' gaming capital. It does not recontextualize the game; however, the "unique nature of fan translation of games is characterized by a fan's technical knowledge and intensive interest in the game development" (O'Hagan 2009:19) and such technical knowledge is displayed there. The enhancement of visuals, sound and graphics is a more surprising aspect of the technical contents. If there is a large gap between the release date and the patch date, then the visuals, setup files, or sound files may need to be improved. This practice is mostly exemplified in the conversion of the graphics into high-definition versions. For instance, the fan paratext on "Tomb Raider 3" notes that "cinematics in the game were converted into HD ones" (Oyunceviri 2019h). On another one, the team leader announces that "The Tomb Raider 1" patch will automatically set up "Unfinished Business" content (Oyunceviri 2019g). The latter is an exclusive type of improvement because the language patch modifies the game content and shapes the gamers' gaming experience. On the dedicated page, "Fahrenheit: Indigo Prophecy Remastered" was labelled "the best patch possible due to the character and storage limit" (Oyunceviri 2019b), highlighting the technical skill of the team. The prosumer has stepped in and showcased his domain-specific knowledge and technical skills (O'Hagan 2009: 21) and his technical knowledge is embodied as gaming capital.

Contextual content includes personal gaming histories, user opinions on the game patched, notes on the localization process, and personal localization histories. Such paratexts essentially materialize gaming capital, and they demonstrate how the non-professional translator contextualizes the game or patch. These paratexts demonstrate the projects' origins. Contextual content is extremely personal, and it can reveal the translator's gaming history, personal experiences, fan attitudes or taste.

The showcase function of paratexts can be best illustrated briefly in "Knight Rider: The Game 2" patch. The game inspired by the popular TV series "Knight Rider" was translated by the project leader 15 years after the game was released. The project leader explains the localization process:

> Memories do not die. Childhood memories, school memories, military service memories, and such ... Knight Rider has a unique spot in my childhood memories. I had watched KITT, the self-driving, talking, bullet-proof car in joy. The car captured us before the TV in 1980s. I prepared the patch for "Knight Rider: The Game 2" to retrieve the memories. I think anyone who loves oldies but goldies will play the game.
> (Oyunceviri 2019c)

Knight Rider was broadcasted under the title "Kara Şimşek" in 1980s by Turkish Radio and Television Corporation (TRT) and attracted a great deal of public interest. The translation process of a game with an expired shelf life was inspired by the childhood memories of a community member.

On the other hand, fandom can also be at the heart of the localization projects as well. "Star Wars the Force Unleashed 2" released in 2010 was patched in 2019. The project leader Ahmet Kökyar notes that "he translated the game as he is a fan of Star Wars Universe" (Oyunceviri 2019f)

Contextual content also includes team members' personal opinions on the game. "Clive Barker's Undying" is a notable example. The game is branded "top ranking in best games of horror game history" by the project team. In a similar vein, the patch of "Oddworld: Abe's Oddysee" released in 1997 by Oddworld Inhabitants was labelled "one of the best and most famous platformers of all time" (Oyunceviri 2019d) by the team. The language patch was released in 2019 with a note that "this game causes insomnia, tears in eyes, severe headache and addiction" (Ibid.)

Personal remarks about the translator's gaming background are another important component of the contextual content. The accumulated gaming capital is materialized in the gaming experience and the team leader, or the team presents such in the paratext. Such display is evident in "Clive Barker's Undying". A note from the project team serves as the guide for the language patch for the well-known horror game: "We advise you to read Clive Barker's Undying Guide in Turkish and diary notes in the game" (Oyunceviri 2019a). The note emphasizes the translation team's "gaming history," which shapes the gameplay experience.

KOTOR Project diaries is among the best-selling examples of how gaming capital is materialized. "Star Wars the Knights of the Old Republic" (Bioware Austin 2003) is an accomplished sci-fi, role-playing and online multiplayer video game, later to be modded by fans to Star Wars-Aperion (Spry). The game released in 2003 for iPad, iPhone, MAC and PC platforms is a bestseller and rated "popular and legendary" by the game media and critics.

Computer Game World (Green 2004: 61) introduced the game as "a masterpiece and probably the best Star Wars game ever". The game was adored as "the best Star Wars game ever" (Grandshaw, 2017) even in 2017, which is surprising for a video game, a product that often has a short shelf life.

The game was translated into Turkish through a non-commercial project by Said Sürücü. Sürücü is a prominent figure in the Turkish localization community. He was the project director for the localization projects "Assassin's Creed Brotherhood", "Assassin's Creed – Revelations", "Call of Duty: Modern Warfare 2" with Oyunceviri and he is currently a professional in the localization industry.

With a duration of 1,063 days, the KOTOR Project is one of the longest running fan localization projects. The language patch was released in 2013, ten years after the game's initial release date. Sürücü kept a blog dedicated to the localization process.

It is evident in the diary entries that the KOTOR translation project is a fan-initiated, leisure-time project based on the free participation principle. KOTOR is identified as a personal localization project motivated by "Sürücü's desire to fill his leisure time" (Sürücü). According to his blog entries, he was inspired by large-scale RPG localization projects, so he decided to start a localization project for KOTOR, which he "loved" (Ibid.). The project was initially launched within the Oyunceviri community; however, Sürücü soon left the community, and he designed and completed the translation project on his own.

The project director worked on it for two years and then "had a draft of KOTOR language patch in summer 2013" (Ibid.). He claims that the project was defective and misdirected, and he had "gained much more experience" by that time. In fact, the project was completed in January 2014.

Sürücü personally tested the game, updated the page based on his quest in the game, and released the patch on 5 January 2014. Sürücü chose KOTOR to localize because he was a fan of the role-playing game. His love for Star Wars is obvious; he thanks "George Lucas," the creator of this universe (Ibid.), the project's contributors and the patient followers of the language patch, and the members of Yildizsavaslari.com, who promoted the project at the end.

Oyunceviri and Yildizsavaslari.com contributed to the localization project. According to a notice on Yildizsavaslari.com, Turkey's online Star Wars franchise fan community, "the community calls for any kind of help from members," and "KOTOR is translated by a group of fans, and various members of Yildizsavaslari also contribute to the process" (yildizsavaslari.com). The forum also mentions that the project is finished and that members can now "play the game in their native language" (yildizsavaslari.com).

What makes the KOTOR project intriguing is how Sürücü contextualizes it. As previously discussed, any member-initiated project provides a clear account of each member's contributions. KOTOR is a fully-fledged RPG and is heavily story-oriented which translates it is packed with enormous amount of text (134.806). As a result, the list of contributors includes a diverse range of individuals with diverse skill sets (dubbing, subtitling, programming, interface design, dialogue translation). Unlike other paratexts, the blog also documents the non-professionals who promised to contribute but did not, or volunteers who dropped out before the project was completed. It is a good example of the effect of "the free participation principle" on localization practices; even a single non-professional driven project with a dedicated team can fail to set strict deadlines in workflow.

Sürücü published regular updates on the localization process, failure to meet deadlines, and the current project phase. In rare cases, the project team offered excuses for missing deadlines, such as their exam period, health issues, or freelance projects at hand.

Technical documentation may include the platforms supported by the patch, the number of strings that remain untranslated, the total time spent, and the testing progress. The test procedure is interesting and detailed; Sürücü played "the entire game with all endings and all characters" (Sürücü), and the test progress is also delayed.

The KOTOR project is clearly a well-documented history of a long-running non-commercial localization project that exemplifies how a localization project is driven by a translator's gaming capital.

The findings from paratextual analysis, broadly interpreted, imply that non-professional translators construct a shadow circulation system. The system is shaped by the interaction between free and skills-based participation and gaming capital. The translators are free to start their own projects in a decentralized non-profit production cycle. In this cycle, the translators can translate a game years after its initial release date, or a patch can last for longer periods of time (as exemplified in KOTOR project), both of which would be unacceptable in a profit-driven cycle.

They are also empowered to contextualize their own patches, which means that it is the translators who contextualize the patch and the game for distribution. Traces of contextualization can be detected in paratexts.

Non-professional translators' practices move beyond the borders of translational intervention as they are empowered to contextualize content. On a technical level, they improve visuals, insert new content into the game, and create self-installing files. On a discursive level, they criticize the game, offer advice to peers, frame the game, or recount their own gaming experiences. Their practice illustrates that the translators recontextualize the games for circulation. The games without commercial value are recirculated depending on the non-professional translators' efforts. They are recirculated with the gaming capital of translators. The games are circulated with fancy graphics, if the translator has the appropriate technical skills, or they are circulated with a game bible, if the translator has gaming experience.

The fan paratexts appear to work in the way that Mia Consalvo described. The fan paratexts also "instruct the player in how to play, what to play, and what is cool (and not) in the game world" (Consalvo 2007: 22). In the context of Turkey, it is translators empowered by the community who instruct the user, and not the paratextual industries. The circulation practice is not commercial; it is driven by non-professionals' gaming capital.

This chapter attempts to explore the phenomenon of *belated localization*, which refers to the non-commercial translation of games whose shelf life has expired. In the belated localization process, the gap between the release and localization dates of the game is wide and the game may have lost commercial value by the date of localization. Focusing through a sociological lens on the non-commercial and non-professional production-distribution of language patches by Turkish translators, this chapter outlined the practices of non-professional translators, who act as culture brokers and "make games into something not just comprehensible but also enjoyable for players in other countries who speak other languages" (Consalvo, 2016: 123). When commercial localization is unavailable, non-professional translators step in to translate for the community, eventually empowering them to recontextualize the localization process and the game itself. Accordingly, this chapter argues that these non-professional translators not only act as culture brokers but also create an alternative production cycle in which games with an expired shelf life are translated, recontextualized and recirculated.

Drawing theoretical implications from the concept of *gaming capital*, the reworking of the Bourdieu's notion of cultural capital by Mia Consalvo to reveal "how individuals interact with games, information about games and the game industry, and other game players" (Consalvo, 2007: 4), this chapter posits that the non-professionals with a passion for games, gaming backgrounds or roots in gaming communities are the ones who initiate these non-profit-driven practices. The patches are then promoted and distributed through web pages, which host fan paratexts that showcase the translators' gaming capital and the analysis of these paratexts may shed light on how the game or localization process is recontextualized.

Concerning paratextual analysis, this chapter constructs *a local sociology of production* and illustrates that the practices of belated localization are shaped by translators' gaming capital, which encompasses fandom, gaming histories and childhood memories. Non-professional translators select and translate games based on their own preferences, without necessarily considering their commercial value and they are empowered to showcase their gaming capital in the paratexts which eventually recontextualize the game.

This study is among the first to comprehensively investigate non-commercial translation practices by focusing on the agents who actually translate the games, as previous research has focused predominantly on communities. The insights gained from this study can help further our understanding of the roles of individuals in alternative networks of circulation and how their gaming capital shapes translation practices. The findings from this research may also provide insights into the roles of individuals in alternative networks of circulation.

The relationships between non-professional translators and non-commercial translation practices require further investigation in various different contexts as well. As this chapter focused on the Turkish localization sphere, future research on other localization spheres could benefit from exploring the role of translators and their gaming capital in non-commercial practices.

## References

Al-Batineh, Mohammed, and Alawneh Razan . 2021. "Translation Hacking in Arabic Video Game Localization: The History and Current Practices." *Translation Spaces*. 10.(2):202–230.

Consalvo Mia. 2007. *Cheating: Gaining Advantage in Videogames*. Cambridge, Massachusetts: The MIT Press.

Consalvo Mia. 2012. "A Localization's Shop Tale: Bringing an Independent Japanese Role-playing Game to North America." In *The Participatory Cultures Handbook*, ed. by Aaron Alan Delwiche and Jennifer Jacobs Henderson, 59–10. New York. Routledge.

Consalvo Mia. 2013. "Unintended Travel: ROM Hackers and Fan Translations of Japanese Video Games" In *Gaming Globally: Production, Play, and Place*, ed. by Nina B. Huntemann and, Ben Aslinger, 119–141. New York: Palgrave Macmillan.

Consalvo Mia. 2016. *Atari to Zelda: Japan's Videogames in Global Contexts*. Cambridge, Massachusetts: The MIT Press.

Dietz, Frank. 2007. ""How Difficult Can That Be?" – The Work of Computer and Video Game Localization" *Revista Tradumàtica – Traducció i Tecnologies de la Informació i la Comunicació*. 5: http://www.fti.uab.cat/tradumatica/revista

Dovey, Jon, and Helen W. Kennedy. 2006. *Game Cultures: Computer Games As New Media*. Berkshire: Open University Press.

Fernández Costales, Alberto. 2013. "Crowdsourcing and collaborative translation: Mass phenomena or silent threat to translation studies?" *Hermes* 15: 85–110.

Fraysse, Olivier, and Mathieu O'Neil. 2015. "Introduction: Hacked in the USA: Prosumption and Digital Labour" In *Digital Labour and Prosumer Capitalism The US Matrix* ed. by Olivier Fraysse and Mathieu O'Neil, 1–20. New York: Palgrave Macmillan.

Genette, Gérard. 1997. *Paratexts: thresholds of interpretation*. Cambridge: Cambridge University Press.

Green, Jeff. 2004. "Knights of The Old Republic." *Computer Gaming World* 225: 60–61.

Guo, Ting and Jonathan Evans. 2020. "Translational and Transnational Queer Fandom In China: The Fansubbing of *Carol*." *Feminist Media Studies*. 20(4): 515–529.

Haythornthwaite, Caroline. 2009. "Crowds and Communities: Light and Heavyweight Models of Peer Production," In 42nd Hawaii International Conference on System Sciences: 1–10,

Jimenez-Crespo, Miguel A. 2017. *Crowdsourcing and Online Collaborative Translations: Expanding the Limits of Translation Studies*. Amsterdam, Philadelphia: John Benjamins.

Karagöz, Selahattin. 2019. "Amateurs, experts, explorers: Video game localization practices in Turkey" PhD Thesis. Istanbul, Yıldız Technical University.

Khoshsaligheh, Masood, Saeed Ameri, and Milad Mehdizadkhani. 2018. "A Socio-Cultural Study of Taboo Rendition in Persian Fansubbing: An Issue of Resistance", *Language and Intercultural Communication*. 18(6): 663–680.

Li, Dang. 2021. "The Transcultural Flow and Consumption of Online *Wuxia* Literature through Fan-based Translation." *Interventions*. 23:7:1041–1065.

Mangiron, Carme. 2018. "Game on! Burning Issues in Game Localisation". *Journal of Audiovisual Translation*. 1(1):122–138.

McDonough Dolmaya, Julie. 2011. "A Window into the Profession." *The Translator*. 17:1, 77–104.

Muñoz Sánchez, Pablo. 2009. "Video Game Localisation for Fans by Fans: The Case of Romhacking." *The Journal of Internationalization and Localization* 1 (1): 168–185.

Norris, Craig. 2014. "FCJ-171 Expectations Denied: Fan and Industry Conflict Around The Localisation of the Japanese Video Game Yakuza 3." *The Fibreculture Journal*, 23: 73–95

O'Hagan, Minako. 2009. "Evolution of User-generated Translation: Fansubs, Translation Hacking and Crowdsourcing." *Journal of Internationalisation and Localisation*. 1 (2009): 94–121.

O'Hagan, Minako. 2017. "Seeking delocalization: Fan community and game localization in the age of user empowerment." *Journal of Internationalization and Localization*. 4: 183–202.

O'Hagan, Minako, and Chandler Heaher. 2016. "Game Localization Research and Translation Studies: Loss and Gain Under An Interdisciplinary Lens" In *Border Crossings Translation Studies and Other Disciplines* ed. by Yves Gambier, and Luc van Doorslaer, 309–331. Amsterdam/Philadelphia: John Benjamins.

Öncü Yılmaz, Tutku and, Emre Canbaz . 2019. "The Role of Translation in Story Driven Video Games: An Evaluation of The Last of Us" *Çeviribilim ve Uygulamaları Dergisi Journal of Translation Studies*. 26: 77–103.

Önen, Seçkin İlke. 2018. "Approaches and Strategies to Cope with the Specific Challenges of Video Game Localization." Master's thesis, Ankara, Hacettepe University.

Pérez González, Luis. 2007. "Fansubbing Anime: Insights into The 'Butterfly Effect' of Globalisation on Audiovisual Translation." *Perspectives*. 14:4, 260–277.

Piróth, Attila and Mona Baker . 2020. "The Ethics of Volunteerism in Translation: Translators without Borders and the Platform Economy." *Journal of Foreign Language Teaching and Translation Studies*. 5(3): 1–30.

Ritzer, George and Nathan Jurgenson. 2010. "Production, Consumption, Prosumption: The Nature of Capitalism in the Age of the Digital 'Prosumer'." *Journal of Consumer Culture*. 10(1): 13–36.

Saadat, Shabnam. 2017. "Translaboration". *Translation and Translanguaging in Multilingual Contexts*. 3(3): 349–369.

Sánchez, Pablo Muñoz. 2009. "Video Game Localisation for Fans by Fans: The Case of Romhacking." *The Journal of Internationalization and Localization* 1: 168–185

Sarıgül, Semih and Jonathan Ross . 2020. "Volunteer vs. Professional Community Translation in Video Game Localization: The Case of the Steam Translation Server in Turkish", *Translogos*. 3(2): 1–22.

Tapscott, Don and Anthony D. Williams. 2006. *Wikinomics: How Mass Collaboration Changes Everything*. New York: Portfolio.

Terranova, Tiziana. 2000. "Free Labor: Producing Culture for Digital Economy", *Social Text*, 18(2): 33–58.

Walsh, Christopher and Thomas Apperley. 2009. "Gaming Capital: Rethinking Literacy." In: *Changing Climates: Education for Sustainable Futures. Proceedings of the AARE 2008 International Education Research Conference*, 30 Nov 4 Dec 2008, Queensland University of Technology.

Wongseree, Thanda, Minako O'Hagan, and Sasamoto Ryoko . 2019. "Contemporary Global Media Circulation Based on Fan Translation: A Particular Case of Thai Fansubbing." *Discourse, Context and Media*. 32: 1–9.

Zan, Arman. 2018. "Domestication and Foreignization in the Turkish Translation of Video Games." Master's thesis, Ankara, Hacettepe University.

Zimmerman, Joshua J. 2019. "Computer Game Fan Communities, Community Management, and Structures of Membership." *Games and Culture*. 14(7–8): 896–916.

Zwischenberger, Cornelia. 2021. "Online Collaborative Translation: Its Ethical, Social, and Conceptual Conditions and Consequences." *Perspectives*

## Online resources

Akdoğan, Adem. 2014. Oyun çevirileri hakkında Genel bilgilendirme ... OYUNCEVİRİ. Accessed September 2, 2021. https://oyunceviri.net/oyun-cevirileri-hakkinda-genel-bilgilendirme/.

EF English Proficiency Index. 2020. *EFI*. Accessed September 2, 2021. https://www.ef.com/wwen/epi/regions/europe/turkey/.

Eliaçık, Erdi. 2013. Site Yöneticimizden Bir Açıklama. *OYUNCEVİRİ*. Accessed September 2, 2021. https://oyunceviri.net/site-yoneticimizden-bir-aciklama/.

Eliaçık, Erdi. 2013b. Önemli Bir Duyuru! – (Lütfen tüm takipçilerimiz okusunlar.) *OYUNCEVİRİ*. Accessed September 2, 2021. https://oyunceviri.net/onemli-bir-duyuru-lutfen-tum-takipcilerimiz-okusunlar/.

GOG. 2021. Oddworld: Abe's Oddysee. GOG. Accessed October 2, 2021. https://www.gog.com/game/oddworld_abes_oddysee.

Grandshaw, Lisa. 2017. "The Unexpected Reveal in Star Wars: Knights of the Old Republic." SYFY.com. Accessed October 20, 2018. https://www.syfy.com/syfywire/stuff-we-love-the-unexpected-reveal-in-star-wars-knights-of-the-old-republic.

Kasavin, Greg. 2001. Clive Barker's Undying Review. *GAMESPOT*. Accessed October 2, 2021. https://www.gamespot.com/reviews/clive-barkers-undying-review/1900-2687131/.

Oyunceviri. 2017. Sıkça Sorulan Sorular. *OYUNCEVİRİ*. Accessed September 9, 2017. https://oyunceviri.net/sss/.

Oyunceviri. 2019a. Clive Barker's Undying Türkçe Yama. *OYUNCEVİRİ*. Accessed October 2, 2021. https://www.oyunceviri.net/clive-barkers-undying-turkce-yama/.

Oyunceviri. 2019b. Fahrenheit: Indigo Prophecy Remastered Türkçe Yama v1.0. *OYUNCEVİRİ*. Accessed October 2, 2021. https://www.oyunceviri.net/fahrenheit-indigo-prophecy-remastered-turkce-yama-v1-0/.

Oyunceviri. 2019c. Knight Rider the Game 2 Türkçe Yama. *OYUNCEVİRİ*. Accessed October 2, 2021. https://www.oyunceviri.net/knight-rider-the-game-2-turkce-yama-v1-0/.

Oyunceviri. 2019d. Oddworld – Abe's Oddysee – %100 Türkçe Yama. *OYUNCEVİRİ*. Accessed October 2, 2021. https://www.oyunceviri.net/oddworld-abes-oddysee/.

Oyunceviri. 2019e. Prince of Persia Warrior Within – %100 Türkçe Yama. *OYUNCEVİRİ*. Accessed October 2, 2021. https://www.oyunceviri.net/prince-of-persia-warrior-within/.

Oyunceviri. 2019f. Star Wars The Force Unleashed 2 – %100 Türkçe Yama. *OYUNCEVİRİ*. Accessed September 2, 2021. https://www.oyunceviri.net/star-wars-the-force-unleashed-2/.

Oyunceviri. 2019g. Tomb Raider I Türkçe Yama v 1.0. *OYUNCEVİRİ*. Accessed September 2, 2021. https://www.oyunceviri.net/tomb-raider-i-turkce-yama-v1-0/.

Oyunceviri. 2019h. Tomb Raider 3 – Türkçe Yama v 2.0. *OYUNCEVİRİ*. Accessed September 2, 2021. https://www.oyunceviri.net/tomb-raider-3-turkce-yama-v1-0/.

Oyunceviri. 2020. Crysis – %100 Türkçe Yama. *OYUNCEVİRİ*. Accessed October 2, 2021. https://www.oyunceviri.net/crysis-o-turkce-yama/.

Spry, Jeff. Star Wars: Knights of the Old Republic Set to Score a Modern Fan Makeover. SYFY.com. Accessed October 20, 2018. https://www.syfy.com/syfywire/star-wars-knights-old-republic-set-score-modern-fan-makeover.

Sürücü, Said. KOTOR. Accessed October 20, 2018. http://www.kotorprojesi.com/.

Yıldızsavaşları. 2011. KOTOR Artık %100 Türkçe. *YILDIZSAVASLARI*. Accessed October 2, 2021. http://yildizsavaslari.com/2014/01/26/kotor-artik-o-turkce/.

Yıldızsavaşları. 2011. Türkçe Kotor Projesi Desteğinizi Bekliyor. *YILDIZSAVASLARI*. Accessed October 12, 2021. http://yildizsavaslari.com/2011/08/22/kotor/.

## List of the games

Assassin's Creed – Revelations. 2011. Ubisoft Montreal.
Assassin's Creed Brotherhood. 2010. Ubisoft Montreal.
Call of Duty: Modern Warfare 2. 2009. Infinity Ward.
Colin McRae DIRT 2. 2009. Codemasters.
Crisis. 2007. Cybertek.
Fahrenheit: Indigo Prophecy Remastered. 2015. Aspyr
Formula I 2011. 2010. EA Sports
Knight Rider: The Game II. 2002. Tri Synergy.
Oddworld: Abe's Oddysee. 1997. Oddworld Inhabitants.
Postal I. 1997. Running with Scissors
Prince of Persia: Warrior Within. 2004. Ubisoft Montreal.
Star Wars The Force Unleashed II. 2010. Aspyr
The Clive Barker's Undying. 2001. DreamWorks Interactive
The Tomb Raider I. 1996. Core Design
The Tomb Raider III: Adventures of Lara Croft. 1998. Core Design

CHAPTER 7

# Nollywood and indigenous language translation flows
A systems perspective

Maricel Botha
North-West University Potchefstroom

Africa's multiplicity of languages has seen little manifestation in large-scale translation flows of the indigenous African languages in the post-independence period, largely because of the hegemony of ex-colonial languages. Against this background, Nollywood's stimulation of translation from and into indigenous African languages in a way that crosses national borders and exhibits some "velocity" is exceptional. This chapter investigates Nollywood's relationship with indigenous language translation and accounts for the conditions that promote indigenous language use in inter-societal information flows. The investigation employs the concepts of selective mediation and permeability as described in Sergey Tyulenev's application of Niklas Luhmann's social systems theory to explore how Nollywood-stimulated indigenous language translations can pierce through language barriers, while operating selectively under the influence of social and ideological conditioning.

**Keywords:** Nollywood, translation, subtitling, interpreting, indigenous African languages, social systems theory, Niklas Luhmann

## Introduction

If translation flows are understood as trends in inter-lingual mediation that exhibit some degree of volume and velocity, then translation practices involving indigenous African languages can perhaps be described as a trickle. The hegemony of ex-colonial languages, especially in written, prestigious and formal social domains, has stifled the use of indigenous languages in these domains, and language policy and translation have been inadequately employed to facilitate linguistic representation and access (Adejunmobi 2013: 19–25; Beukes 2006). This situation prevails despite widespread functional illiteracy in former colonial languages (Thiong'o

2018: 125) and the obvious value of indigenous language translation in relation to symbolic and material social inclusion (Botha 2019). The effect of merely tokenistic recognition of indigenous languages in African language policies (Kamwangamalu 2016: 157) is further aggravated by prevailing language attitudes. Ngũgĩ wa Thiong'o (2018: 125) sums up dominant language attitudes as involving esteem for English (and other ex-colonial languages) as "the gate to progress and modernity" and a view of indigenous languages as "barriers to this glittering thing called progress and modernity". This attitude aligns with global trends of favouring world languages as vehicles of progress, but it is particularly pronounced given the colonial delegitimisation of the indigenous languages and nefarious post-colonial language politics. Regarding the latter, there tends to be a disjunction between what "governing elites are obliged to do [...] and what they prefer to do based on their interests and the convenience of inertia" (Alexander in Mesthrie 2006: 154). The impracticality of multilingualism and financial constraints offer useful excuses for de facto endorsement of monolingual language practices and neglect of indigenous language translation (Kruger et al. 2007: 36). To some sceptics this endorsement purposefully perpetuates status hierarchies and economic models based on cheap labour, and to more moderate critics it simply hides administrative incapacity.

Despite a general devaluation of their progressive utility, however, there is a high regard for indigenous languages as expressions of identity. Indigenous African languages enjoy significant vitality in spoken form (including spoken mass media) in contrast to their comparative scarcity in written forms as a consequence of the factors described above. They are cherished as languages of community, intimacy and solidarity, and their general exclusion as languages of aspiration (Mesthrie 2015: 189) does not threaten their role as identity markers. This oral vitality may suggest a greater degree of translational flow involving indigenous languages in the sphere of spoken discourse. But this is difficult to determine, given not only the often informal nature of interpreting, but also translation studies' bias towards more formalised oral translation practices such as conference and legal interpreting. It may therefore be that many translation flows go unnoticed in the sphere of community interpreting (with interpreting in church and forced immigration contexts perhaps representing especially neglected examples). At least as far as commonly documented African interpreting practices are concerned, the indication of a shortage of formal interpreting and references to the myriad of frustrations to successful interpreting (even in cases not strictly involving indigenous languages) suggests obstacles to the overall categorisation of oral translation as a flow. The same is true of formal written translation in Africa overall, and both are undermined by insufficient recognition (Atanganna Nama 1993: 417; Beukes 2006; Ndlovu 2020), inadequate training of practitioners

(Ndeffo Chene and Chia 2009; Lesch and Ntuli 2020), the use of lay practitioners (Thuube and Ekanjume-Ilongo 2018), unsatisfactory working conditions (Aroga Bessong 2009) and poor-quality translation (Pienaar and Cornelius 2015; Fuentes-Luque 2017), alongside the already-mentioned language policy issues (Kadenge and Nkomo 2011).

The large-scale translation from and into indigenous African languages of films produced by the Nigerian film industry, Nollywood, offers a welcome contrast to the general dearth of translation, and especially indigenous language translation, sketched very briefly above. Around half of Nollywood's prolific film output (surpassing Hollywood, but second to Bollywood) consists of indigenous-language films, and subtitling into English, French and even indigenous languages have been employed since the early 1990s to ensure film distribution locally, but also across Sub-Saharan Africa and abroad (Fuentes-Luque 2017). Nollywood films are also frequently interpreted live into indigenous languages at film screenings and oral translations into indigenous languages are recorded onto DVDs. These cases of translation involving indigenous languages exhibit a degree of momentum and dynamism which may be described as "organic" in that they are prompted by grassroots motivation and popular consumption trends rather than policy obligations. It is also worth noting their designation as part of the informal economy. (In this respect, this research responds to a call by Marais and Feinauer (2017) for African translation studies to pay more attention to this neglected yet predominant sector of the African economy.) The instrumentality of indigenous African languages as vehicles of cultural expression and disruptors of linguistic imperialism is displayed in Nollywood's indigenous language translation trends – something many African scholars have longed to see.

In the analysis of Nollywood as a catalyst of indigenous language translation flows, this research employs Niklas Luhmann's social systems theory (SST), which has enjoyed some attention within sociologically informed translation research (see Botha 2020; Hermans 1999; Hermans 2007a and b; Tyulenev 2009; Tyulenev 2012a, b and Tyulenev 2013), although its value, particularly in macro-level translation research, has perhaps been underappreciated (see Tyulenev 2012a: 164–165). Macro-level translation research investigates broad translation trends (or flows) and large social structures such as entire regions, societies or social systems, rather than smaller structures such as communities or organisations, or individual texts or translators. Social theories that focus on macro-structures are helpful in studying the nature and operation of translation as a social practice, since they reflect "translation's natural social habitat" (Tyulenev 2014a: 164). The social habitat that Luhmann describes is one that consists of interacting systems of communication, which, at the broadest levels, may include societies or societal function systems such as the law, politics, education or mass media, which Luhmann sees as the main organising components of modern society. These systems provide stimuli which condition the behaviour of other systems, but they do not directly control one another. Rather, each system functions according to its own internal order to reproduce itself and selects from the environment what it needs, reducing environmental complexity to achieve its own communicative reproduction. In this regard, systems operate similarly to biological cells. Sergey Tyulenev (2009; 2012a, b; 2013) inserts translation into this environment as a system itself, which "services" other systems by mediating communication flows across language barriers. It assumes a boundary position around systems and selectively filters information into those systems in response to various stimuli, of which ideological stimuli are particularly important. In this regard, its selective operation in the service of other systems is likened to the functioning of a semi-permeable cell membrane.

As a social theory which is on the extreme structural end of the structure-agency continuum, SST has been justifiably critiqued for a lack of attention to human agents and an abstractionist tendency to focus on structures. Yet Luhmann's biologically inspired approach possesses a particular capacity to focus attention on communication and information flows, and in the context of this volume its scientific "peculiarities" and concentration on processes rather than persons render it an analytical advantage rather than a hindrance. Relying on Tyulenev's application, translation is seen in this chapter as functioning to mediate communication flows across language barriers between societies (African and foreign) in the contexts of Nollywood film distribution by assuming a boundary position around the mass media systems of receptor societies. It is also seen to mediate on the part of the donor society, Nigeria, as a means to facilitate intersocietal information exchange. The latter view is my own and departs somewhat from Tyulenev's original description, which focuses on mediation by receptor societies, but it relies on his insights nonetheless. In both cases the nature of translational mediation is ideologically conditioned. Translation's particular systemic qualities are only explained here as far as is necessary to describe its facilitation of interlingual information flows in relation to mass media systems. The focus here is thus on translation's servicing of these systems rather than its own operation as a focus in itself. Viewing translation in terms of its selective perforation of language barriers under the influence of ideological stimuli and under the conditioning of the social environment provides a very useful perspective for understanding Nollywood translation flows, since it emphasises the conditions which allow indigenous language mediation to occur across system boundaries against the backdrop of its general non-occurrence. The intention is to demonstrate that the conditioning of translation by a certain configuration of ideological and environmental impulses provides an enabling environment for indigenous language translation in this case. This includes translation's evasion of certain constraints that typically limit indigenous language translation. The analysis of these conditions might suggest routes along which indigenous language translation trickles might gain momentum in other social spheres in the future.

In the following section, SST is explained relatively succinctly only insofar as it pertains to the aims of this chapter. Thereafter SST is applied in the discussion of Nollywood's stimulation of translation flows from and into indigenous languages respectively, before concluding with a consideration of the relevance of the findings.

## Social systems theory

One peculiarity of Luhmann's SST is that it views society as consisting of communication networks, rather than focusing on people or actions (Luhmann 2012: 7–12). The function systems mentioned above as the major orienting systems of modern society, as well as all other social systems (programmes and organisations, which are not relevant here), are therefore systems of communication from Luhmann's perspective. These are dependent on human consciousness, but humans are seen to exist outside of society and outside of these systems. Function systems are conceived as self-reproducing, or autopoietic, in their operation similarly to biological cells (Seidl 2004: 2–3). They depend on a social environment (consisting of other social systems) as well as on a psychic and physical environment (consisting of human consciousness and the physical world respectively). They receive input from this environment, just as cells receive energy and matter from the environment, but their operation is not determined directly by the environment (Seidl 2004: 3), which renders them autopoietic (self-reproducing) rather than allopoietic (direct products of the environment). The internal order of function systems is described using binary codes, such as aesthetic/non-aesthetic for the art system, or immanent/transient for the religious system. These codes summarise the ways in which different systems make sense of or respond to environmental stimuli according to their internal organisation and function for society (Hermans 2007a: 65). Whereas the economic system may interpret a film in terms of profitability, for example, the political system may interpret it in relation to power based on its governing code. The relationship between the environment and the systems produces what is known as structural coupling. If systems can be structurally coupled with the environment, this means that they can adjust themselves based on significant environmental stimuli (Tyulenev 2013: 44).

Luhmann understands the communication of systems inferentially as a combination of three elements: information, utterance and understanding (see Seidl

2004:7). Information relates to message content and involves selecting what needs to be communicated from everything that could possibly be communicated. Utterance refers to the way in which a message is communicated and the reason for its communication and it also relies on selection out of a set of possible utterances. Understanding involves distinguishing between information and utterance and is derived from an *interpretation* of them (see Hermans 2007a: 63).

This communication model has implications for the description of the various functions of the mass media system. This system is exceptionally comprehensive, including all forms of technologically mass distributed communication (Luhmann 2000: 3). Mass distribution implies the absence of direct feedback from the message recipient to the message creator, and thus the necessity of generalised communication (Bechmann and Stehr 2011: 143). It is internally differentiated to include "programmes", including journalism, advertising and entertainment. These are considered programmes rather than separate function systems, because they all operate using the binary code information/non-information and direct society's self-observation by providing a construction of reality (Luhmann 2000: 5). The description of the code of the mass media system as information/non-information might suggest a bias towards journalism, but Luhmann compares the function of entertainment with that of games to explain the relevance of information to entertainment and the socially reflective role of entertainment within the media system. A sports game constructs a reality which "conforms to certain conditions and from which perspective the usual ways of living life appear as real reality" (Luhmann 2000: 51). Similarly, entertainment, such as films, designates a "second reality" visually and acoustically, and this framing "releases a world in which a fictional reality of its own applies" (Luhmann 2000: 52). Yet, unlike a game, entertainment does not require rules, but information (Luhmann 2000: 52–53). These are the familiar details which produce unity in the story told and "facilitate a conceptual leap to a (likewise constructed) personal identity of the viewer" (Luhmann 2000: 54). Although entertainment relies on information, it derives its value from a greater emphasis on utterance than on information, in contrast to journalism (Görke 2001: 220). In other words, the way in which information is communicated gains particular value in the entertainment programme.

Regarding translation as a social system, Tyulenev suggests the code mediation/non-mediation (which does not include only inter-lingual mediation, although I will focus on this type of mediation here). This mediation relies on Luhmann's communication model in that it consists of the selection of information and utterance on the part of the message producer, followed by understanding on the part of the mediating (translating) party. This results in a second level of information and utterance, which is interpreted to produce understanding in the receiving party (Tyulenev 2013:162). The term *mediation* evokes active intervention in the communicative act by the translation system to ensure successful or purposeful communication. It also foregrounds structural coupling to a greater extent than Hermans's suggested term "representation" does and is therefore better able to explain translation's function in relation to other systems. Tyulenev describes translation, as a boundary phenomenon that functions to reduce information into a form that can be comprehended by the commissioning system and to introduce that information into the system's internal communication. In this sense, translation also facilitates coupling between the human (psychic) realm and the social realm by reducing information to a form that makes it generally consumable by human participants in a particular society who are limited by the languages they understand. As soon as the translation system assumes a boundary position around a particular system (at any time mediation is required), the commissioning system contextualises the operation of translation. Thus, whereas the study of translation merely as an autonomous function system takes the system as the sphere of observation (see Hermans 2007a), studying translation in its boundary function in relation to other systems includes the commissioning system in its scope. The norms and discourses of the commissioning system are thus studied in relation to the way in which they determine translation activities (Tyulenev 2009:156).

In this regard, ideology becomes an important consideration. Tyulenev (2009:156) considers the constitutive elements of the translation system to be translations themselves as well as other phenomena of social discourse, particularly ideologemes. Ideologemes are manifested in the communication of virtually any system and can be distinguished from ideologies (as psychological phenomena) by their existence in the social sphere as units of ideological expression in communication. The ideologies prevalent in a particular system, which often reflect its particular operation, but may also be societally widespread, thus contextualise translation practices as soon as translation assumes a boundary position around that system.

In Africa, the degree of systemic differentiation of translation is lower than in the West, but arguably comparable with other developing regions. Translation typically emerges as a system in response to society's increasing functional differentiation and tends to take place once translation begins to undergo a degree of professionalisation. Its systemic development is reflected in the "clustering" of translational communication and the development of specialised bodies such as professional associations, government departments, training institutions, etc. It is also expressed in translation's self-reflection on its operations in translation scholarship. In Africa, this type of development generally occurred after liberation and was spurred on by the establishment of new pan-African political and economic associations. However, continued language imperialism has resulted in slow development, as was implied in the introduction. Therefore, translation can be considered a somewhat poorly differentiated system in most African countries.

In the interpretations that follow, this simplified explanation of SST will be applied to African mass media systems following an approach that recognises national manifestations of these systems. This represents a departure from Luhmann's original theorisation. Luhmann (2012: 9) considered the drawing of national boundaries an arbitrary phenomenon, unable to account for the boundaries of society. Yet localised differences in systemic behaviour within a national delineation remain distinctly observable despite interconnections. Thus, although communication transcends national boundaries, the tendency for communication to be clustered differently in various national contexts provides not only a justification for this approach, but also makes the implementation of SST fruitful.

## Nollywood as a stimulator of translation flows

Nollywood came into existence in Nigeria in the early 1990s after the collapse of the local film industry under the negative economic impact of the Ibrahim Babangida regime. Cheap and accessible video film technology saw a mushrooming of amateur films, which became a booming "all comers' affair" (Ayakoroma 2014: 21). In terms of SST, political and economic stimuli thus negatively conditioned the media system by limiting its conventional offerings. This stimulated cheap and informal film production (allowed by new developments in the science/technology system) to meet entertainment needs. The crisis within the entertainment programme of the mass media system led to a democratisation of film production, i.e. a change in coupling with the systems of human consciousness (psychic systems) to include ordinary citizens, and a necessary subversion of institutionalised production and distribution practices (Mistry and Ellapen 2013: 46). Films were produced by businessmen ranging from electronic equipment dealers to cement sellers in a highly unregulated atmosphere in terms of taxation, production standards, etc. (Ayakoroma 2014: 21). Films were initially sold or rented as VHS tapes in video parlours and were spread informally among friends and family. DVDs replaced VHS tapes over time and the internet became an important dissemination site alongside television channels, DVD outlets, and continued informal exchange. During both periods piracy represented a major form of distribution – with debilitating consequences for the growth potential of the market. Thus, in terms of both production and distribution, Nollywood's practices are characterised by comparative freedom from the host of environmental constraints that typically condition film production (and render it a fairly exclusive practice) and by the formation of new, often less rigid types of coupling with environmental systems. The Nigerian entertainment programme's typical patterns of communication and its self-reproductive behaviour were thus reconfigured with the emergence of Nollywood and it was reorganised to make provision for new communicative contingencies.

A significant aspect of this reorganisation was novel thematic developments, which set Nollywood further apart from institutionalised African cinema and reflected new forms of coupling with psychic systems. The themes of Nollywood productions are often distilled to melodramatic representations of witchcraft, family squabbles, marriage and infidelity. These are contrasted with the progressive and overtly ideological themes of institutionalised African cinema, which has been critiqued for its "literariness or symbolic specificity that has made itself elusive to mainstream (popular) African audiences" (Mistry and Ellapen 2013: 52) and has rendered it appealing mainly to an educated elite and foreign audiences. Mistry and Ellapen (2013: 54) describe Nollywood themes as unreflexive and regressive in their perpetuation of stereotypes and disregard for "the complex critical project of filmmaking practices, especially in the canonized tropes of African cinema and 'its struggle against cultural imperialism'". But the authors explain that this "audacity" is precisely what supports Nollywood's claim to authenticity and representativeness. The distinctly African "dynamics of domesticity and familiarity" (Mistry and Ellapen 2013: 52) that characterise Nollywood productions awards capital to the mass media system's function of reconstructing social reality. They represent a selection of information that apparently quite successfully facilitates the conceptual leap from entertainment to viewers' reality and identity by creating a world that is relatable, and intriguing or amusing for that reason. (Of course, depictions of the "exotic" possess another type of appeal.) The proximity of Nollywood's themes to familiar everyday experiences and their "Africanity" (see Krings and Okome 2013; McCall 2007; Pype 2013) renders them immensely appealing in neighbouring West African societies, among the West African diaspora, across Sub-Saharan Africa and even in the West Indies. In this regard, Nollywood challenges the assumption that Western hegemony in globalised world politics directs the movement of cultural products mainly in a North-South direction (see Pype 2013: 202). Nollywood's disruption of global MacDonaldisation through its stimulation of disparate trends in cultural transfer has been lauded by academics for its reflection of a welcome form of post-colonial cultural pan-Africanism (see Marston et al. 2007; McCall 2007; Pype 2013). McCall (2007: 96) boldly claimed that Nollywood "created a Pan-African forum that makes speaking of [...] pan-African culture possible for the first time". The question of interest here is how the translation of indigenous language products fits into this web of inter-societal media diffusion and what practical and ideological conditions engage indigenous languages in this "pan-African forum" and its international outposts.

Before the position of the indigenous languages is investigated, it should be noted that the instrumental value of English film production has accounted in part for Nollywood's transportability (Fuentes-Luque 2017:145) and that the most popular and well-funded Nollywood films are generally produced in English. Yet equally noteworthy is Nollywood's typical employment of indigenised English (Nigerian English and Pidgin) and its use of code-switching involving local languages and even film production in various languages simultaneously (see Adeoti and Lawal 2014:189–190). The use of English is therefore not merely a tactic to promote foreign marketing (although the proportionately few well-funded and Hollywood-influenced blockbusters do tend to employ a more international and understandable version of English as an economic coupling mechanism). Rather, the authentic use of English reflects social realities in a way that ties in with the authenticity of Nollywood themes described earlier.

Nevertheless, McCain (2013:26) points out that researchers' focus on English-language films "risks missing the ways that Nigerian-language films are also crossing borders and appealing to transnational audiences". In this regard, it is important to note the large proportion of Nollywood films produced in indigenous languages. An often cited 1997–2003 UNESCO survey indicated the following language distribution among the total films produced in that period (UIS 2009:9): English 44%; Yoruba 31%; Hausa 24%; Igbo 1%; other languages >1%. McCain (2013:32–33) indicated an increasing proportion of indigenous language films in the early 2000s and a significant spike in indigenous language film production in 2010 (McCain 2013:33). Unfortunately, more recent statistics are not available, but it is likely that a sizeable proportion of indigenous language films continues to be produced, particularly in the light of McCain's (2013:36) explanation of the profitability of these films in comparison with English films within local, small-scale and informal marketing and distribution models, which are less threatened by piracy. This profitability probably accounts for the spikes mentioned earlier.

## Subtitling of indigenous language Nollywood films

Subtitling has represented an important mechanism for the flow of indigenous language films primarily within Nigeria, but also abroad, ever since the success of what some consider the first Nollywood film, the Igbo production *Living in Bondage* (1992). Subtitling is generally done unprofessionally and informally by Nigerian film producers themselves or it is cheaply commissioned by producers (Fuentes-Luque 2017:145). When translators are commissioned, they are paid a small fee (less than US$50 per film) for films translated within a very short time (ca. 24 hours) and have "neither a contract nor a steady flow of work" (Fuentes-Luque 2017: 145–146). The hand-to-mouth nature of subtitling characterises it as part of the informal economy. Given this approach, it is unsurprising that subtitling practices show little regard for the conventional patterns and standards of translation established within translation theory. The translation system's theoretical impact on these practices is thus rather weak. The relative underdevelopment of the Nigerian translation system may be blamed for this, as is suggested by Fuentes-Luque's (2017: 146) reference to poor training infrastructure in the region as an explanation for poor quality. Yet SST helps to indicate that informality and poor quality are probably instead reflective of Nollywood's evasion of the constraints which generally affect film production – a tactic shown to be an economic requisite for its very existence. It is therefore likely that the presence of well-developed local audio-visual translation infrastructure and the availability of well-trained subtitlers would not affect Nollywood subtitling practices at all.

Cheap and quick subtitling represents a strategy to viably overcome local intelligibility barriers, on the one hand. In this regard, translation surmounts local language barriers. But this type of mediation also establishes coupling with foreign media systems, which is of greater interest here. Translation assumes a boundary position around the Nigerian mass media system in these cases by allowing it to direct stimuli to specific destinations within the environment. It does this by linguistically manipulating its offerings to allow penetration of certain foreign systems without the need for linguistic mediation on their part, which is an economic benefit for receiving systems. English subtitles produced by the Nigerian translation system also sometimes contain evidence of cultural mediation. Fuentes-Luque (2017: 145) notes the frequent absence of subtitles in witchcraft scenes, for example, which suggests that Nigerian translation facilitates message absorption (probably abroad) by moderating potentially offensive themes. Although the Nigerian media system cannot directly determine what films penetrate inter-societal barriers, as this is determined by the receiving systems' own autopoiesis, translation offers enabling stimuli and facilitates inter-societal coupling based on its knowledge of the linguistic modes employed by, and cultural norms prevalent in, specific environmental systems.

Subtitling, as a specific mediational choice, represents a practical selection strategy in that it enables simultaneous film distribution to audiences who understand the spoken dialogue and those who do not. Additionally, it facilitates preservation of the "cultural and linguistic taste of national films" (Olukayode 2017: 27), which accounts for their appeal within Nigeria and among the Nigerian diaspora particularly. It therefore allows for a particular type of cultural mediation, which relates to translational utterance as a particular framing or "performance" of an original (Hermans 2007a: 68–69). The foregrounding of the indigenous language dialogue which occurs during subtitling (as opposed to dubbing) carries the implication that the original performance holds significance, which directs the eventual understanding of the information. Olukayode (2017: 27) explains in this regard that subtitling of local languages plays a particular role in propagating African tradition and Nigerian cultures and norms abroad. African languages express an authenticity and indigeneity that add meaning to the filmic experience, even when comprehensible only in translation. Nollywood director Tunde Kelani's very purposeful and educational use of Yoruba is seen by Olusegun Soetan (2018: 6) in this light when he designates it as a way "to confer agency on African languages so that Africans may own their indigenous languages and project the culture embodied by the language to the world". While Kelani's employment of indigenous languages is more purposeful than that of other directors, a similar desire for cultural expression arguably undergirds most indigenous language productions.

It is worth noting that African mass media systems, and particularly their entertainment programmes, offer positive conditions for the expression of cultural esteem via indigenous languages that are absent in many other systems. Whereas African social functions such as the law, science, literature, higher education, healthcare, politics, etc. are, relatively speaking, not conducive to indigenous language promotion and their employment in elevated and formal contexts, African mass media systems are more accommodating. This perhaps relates to their relationship with reality construction and their greater partiality to "the masses". The entertainment programme, in particular, is not constrained by a strong association with development, while its incorporation of daily realities as information into its autopoietic operation allows significant room for indigenous language expression. It is thus better positioned to accommodate positive ideologies with regard to indigenous languages than certain other systems. African mass media systems thus represent a realm of comparative freedom. Nevertheless, the ability for indigenous language products to transcend national boundaries remains a peculiarity associated with Nollywood.

The Nigerian translation system's decision to provide subtitles mainly in English, but also in French, counteracts the regional restrictions that the use of indigenous languages imposes. This choice is clearly strategic (and expressive of selective coupling) given the position of English and French in Sub-Saharan Africa and among African diasporic communities in the West – the main destinations of indigenous language exports. Indigenous language exports apparently constituted around 35% of the total Nollywood export market in 2007 (Marston et al. 2007: 64), yet the lack of research and statistics as well as the informal nature of Nollywood distribution complicate quantification and cast doubt on the ability to provide accurate estimations. Among the Nigerian diaspora in the West, subtitling of indigenous language Nollywood films facilitates not only access, but also language learning among an increasingly Europhone diasporic population (McCain 2013: 45). Here, indigenous languages play a particular role in maintaining homeland ties because of their high authenticity value, but potentially also because of the tendency for indigenous language films to "stay closer to the aesthetics and moral vision of the grassroots", while a proportion of English films becomes increasingly conditioned by Hollywood's filmic requirements (McCain 2013: 45). There are suggestions that indigenous language films may even be more popular in certain foreign destinations than English films (McCain 2013: 45). Abroad, indigenous language Nollywood films are often consumed via internet distribution platforms. Irokotv, a major Nollywood subscription platform, caters predominantly for diasporic communities, with the top destinations including the United States, the United Kingdom, Canada, Germany and Italy (Adegoke 2012). It provides subtitles for all its indigenous language films, suggesting that these are frequently viewed by non-speakers of those languages. Besides English subtitles, it also provides subtitles in French and Swahili to broaden its viewership in Africa, but has struggled to build a viable base of subscribers here for economic reasons (Künzler 2019: 8).

The popularity of indigenous language Nollywood films in societies neighbouring Nigeria results partly from shared languages (e.g. Hausa in Niger, Chad and Cameroon, and Yoruba in Benin and Togo). Yet, satellite television service DStv's Africa Magic channels in Yoruba, Hausa and Igbo are broadcast throughout West, Central and East Africa (The Eagle Online 2021), furnished with poor quality subtitles, explained earlier to be a hallmark of Nollywood productions. Broad dissemination suggests a notable market for translated indigenous language content across a large area. In support of this deduction, Olukayode (2017: 25) observes that in nearby Francophone countries, indigenous languages help to boost Nollywood's offerings. However, Olukayode (2017: 25) explains that while Nigerian film makers have been subtitling into French for nearby African countries since the 1980s, dubbing is the preferred mediation strategy of African Francophone societies. This is probably because of funding for dubbing from the French government, which supports dubbing rather than subtitling for various social reasons which include better promotion of the French language. The foregrounding of indigenous languages as symbols of authenticity seen in Nigerian subtitling practices can be contrasted with the masking of foreignness and homogenisation typically observed with dubbing practices (Olukayode 2017: 28), highlighting the selectivity of translation practices amid differing forms of ideological conditioning.

### Interpreting of Nollywood films into African indigenous languages

Trends of orally interpreting Nollywood films into indigenous African languages reflect a complex negotiation between the foreign and familiar. Such oral translations are usually initiated by receiving systems and showcase translation ability to facilitate selective system permeability. As was the case with Nigerian subtitling practices, these translation practices tend to be carried out informally, i.e. apart from the constraints that typically govern professional translation, and partly because of this, they give rise to unique expressions of domestication or indigenisation. In the Democratic Republic of Congo, for example, Nollywood films expressing a Pentecostal Christian worldview are immensely popular and are consumed either untranslated, in which case the English or indigenous language dialogue is often unintelligible (Pype 2013: 203), or they are interpreted from English to Lingala and kiKinois (Kinshasa street-Lingala) by "dubbers". These dubbers, who work for local television stations and interpret all roles, sometimes periodically call out names of local politicians while interpreting in line with local cultural practices (where such inserted declarations of support or praise, known as *mabanga*, or diamonds, elicit financial reward) (Pype 2013: 217). Dubbers also interpret or contextualise film content in a way that ascribes "a series of local significances to these films' narratives and images, thus permitting their integration into various local strategies of reception" (Pype 2013: 217). One example of this is inserting a Pentecostal Christian interpretation and moral instruction where these are absent in the original film (Pype 2013: 217). In Tanzania, a similar approach is followed, where live oral interpreting of Nollywood films into Kiswahili takes place at public screenings. Here, while "[a]d-libbing and adding observations with local inflections and personal commentary to 'spice up' the movies", the narrators adapt "the stories to a local hermeneutic framework" (Krings and Okome 2013: 8; see also Krings 2010). Similarly, in Togo, Nollywood film interpetations by a prominent pastor and television station owner into Ewé contain commentary and comparisons with the local cultural and political scene (Krings and Okome 2013: 8). In Kenya and Uganda similarly free types of "dubbing" and live interpretation into local languages are applied to a wide range of films (Künzler 2019). Although Nollywood films are less popular here than in societies closer to Nigeria, they are also screened live and on television with liberal, indigenising forms of translation (Künzler 2019: 18). A very loose form of translation is associated with the so-called VJs ("videojockeys" or "videojokers") responsible for indigenous-language dubbing of DVDs for vendors in Kenya and Uganda. Künzler (2019: 18) refers to them as "translators" (in quotation marks) and notes that some even interpret films in languages they do not know, meaning that they guess or invent the meaning of dialogue based on the imagery.

Oral translation offers a strategic indigenising response from receiving systems, since it allows more room for interpretation than the space restriction of subtitling allows. It also helps overcome illiteracy barriers and thus responds to educational stimuli. The informal nature of these practices further renders them affordable in comparison with professional dubbing and even subtitling, and economic limitations are thus overcome. Since these oral forms of translation often involve live or voice-over techniques, where the original dialogue is audible, they represent a different form of mediation to traditional dubbing, since the act of "rendering" or "performing" the original is more overt. Through obvious acts of localisation, allowed by direction towards particular, small-scale audiences, the distinction between information and utterance and the mediatory role of the translator are also more pronounced. Nollywood films are thus marked as foreign, while undergoing obvious cultural mediation and selective introduction into the target system.

These translation trends prove that "[t]hough Nigerian video films have assumed a transnational existence, depending on the context, their accessibility in cultural and linguistic terms may still be limited, and the films therefore warrant one form of mediation or the other" (Krings and Okome 2013: 8). The interpretation of Nollywood films into indigenous languages reflects attempts at overcoming both cultural and linguistic unintelligibility. This involves changes not only at the level of utterance, but interference at the level of information, by which information in the form of interpretations and explanations are added to facilitate understanding. Translation's function as a selectively permeable membrane is contingent upon the selection of Nollywood films by film distributors out of all possible films (based on their perceived entertainment value and relevance) at the most basic level. Then it involves rendering that information in a culturally relevant manner. Translation thus serves as an active linguistic and cultural/ideological broker between the environment and the commissioning system.

## Conclusion

The consumption of indigenous language films inter-societally via translation implies a realm of opportunity for indigenous language cultural commodities (films, literature, theatre productions, etc.) by showcasing their potential to transcend local realms of relevance. This challenges common assumptions about indigenous language products and their scope and appeal. In this regard, I would like to comment, in relation to Nollywood, on the following statement by Nhlanhla Maake (2015: 14) about indigenous language literature:

> The question of choice of language is an act of entering into canonised spaces which also implies both freedom and at the same time limitation and fixity of boundaries of identity – a paradox which dictates painstaking negotiation. [...] [T]here is always the challenge of speaking to or writing for a specific community and remaining within the setting, milieu and context of that community, which speaks a particular language, thus circumscribing one's freedom of social communions and linguistic mobility, so to speak.

The freedom Maake speaks of in the first sentence is that of expression, by which indigenous languages allow creators supreme mastership over their narratives (Maake 2015: 15). It may also be broadened to refer to freedom of cultural expression. Nollywood translation practices suggest that there is room to capitalise on the creative liberties and expressive advantages that indigenous languages allow by demonstrating that translation can indeed overcome the "fixity of boundaries" mentioned in the quotation.

Of course, this does not mean that all indigenous language commodities will find an audience elsewhere. In this regard, Nollywood's ability to project a relatable African identity and to address themes with broad relevance to Africans proves instructive. Nollywood's pan-African thematic relevance enhances its ability to export indigenous language films, and indigenous languages in turn underscore its popular Africanity. This suggests that the current African ideological climate might indeed be conducive to indigenous language translation flows and translational exchanges in the cultural realm, particularly if products are able to capitalise on key commonalities.

The Nollywood model's democratic nature was evident in its employment of indigenous languages. Its grassroots nature and ability to overcome its economic limitations, which have always tended to foster linguistic imperialism, are central to fostering indigenous language translation flows. Nollywood's affordability, along with its thematisation of daily African realities, described above, makes it broadly accessible in contrast to the exclusiveness of institutionalised African cinema. The accessibility of Nollywood productions reflects their effective response to societal characteristics that translate into a large market for indigenous language products and their translations – something which has generally been deemed unlikely.

While the informality of Nollywood subtitling and the resultant poor quality are not conducive to optimal understanding or high cinematic regard, subtitling was nevertheless shown to operate strategically and to be an effective responsive to environmental conditions in terms of overcoming economic barriers, achieving cultural expression, catering to different audiences simultaneously and establishing coupling with particular foreign societies.

In the case of Nollywood film interpreting, the use of indigenous languages and the occurrence of informal interpreting practices point toward the democratisation of film screening and subtle subversion of linguistic imperialism. While non-professional interpreting reflects weak conditioning by the quality requirements of translation systems, interpreting was nevertheless seen to operate strategically to ease the tension around Nollywood's "ambiguous positions on the boundaries of the familiar and the strange" (Pype's 2013: 202). In this regard, interpreting practices exemplify the selectively permeabilising function of translation as a boundary phenomenon, by which the translation system serves to make information comprehensible and relevant within specific societal contexts. Local languages facilitate the addition of local relevance in these cases of cultural exchange.

Where there is pronounced multilingualism, dominant indigenous languages may play an important role in the likelihood of indigenous languages functioning as culturally mediating receptor languages outside the Nollywood realm. Yet the informal nature of interpreting perhaps suggests room for the adoption of even minor indigenous languages in more localised informal translation practices. The fact that indigenous languages are employed in donor and receptor roles (although in combination with an ex-colonial language in most cases) further showcases the utility of indigenous languages in the realm of entertainment. It also expresses the presence of a form of linguistic agency at the grassroots level involving a full embrace of the relevance of indigenous languages as identity markers.

Luhmann's model fosters an appreciation of the social environment of Nollywood translation and the constellation of stimuli that condition its selective operation. While some of these stimuli were shown to be constraining, others suggest realms of freedom. Overall, an SST approach has shown that Nollywood translation has positive implications for the feasibility of inter-societal information flows involving indigenous language translation by highlighting ways in which indigenous language translation may forge channels for pan-African information flows amid the restrictions present in developing economies.

## References

Adegoke, Yinka. 2012. "African Web Video Service Iroko Raises More Funds, Targets Cable TV." Accessed November 19, 2022. https://web.archive.org/web/20120718191123/http://blogs.reuters.com/mediafile/2012/07/16/african-web-video-service-iroko-raises-more-funds-targets-cable-tv.

Adejunmobi, Moradewun. 2013. "Literary Translation and Language Diversity in Contemporary Africa." In *Intimate Enemies: Translation in Francophone Contexts*, ed. by Kathryn Batchelor and Claire Bisdorf, 17–35. Liverpool: Liverpool University Press.

Adeoti, Gbemisola, and Abdullahi Lawal. 2014. "Nigerian Video Film and the Conundrum of Language: Observatory Notes on Kunle Afolayan's Araromire and Irapada." In *Auteuring Nollywood. Critical Perspectives on The Figurine*, ed. by Adeshina Afoyalan. Ibadan: University Press, Nigeria.

Aroga Bessong, Dieudonné P. 2009. "Les conditions socio-historiques et juridiques de l'exercice de la profession de traducteur /interprète dans la fonction publique camerounaise: Problèmes et perspectives." In *Perspectives on Translation and Interpreting in Cameroon*, ed. by Emmanuel N. Chia, Joseph C. Suh, and Alexandre Ndeffo Tene, 125–145. Bamenda: Langaa RPCIG.

Atanganna Nama, Charles. 1993. "Historical, Theoretical and Terminological Perspectives of Translation in Africa." *Meta* 38 (3): 414–425.

Ayakoroma, Foubiri. 2014. *Trends in Nollywood: A Study of Selected Genres*. Ibadan: Kraft Books.

Bechmann, Gotthard and Nico Stehr. 2011. "Niklas Luhmann's Theory of the Mass Media." *Sociology* 48: 142–147.

Beukes, Anne-Marie. 2006. "Translation in South Africa: The Politics of Transmission," *Southern African Linguistics and Applied Language Studies* 24 (1): 1–6.

Botha, Maricel. 2019. "Translation and Development: (Non-)Translation and Material Exclusion in South Africa." *Southern African Linguistics and Applied Language Studies* 37 (3): 247–261.

Botha, Maricel. 2020. *Power and Ideology in South African Translation: A Social Systems Perspective*. Cham: Palgrave Macmillan.

Fuentes-Luque, Adrián. 2017. "Nollywood Stands Up: Mapping Nigeria's Audiovisual Sector." In *Translation Studies Beyond the Postcolony*, ed. by Kobus Marais and Ilse Feinauer, 130–153. Cambridge: Cambridge Scholars.

Görke, Alexander. 2001. "Entertainment as Public Communication: A Systems-Theoretic Approach." *Poetics* 29: 209–224.

Hermans, Theo. 1999. *Translation in Systems: Descriptive and System-Oriented Approaches Explained*. Manchester: Saint Jerome.

Hermans, Theo. 2007a. *The Conference of the Tongues*. Manchester: Saint Jerome.

Hermans, Theo. 2007b. "Translation, Irritation, Resonance." In *Constructing a Sociology of Translation*, ed. by Michela. Wolf and Alexander Fukari, 57–78. Amsterdam and Philadelphia: John Benjamins.

Kadenge, Maxwell and Dion Nkomo. 2011. "Language Policy, Translation and Language Development in Zimbabwe." *Southern African Linguistics and Applied Language Studies* 29 (3): 259–274.

Kamwangamalu, Nkoko. M. 2016. *Language Policy and Economics: The Language Question in Africa*. London: Palgrave Macmillan.

Krings, Matthias. 2010. "Nollywood Goes East: The Localization of Nigerian Video Films in Tanzania." In *Viewing African Cinema in the Twenty-First Century – Art Films and the Nollywood Video Revolution*, ed. by Mahir Şaul and Ralph. A. Austen, 74–91. Athens: Ohio University Press.

Krings, Matthias and Okome, Onookome. 2013. "Nollywood and its Diaspora: An Introduction." In *Global Nollywood: The Transnational Dimensions of an African Video Film Industry*, ed. by Matthias Krings and Onookome Okome, 1–22. Bloomington and Indianapolis: Indiana University Press.

Kruger, Jan-Louis, Haidee Kruger, and Marlene Verhoef. 2007. "Subtitling and the Promotion of Multilingualism: The Case of Marginalised Languages in South Africa." *Linguistica Antverpiensia* 6: 35–49.

Künzler, Daniel. 2019. "Movies on the Move: Transnational Video Film Flows and the Emergence of Local Video Film Industries in East Africa." *Vienna Journal of African Studies* 36 (19): 5–26.

Lesch, Harold M. and Thomas Ntuli. 2020. "In Search of Quality Interpreting Services – The National Parliament of South Africa as a Case Study," *Nordic Journal of African Studies*, 29 (1):1–26.

Luhmann, Niklas. 2000. *The Reality of the Mass Media*, trans. by Kathleen Cross. Stanford, CA: Stanford University Press.

Luhmann, Niklas. 2012. *Theory of Society* (Volume 1), trans. by Rhodes Barret. Stanford: Stanford University Press.

Maake, Nhlanhla. 2015. "Negotiating Ironies and Paradoxes of Mother Tongue Education: An Introspective and Retrospective Reflection." *South African Journal of African Languages* 35 (1): 11–17.

Marais, Kobus and Ilse Feinauer. 2017. "Introduction." In *Translation Studies Beyond the Postcolony*, ed. by Kobus Marais and Ilse Feinauer, 1–6. Cambridge: Cambridge Scholars.

Marston, Sallie A., Keith Woodward, and John Paul Jones. 2007. "Flattening Ontologies of Globalization: The Nollywood Case." *Globalizations* 4(1): 45–63.

McCain, Carmen. 2013. "Nollywood and its Others: Questioning English Language Hegemony in Nollywood Studies." *The Global South* 7(1): 30–54.

McCall, John. 2007. "The Pan-Africanism We Have: Nollywood's Invention of Africa." *Film International* 5 (4): 92–97.

Mesthrie, Rajend. 2006. "Language, transformation and development: a sociolinguistic appraisal of post-apartheid South African language policy and practice." *Southern African Linguistics and Applied Language Studies* 24 (2): 151–163.

Mesthrie, Rajend. 2015. "English in India and South Africa: Comparisons, Commonalities and Contrasts." *African Studies* 74: 186–198.

Mistry, Jyoti and Jordache A. Ellapen. 2013. "Nollywood's Transportability: The Politics and Economics of Video Films as Cultural Products." In *Global Nollywood: The Transnational Dimensions of an African Video Film Industry*, ed. by Matthias Krings and Onookome Okome, 46–69. Bloomington and Indianapolis: Indiana University Press.

Ndeffo Chene, Alexandre and Emmanuel N. Chia. 2009. "Traduction pédagogique et traduction professionnelle: Une mise au point." In *Perspectives on Translation and Interpreting in Cameroon*, ed. by Emmanuel N. Chia, Joseph C. Suh and Alexandre Ndeffo Tene, 125–145. Bamenda: Langaa RPCIG.

Ndlovu, Eventhough. 2020. "Interpretation and Translation as Disciplines and Professions in Zimbabwe: A Critical Appraisal." *Language Matters* 51 (2): 129–147.

Olukayode, Babatunde. 2017. "Audio-visual Translation and Nigerian Cinematography: Subtitling and Dubbing from English and Indigenous Languages in Favour of French." *International Journal of Applied Linguistics and Translation* 3 (2): 24–31.

Pienaar, Marné and Eleanor Cornelius. 2015. "Contemporary Perceptions of Interpreting in South Africa." *Nordic Journal of African Studies* 24 (2):186–206.

Pype, Katrien. 2013. "Religion, Migration, and Media Aesthetics: Notes on the Circulation and Reception of Nigerian Films in Kinshasa." In *Global Nollywood: The Transnational Dimensions of an African Video Film Industry*, ed. by Matthias Krings and Onookome Okome, 199–222. Bloomington and Indianapolis: Indiana University Press.

Seidl, David. 2004. *Luhmann's Theory of Autopoietic Social Systems*. Munich: Ludwig Maximilian University.

Soetan, Olusegun. 2018. "Language, Culture and Politics in the Films of Tunde Kelani." *Polymath* 8 (2): 1–26.

The Eagle Online. 2021. "How MultiChoice Nigeria is Promoting Local Languages, Culture with Africa Magic Channels." Accessed October 14, 2021. https://theeagleonline.com.ng/how-multichoice-nigeria-is-promoting-local-languages-culture-with-africa-magic-channels/.

Thiong'o, wa, Ngũgĩ. 2018. "The Politics of Translation: Notes Towards an African Language Policy." *Journal of African Cultural Studies* 30 (2): 124–132.

Thuube, Raphael and Beatrice Ekanjume-Ilongo. 2018. "Exploring the impact of linguistic barriers on health outcomes: A linguistic analysis of ad hoc medical interpreting in Lesotho hospitals." *South African Journal of African Languages* 38:159–166.

Tyulenev, Sergey. 2009. "Why (Not) Luhmann? On the Applicability of Social Systems Theory to Translation Studies." *Translation Studies* 2 (2): 147–162.

Tyulenev, Sergey. 2012a. *Applying Luhmann to Translation Studies: Translation in Society*. London and New York: Routledge.

Tyulenev, Sergey. 2012b. *Translation and the Westernisation of Eighteenth-Century Russia: A Social-Systematic Perspective*. Berlin: Frank und Timme.

Tyulenev, Sergey. 2013. Social Systems and Translation. In *Handbook of Translation Studies*, ed. by Yves Gambier and Luc Van Doorslaer (Vol. 4), 160–166. Amsterdam and Philadelphia: John Benjamins.

UIS (UNESCO Institute for Statistics). 2009. "Information Sheet No. 1. Analysis of the UIS International Survey on Feature Film Statistics." Accessed October 21, 2021. http://uis.unesco.org/sites/default/files/documents/analysis-of-the-uis-international-survey-on-feature-film-statistics-en_0.pdf.

CHAPTER 8

# Maryse Condé and the Alternative Nobel Prize of 2018

Yvonne Lindqvist
Stockholm University

Inspired by the methodological framework of *histoire croisée*, this paper examines the bibliomigrancy of the French Caribbean author Maryse Condé. To this end, four major causal series of events leading up to her nomination and selection for the 2018 Alternative Nobel Prize in Literature are analyzed. The first causal series of events consists of the translation bibliomigrancy of French Caribbean fiction to Sweden over the past 40 years. The second causal series of events briefly covers the authorship of Maryse Condé and her reception in Sweden. The third causal series follows the effects and repercussions of the cancellation of the Nobel Prize in Literature in 2018, as well as the particular consequences related to the reorganization of the Royal Swedish Academy. The fourth causal series of events entails the foundation of the "New Academy" and the Alternative Nobel Prize in Literature. Closing remarks discuss Maryse Condé's chances of being awarded the regular Nobel Prize in Literature.

**Keywords:** Maryse Condé, the Alternative Nobel Prize of Literature, *histoire croisée*, Caribbean translation bibliomigration, double consecration

## Introduction

With only nine million inhabitants, Sweden is a relatively small country at the northern outer edge of Europe and a comparatively minor literary space in world literature. Swedish literature, however, has been widely translated. In fact, Swedish as a source language held a firm position as the sixth most translated language in the world, according to Index Translationum in 2015 (Lindqvist 2019: 606). Inspired by the methodological framework of *histoire croisée* (Werner and Zimmermann 2003, 2006; D'Hulst 2012; Batchelor 2017; Kullberg 2017), this paper reconstructs four major causal series of events that led up to the nomination and selection of the French Caribbean author Maryse Condé for the 2018 Alternative Nobel Prize in Literature. The notion of *histoire croisée* refers to a history associated with the idea of a nonspecific connection that points to a configuration of events that is to some extent structured by the metaphor of an intersection (Werner and Zimmermann 2003: 16). Simply put, the nonspecific connection reconstructs strings of relational events. As a consequence, connections are not analyzed on the assumption of stable and linked instances. Viewed from a *histoire croisée* perspective, something that is actually happening in instances of intersecting events involves the actual intersection as much as the intersection's effects and repercussions. An event is not limited to the analysis of the point of intersection or a moment of meeting, but instead it takes more broadly into account the processes that may result from it, as the term "history" in the expression "*histoire croisée*" suggests (Werner and Zimmermann 2003: 16). Kullberg (2017: 224) argues that translation studies *per se* constitute a *histoire croisée* since they operate within a similar relational paradigm to that which Werner and Zimmermann present as a basis for their theory. She rightly claims that *histoire croisée* has the advantage of trying to go beyond the binary model that is often the basis for any comparative approach whether in translation or in literary studies. Rather than taking identifiable and comparable entities as the point of departure, it approaches the object of research at the crossroads of perspectives and contextual factors.

Consequently, with regard to Maryse Condé and the 2018 Alternative Nobel Prize, the first causal series of events reconstructed consists of the translation bibliomigrancy of French Caribbean fiction to Sweden during the past 40 years. The second causal series of events briefly covers the authorship of Maryse Condé and her reception in Sweden. The third causal series deals with some of the effects and repercussions of the cancellation of the Nobel Prize in Literature in 2018, specially with the consequences of the reorganization of the Royal Swedish Academy. The fourth causal series of events follows the foundation of the "New Academy" and the Alternative Nobel Prize in Literature.

Bibliomigrancy is an umbrella term that describes the migration of literary works, in the form of books, from one part of the world to another. The term comprises physical migration of books, i.e. production and trade of books, translations, library acquisitions and circulation as well as virtual migration, i.e. adaptations and appropriation of narratives and, in more recent times, the digitization of books (Mani 2014: 289; 2017). Bibliomigrancy promotes and facilitates connections between central, semi-peripheral and peripheral positions in world literary space. As Damrosch (2013: 200) claims, a literary work enters into world literature by circulating out into a broader world beyond its linguistic and cultural point of origin. Bibliomigrancy patterns are also influenced by different literary consecration cultures (Lindqvist 2018a: 289) that enable and shape literary trajectories. The more "pluri-centric" a literary consecration culture is, the more winding and heterogeneous are the literary translation trajectories in the world republic of letters (Lindqvist 2018b). From a *histoire croisée* perspective, each translation event in this study is considered an instance of intersection that creates a larger configuration of events, involving literary institutions, agents, publishers, translators and critics etc. However, the account which follows will not elaborate on each intersection. Instead, the events are narrated as causal series and consequences.

## French Caribbean translation bibliomigrancy to Sweden

Research on translation flows has proliferated during the past two decades, and it unsurprisingly confirms that English-language literature, stemming from English-speaking countries, is the most frequently translated in the world.[1] This is also the case for literary translation into Swedish. The second and third most translated literatures into Swedish are perhaps more surprisingly – due to the existing Scandinavian translation field (Lindqvist 2016) – Danish and Norwegian. In the top-ten list of significant literatures translated into Swedish, German is fourth and French-language literature is fifth. This paper examines a peripheral French-language literature in the world literary space, French Caribbean literature, and its bibliomigrancy to Sweden.

Translation bibliomigrancy of French Caribbean literature to Sweden is marked by the reluctance of Swedish publishers to publish an unknown Caribbean writer, who has not previously been consecrated by literary prizes and awards within the Anglo-American literary space. The success of a peripheral French Caribbean writer in the Swedish literary market thus seems to depend on previous consecration and success within Anglo-American literary culture. Translation bibliomigrancy from the Caribbean to the northern hemisphere, and particularly to Sweden, seems to depend to a large extent on a kind of double consecration – first within the center of the former colonial power and secondly within the centers of Anglo-American literary culture. This double consecration process is decisive for the lion's share of francophone Caribbean literature in Swedish translation (Lindqvist 2010). On the contrary, Anglophone Caribbean writers, regardless of whether they are presented as Haitian writers to the Swedish readers – as in the case of, for instance, the Haitian-American author Edwidge

---

1. See for instance: *Translatio: Le marché de la traduction en France à l'heure de la mondialisation* 2008, *How Peripheral is the Periphery? Translating Portugal Back and Forth* (2015), *Doing Double Dutch* (2017), *Scandinavia through Sunglasses: Spaces of Cultural Exchange between Southern/Southeastern Europe and Nordic Countries* (2019). *Translating the Literatures of Small European Nations* (2020), *Northern Crossings. Translation, Circulation and the Literary Semi-periphery* (2022).

Danticat – do not to the same extent need double consecration in order to be selected for translation into Swedish.[2] This is the result of the substantial Americanization of the Swedish literary space – a long process, which dates back to the beginning of the 20th century (Torgerson 1982). More recently in 2018, 71% of all fiction works published and translated in Sweden were translations from English (National Bibliography 2018). Moreover, when examining the gap between the first publication in an author's original language and its Swedish translation, the works of 'Francophone writers' writings in English migrate faster to Sweden than their French-language counterparts. For instance, the first published novel by Edwidge Danticat, *Breath, Eyes and Memory* (1994), was translated by Dorotee Sporrong and published by the publishing house Natur och kultur in 1996. Regarding the bibliomigrancy of Maryse Condé's novel *Traversée de la mangrove* first published in 1989, Condé's novel was first translated into English by Richard Philcox and published under the title *Crossing the Mangrove* by Doubleday in 1995 and subsequently translated to Swedish by Helena Böhme as *Färden genom mangroven [The Voyage through the Mangrove]* in 2007 by Leopard publishing house. It took 18 years from its initial publication in France, passing through the "duo-centric" Anglo-American literary culture, to finally reach Swedish readers in translation. Comparing the publication gap of *Crossing the Mangrove* within the three studied literary spaces, the translation bibliomigrancy of the novel seems to support the double consecration hypothesis (Lindqvist 2010). Additional support for the necessary double consecration of French Caribbean Literature before it can cross into Swedish literary space is the fact that bibliomigracy patterns of Caribbean Francophone literature form part of the French "mono-centric" literary consecration culture (Casanova 2004: 115) where most authors are *made* in Paris:

> [...] on the literary front France is still institutionally and intellectually the locus princeps. Not only are literary texts, essays and histories published in Paris, but it is first and foremost there that they are commissioned, reviewed and commended. The majority of established Caribbean authors become famous originally in France and the United States has only really courted French Caribbean writers to the extent that Paris has already made their reputation.
> 
> (Gallagher 2002: 206)

---

2. In the Swedish database, Världslitteratur.se, Edwidge Danticat is presented as a Haitian writer to the Swedish audience. https://varldslitteratur.se/person/edwidge-danticat (Accessed July 18, 2022). This presentation might seem confusing, but what is important here is that she is writing in the English language. For a discussion about "Who is considered a Caribbean author?", see Lindqvist (2019: 611).

The literature of the francophone part of the Caribbean translated into Swedish stems from the islands of Haiti, Guadeloupe and Martinique. The database Världs-litteratur.se,[3] which is the most important source for this research, lists 16 authors from this literary space. Of these 16 authors, nine have been translated into Swedish (cf. Table 1).

In this francophone context, Martinique can be singled out as the island of poetry and politics, with important poets such as Aimé Cesaire and Joseph Zabel, and major thinkers such as Édouard Glissant, Franz Fanon and Patrick Chamoiseau, the latter also a Goncourt prize winner.

Table 1. Overview of the Francophone Caribbean literature per region and according to the selection criteria of the study

| Region/ Numbers | Authors presented in världslitteratur.se | Authors in Swedish translation | Translated novels 1980–2020 |
| --- | --- | --- | --- |
| Haiti | 6 | 2 | 5 |
| Guadeloupe | 5 | 2 | 9 |
| Martinique | 5 | 5 | 1 |
| Total | 16 | 9 | 15 |

However, according to the selection criteria of the study at hand, only novels translated during the period 1980–2020 have been retained, which explains why only one novel from Martinique, namely *Texaco,* originally published in 1992, appears in the survey. The only novel from Haiti in the study written in French is *Comment faire l'amour avec un nègre sans se fatiguer* by Dany Laferrière. This novel was first published in 1987 and then translated into Swedish by Tony Andersson in 1991, after an English language translation by David Homel, which appeared in Canada in 1987.

Concerning the French language writers in the Världslitteratur [World literature] database, their tokens of consecration are rather similar as demonstrated by the Gallagher (2002) quote above. They have been published in Paris by prestigious publishing houses, for example, Grasset et Gallimard, and they have received high acclaim in the form of literary prizes and awards, but only Maryse Condé has been frequently translated into English and Swedish (Lindqvist 2010; 2019).

---

**3.** *Världslitteratur.se.* The site is part of a project run by the World Library [Världsbiblioteket] in Stockholm. Its aim is to promote world literature – defined as African, Asian and Latin-American literature – in Sweden.

## The literary production and translation bibliomigrancy of Maryse Condé

Maryse Condé (b. 1937) is today one of the most significant contemporary Caribbean writers writing in French. Her production consists of more than 20 novels, three autobiographical works, eight children's books and a large number of essays and short stories. Maryse Condé is read in many cultures. She is widely translated not only into English, but also into German, Dutch, Italian, Spanish, Portuguese, Japanese and Swedish. According to Sapiro and Bustamante (2009:1), the number of languages that a novel is translated into gives a rough estimation of the consecration of the author within the world literary space. Condé is thus a consecrated author in many parts of the world.

One of the most salient themes in her literary production is the search for "the origin", to understand the past to be able to tackle the future (Duke 2010: 57).[4] In her native Guadeloupe, as in the rest of the Caribbean, black blood symbolizes centuries of oppression and exploitation. Condé's novels narrate tales of abusive colonial power contrasted with resistance from strong women, often in a pseudo-autobiographical form, thus breaking the *autobiographical pact* that defines the relationship between the autobiographer, the text and the reader as a true story narrated in first person (Kullberg 2011: 17).

Maryse Condé is undoubtedly the most successful of the contemporary French language Caribbean writers to establish herself in the Swedish literary market. She has seven translated novels, a translated youth novel and a biography. This far exceeds the one translated novel by Dany Laferrière (Haiti) and one by Patrick Chamoiseau (Martinique). Condé stands out because of her high consecration within Anglo-American literary culture, marked by the American and British literary prizes and awards she has received, which serve as important selection criteria for Swedish translations. In the Anglophone literary space, Condé was awarded the 1993 Puterbaugh Prize and the 2005 Hurston/Wright Legacy Award. In 2015, she was shortlisted for the Man Booker International Prize. These tokens of consecration can probably, apart from her literary skills, be ascribed to her eminent academic career as a literature professor in the USA. Additionally, among her more than 20 novels, 14 have been translated into English. Another contributing factor to her American consecration might be her systematic collaboration with her (second) husband, English translator Richard Philcox. He frequently writes paratexts, for instance, translator's notes not so much explaining his translation strategies when working with Condé's novels, but rather inscribing her within the hyper canon (cf. Damrosch 2009) of world literature by comparing her texts to those of, for instance, Virginia Woolf (Lindqvist

---

4. The theme is also a basic assumption from the critical perspective of *histoire croisée*.

2019).⁵ Paratexts are, as we know, an efficient way of framing foreign experiences for a new audience (Watts 2005).

Furthermore, Condé's *oeuvre* initially needed double consecration to be selected for inscription in the Swedish literary canon by translation. However, after three translated novels, no previous English translation was needed to assure selection for Swedish translation. The bibliomigrancy pattern had changed. Condé had found her way to Swedish readers, which reassured Swedish publishers of her success.⁶ For example, the hardcover edition of *Färden genom mangroven* (*Crossing the Mangrove*) sold very well in Sweden, about 5,000 copies, and the paperback edition was a great success, with 20,000 copies sold, well exceeding market expectations.⁷

The temporal gap between first source publication and translation into Swedish for Condé has thus constantly narrowed during the last decade (Lindqvist 2016). For her latest translated novel into Swedish, *L'Évangile du nouveau monde,* published by Buchet-Chastel in 2021, the temporal gap was hardly a year before the publication in Sweden of *Nya världens evangelium*, published by Leopard publishing house and translated by Ulla Linton. Richard Philcox's English translation of *L'Évangile du nouveau monde,* (*The Gospel According to the New World*) will be published in the UK and in the USA in 2023.⁸ Ever since her first appearance at the Book Fair in Gothenburg in Sweden in 2007, Condé has visited Sweden several times as well as participated in book launches and literary talks, for instance, in 2012 at the International Writers' Stage at the Stockholm Culture House – a literary institution inviting authors from all over the world since 1998.

---

5. For a more detailed account of the cooperation of Maryse Condé and her translator (and husband) Richard Philcox, see Lindqvist 2019: 621.

6. Selected literary production of Maryse Condé. Titles followed by '\*' have been translated into Swedish *Heremakhonon* (1976), *Une saison à Rihata* (1981) Segou: Tome 1: *Les Murailles de terre* (1984)\*, Tome 2: *La Terre en miettes* (1985), *Moi, Tituba sorcière…* (1986) *Haïti chérie* 1986) *Rêves amers* (2005), *La Vie scélérate* (1987), *En attendant le bonheur* (1988), *Hugo le terrible* (1989), *The Children of Segu* (1989), *Tree of Life* (1992), *La Colonie du nouveau monde* (1993), *La Migration des cœurs* (1995), *Traversée de la mangrove* (1989)\*, *Pays mêlé* (1997), *Desirada* (1997)\*, *The Last of the African Kings* (1997), *Windward Heights* (1998), *Le Cœur à rire et à pleurer* (1999), *Celanire cou-coupé* (2000)\*, *La Belle Créole* (2001), *La Planète Orbis* (2002), *Histoire de la femme cannibale* (2005), *Uliss et les Chiens* (2006), *Victoire, les saveurs et les mots* (2006), *Comme deux frères* (2007), *Les Belles Ténébreuses* (2008), *En attendant la montée des eaux* (2010)\*, *La vie sans fards* (2012)\*, *Mets et Merveilles* (2015). *Le fabuleux et triste destin d'Ivan et Ivana* (2017), *L'Évangile du nouveau monde* (2021)\*.

7. In Sweden, a first edition of a rather unknown author is considered a great success if 3,000 copies are sold.

8. https://www.worldeditions.org/product/the-gospel-according-to-the-new-world/ (Accessed July 20, 2022)

Prior to 2018, when she was awarded the Nobel Prize of the New Academy, Condé was frequently mentioned in the Swedish press as a possible candidate for the Nobel Prize in Literature of the Royal Swedish Academy (Flakiersk 2007; Jonsson 2007; Nilsson 2011, Perera 2018).

## The Royal Swedish Academy and the cancellation of the Nobel Prize in literature in 2018

The Royal Swedish Academy is one of the most powerful cultural institutions in Sweden today. It administers a wide range of cultural and literary events, prizes and scholarships. Among them, the Nobel Prize in Literature is the most famous worldwide, probably because of the large sum of money for the prize and to the festivities around the prize-giving ceremony in the City Hall of Stockholm, which is held on 10 December each year.[9] The prize sum of nine million Swedish crowns originates from the provisions of Alfred Nobel's will, which the Royal Swedish Academy administers with the goodwill of the Nobel Foundation. Over more than a hundred years academy members have discussed and decided on what works should be considered high-prestige literature (Espmark 2001) – a task which is not always met with approval by international literary critics. However, Pascale Casanova describes the Nobel Prize in Literature as the strongest consecrating literary power in the world republic of letters, as the definition of "literarity" proper (2004: 147):

> Thus, the greatest of literary consecrations, bordering on the definition of literary art itself, is the Nobel Prize – a European award established at the beginning of the twentieth century that gradually came to enjoy worldwide authority. Today writers everywhere are agreed in recognizing it as the highest honor of the world of letters. There is no better measure of the unification of the international literary field than the effectively universal respect commanded by this prize.
> (Casanova 2004: 147)

The Nobel Prize Laureate in Literature thus immediately becomes a member of what Damrosch (2009: 510) calls the hyper canon of world literature. Kjell Espmark, one of the 18 members of the Royal Swedish Academy, considers that the greatest challenge to be addressed by the Academy is that authors writing in peripheral languages – from a Swedish perspective – should have the same opportunity to be awarded The Nobel Prize in Literature as writers writing in

---

9. The most significant amount of all literary prizes worldwide, according to English (2005: 54).

more central languages (1986: 149). In a retrospective of the work of the Academy in the late 1980s, Espmark underscored the attempts by the Academy to eliminate the distance of the poetry and fiction of "The Other" in a more thorough sense other than just by translations. Judging from the laureates over the 20 past years, this challenge still remains.[10]

The suspension of the Nobel Prize in Literature in 2018 was due to a crisis of trust between the Nobel Foundation and the Royal Swedish Academy. The crisis within the Swedish Academy became known to the general public when cases of sexual harassment, corruption and nepotism among certain academy members and family close to them were disclosed and the code of silence around the esoteric assembly was broken.[11] The crisis resulted in several members of the academy having to resign from their positions, which meant that the Swedish King, Carl XVI Gustav, was compelled to change the protocol of the Academy in order to make the resignations possible.[12] Ever since the foundation of the Academy in 1786, Academy members were appointed for life, with no possibility of resigning from such a privileged position. In the turbulent aftermath of the crises, after several attempts to reconsolidate the reputation of the Academy, appointing new members and reorganizing the selection process for the literary prize, the Academy decided to grant two literature prizes in 2019.[13]

The Royal Swedish Academy then decided to change the working process of the Nobel literature committee and to create an external group to complement the two Academy members Anders Olsson and Per Wästberg, after academy member Horace Engdahl was forced to leave the Nobel literature committee. The group consisted of five new members: authors and translators Kristoffer Leandoer and Gun-Britt Sundström; literary critics Rebecka Kärde and Mikaela Blomqvist; and literary critic and publisher Henrik Petersen. The new members were appointed for a period of two years. With this new configuration, the Academy hoped to restore confidence in the institution as well as regain the respect of Swedish society and the world. This proved to be a rather vain hope, since it took only a year before two of the newly appointed external group members, in fact the translators, announced their resignation.[14] A further measure that attempted to restore the reputation of the Royal Swedish Academy after the public turmoil was to appoint four new female members in 2019: Åsa Wikfors, a university

---

10. An exception to the rule and possibly indicating a new direction in the selection of the Nobel Laureate in Literature is the choice of Abdulrazak Gurnah in 2021.
11. See, for example, Gustavsson. 2019 *Klubben [The Club]* and Frostenson 2019. *K.*
12. Klas Östergren, Sara Danius, Sara Stridsberg, Jane Svenungsen.
13. Olga Tokarczuc, Peter Handke.
14. Kristoffer Leandoer and Gun-Britt Sundström.

professor in Philosophy, and the poets and fiction writers Tua Forsström, Anne Swärd and Ellen Mattson. The implemented changes regarding the rules governing member resignation from the Swedish Royal Academy, the reorganization of the Nobel committee for the Nobel Prize in Literature and the increase of female representation among the members are the present-day results of the causal series of events scrutinized so far in this chapter. Another direct result of the causal series of events up until 2018 was the creation of the New Academy and the Alternative Nobel Prize in Literature.

## The New Academy

The New Academy was born in response to the cancellation of the Nobel Prize in Literature of 2018. It was founded by the journalist and author, Alexandra Pascalidou, as a non-profit organization that was not affiliated with the Nobel Foundation nor the Swedish Academy, but nevertheless claiming the literary prestige associated with the Nobel name. The explicit intention of the New Academy was to emphasize that literature promotes democratic principles, openness, empathy and respect (Perera 2018) and was – in contrast to the traditional selection process of the Royal Swedish Academy – more democratic with a three-step voting procedure for the prize, as well as inviting the participation of the general reading public instead of solely a restricted number of Academy members. As the critic Erika Harlitz-Kern remarks:

> For the Nobel Prize in Literature to regain its international reputation, the ivory tower that the Swedish Academy has become needs to come down. The New Academy is not intended to be the solution to the crisis surrounding the Nobel Prize in Literature. But it can be an important step on the way towards a rejuvenation of the Nobel Prize. (Harlitz-Kern 2018)

At the start of the New Academy's selection process, librarians in Sweden were asked to nominate two authors of their choice. The result of this first step was a list of 47 authors based on the number of nominations received. This list consisted of 30 women and 17 men. Names from Sweden and the United States had most of the nominations, with twelve nominations each. The United Kingdom followed with 5 nominations. Of the American authors nominated, five were women working within a wide span of literary genres, for instance, Jamaica Kincaid, Patti Smith and Donna Tartt. Statistically, the Nobel Prize in Literature favors white, male and French authors. In contrast to this bias, on the librarian's list France was represented by one male writer, Édouard Louis, and two female writers, Nina Bouraoui of North African decent, and Maryse Condé from Guadeloupe. Some of the Swedish authors nominated were Johannes Anyuru, Jonas Hassen Khemiri and Agneta Pleijel, also defying the Nobel norm.

The public then voted for their favorite author on the web site of the New Academy. More than 30 000 people voted. And thirdly, a panel made up of the editor and independent publisher Ann Pålsson, the literature professor Lisbeth Larsson, the literary critic and translator Peter Stenson and the library director Gunilla Sandin then appointed the winner from a short-list of two female and two male writers. The short-listed writers were Haruki Murakami, Kim Thúy, Maryse Condé and Neil Gaiman. Haruki Murakami, however, declined his nomination, leaving three candidates remaining for the prize. The reason for Murakami's renouncement probably was – one could suspect – his desire to be selected for the ordinary Nobel Prize in Literature sometime in the future (Wrede 2018). Nevertheless, on 9 December 2018 Maryse Condé received the Alternative Nobel Prize in Stockholm. In an interview, Condé emphasized that for her there is no difference between the Nobel Prize and the Alternative Nobel Prize. She considers the prize she received to be a great honor (Wrede 2018). Two days after the prize ceremony, the New Academy was dissolved, having served its purpose.

## Conclusions

Inspired by the methodological framework of *histoire croisée*, this paper has reconstructed four major causal series of events leading to the nomination and selection of the French Caribbean author Maryse Condé for the 2018 Alternative Nobel Prize in Literature. The first causal series of events consisted of the translation bibliomigrancy of French Caribbean fiction to Sweden over the past 40 years. Each translation event mentioned in the paper is considered an instance of intersecting occurrences, thus creating a larger configuration of events, which in turn produce bibliomigrancy patterns. The study showed that French Caribbean literature constitutes a minor literary flow to Sweden. Only nine French Caribbean novelists and 15 novels made up this minor literary flow during the past 40 years. It was shown that the lion's share of these translated novels was written by Maryse Condé and that the bibliomigrancy patterns of her novels to Sweden were initially facilitated by the double consecration process, i.e. her novels first had to be translated from French into English in order to be selected for translation into Swedish.

The second causal series of events briefly covered the authorship of Maryse Condé and her reception in Sweden. It reconstructed some of her translation events and appearances in book fairs and at literary promotion talks. The third causal series of events dealt with the steps leading to the cancellation of the Nobel Prize in Literature in 2018 and to some of the effects and repercussions of the turmoil affecting the Royal Swedish Academy, notably consequences concerning the reorganization of the Academy. The Nobel Committee was reorganized to include external literary critics and literary translators, and the protocols of the Academy were changed, permitting the resignation of its appointed members. Moreover, female representation among the members was reinforced with the appointment of five[15] new female members to the Academy to fill the chairs of the members who had resigned, an excluded member and two deceased members.

The fourth causal series of events led to the establishment of the "New Academy" and the nomination process of the Alternative Nobel Prize in Literature, which was awarded to Maryse Condé in 2018. The causal series of events leading up to the Alternative Nobel Prize in Literature consisted of its genesis, its more inclusive nomination process, the withdrawal of one of the award's nominees, the winner of the prize and finally the dissolution of the New Academy. These multi-intersectional series perhaps allude to a democratic overlap with Swedish readership. If this is the case, then this democratic processing stands in contrast to the esoteric and mysterious regime of literary prestige that is still promoted by the Royal Swedish Academy. On the one hand, whether the Royal Swedish Academy will succeed in restoring its former glory remains an open question. On the other hand, whether Maryse Condé still has the chance to become a future Nobel Prize Laurate of the Royale Swedish Academy, or if her winning of the Alternative Prize in 2018 has considerably lowered this possibility, is not such an open question.

## References

Batchelor, Kathryn. 2017 "Introduction: *Histoire croisée*, microhistory and translation history", in Kathryn Batchelor and Sue Ann Harding (eds.) *Translating Frantz Fanon across Continents and Languages*, London: Routledge, 1–16.

Brems, Elke, Orsolya Réthelyi, and Ton van Kalmthout (eds). 2017. *Doing Double Dutch. The International Circulation of Literature from the Low Countries*. Leuven: Leuven University Press.

Casanova, Pascale. 2004. *The World Republic of Letters*. Translated by Malcolm DeBevoise. Cambridge, MA: Harvard University Press.

Chitnis, Rajendra, Jakob Stougaard-Nielsen, Rhian Atkin, and Zoran Milutinovic (eds). 2020. *Translating the Literatures of Small European Nations*. Liverpool: Liverpool University Press.

Damrosch, David. 2009. "Framing World Literature". In: Simone Winko, Jannidis Fotis, and Gerhard, Lauer (eds.). *Grenzen der Literatur. Zum Begriff und Phänomen des Literarischen*. Berlin/Boston: De Gruyter. 496–515.

---

15. The Iranian-Swedish poet Jila Mossaed was appointed in 2018 in the aftermath of the Academy scandals.

Duke, Yukiko. 2010. "Jag kände mig vit och fransk när jag var barn" [I felt white and French when I was a kid]. *Vi läser*. 4. 54–58.

D'Hulst, Lieven. 2012. "(Re)locating Translation History: From Assumed Translation to Assumed Transfer". *Translation Studies* 5 (2): 139–155.

English, James. F. 2005. *The Economy of Prestige. Prizes, Awards and the Circulation of Cultural Value*. Cambridge, Massachusetts/London: Harvard University Press.

Espmark, Kjell. 1986. *Det litterära Nobelpriset. Principer och värderingar bakom besluten*. [The Nobel Prize of Literature. Principles and Valuations behind the Decisions]. Stockholm: Norstedts.

Espmark, Kjell. 2001. *Litteraturpriset : hundra år med Nobels uppdrag*. [The Literature Prize – A Hundred Years Mission]. Stockholm: Norstedt.

Flakiersk, Gregor. 2007. Nobelpris till Karibien? [Nobel Prize to the Caribbean?] *LO-tidningen*. October 5.

Gallagher, Mary 2002. *Soundings in French Caribbean Writing since 1950. The Shock of Space and Time*. Oxford: Oxford University Press.

Harlitz-Kern. Erika. 2018. A closer look at the Alternative Nobel Prize in Literature longlist. *Book Riot*. https://Bookriot.com2018/08/29Alternative-nobel-prize-in-literature-shortlist/ (Accessed 2020-02-03).

Jonsson, Stefan. 2007. "Maryse Condé: Färden genom mangroven. *Dagens Nyheter*". Kultur. September 18.

Kullberg, Christina. 2011. "Ett 'jag' som sträcker sig utåt". [An 'I' which reaches outwards] *Karavan*. 4. 16–19.

Kullberg, Christina. 2017. "Fanon in Scandinavia. Words and Actions". In: *Translating Frantz Fanon Across Continents and Languages* (eds). Kathryn Batchelor and Sue-Ann Harding. London: Routledge. 222–248.

Lindqvist, Yvonne. 2010. "Dubbel konsekration – en förutsättning för svensk översättning av utomeuropeisk litteratur? Maryse Condé som exempel". [Double Consecration – A Prerequisite for Translation of Literary Peripheries? Maryse Condé as an Example] In: *Språk och stil*. Nr 2. 40–170.

Lindqvist, Yvonne. 2016. "Det skandinaviska översättningsfältet – Finns det?" [The Scandinavian translation field – Does it exist?]. *Språk och stil*. 25. 69–87

Lindqvist, Yvonne. 2018a. "Introduction to Lost and Found: Translation and Circulation". *World Literatures: Exploring the Cosmopolitan-Vernacular Exchange*. (eds) Stefan Helgesson, Annika Alling Mörte, Yvonne Lindqvist, and Helena Wulff. Stockholm: Stockholm University Press. 289–295.

Lindqvist, Yvonne. 2018b. "Translation Bibliomigrancy: The Case of Contemporary Caribbean Literature in Scandinavia". In: *World Literatures: Exploring the Cosmopolitan-Vernacular Exchange*. (eds.). Stefan Helgesson, Yvonne Lindqvist and Helena Wulff. Stockholm: Stockholm University Press. 295–309.

Lindqvist, Yvonne. 2019. "Translation Bibliomigration. The Case of French Caribbean Literature in Sweden". *Meta. International Journal for Translation Studies*. 64 (3). 600–630.

Mani, Venkat. 2014. "Bibliomigrancy: Book Series and the Making of World Literature". In: Teo D'haen, David Damrosch, and Djelal Kadir (eds) *The Routledge Companion to World Literature*. London/New York: Routledge. 283–296.

Mani, Venkat. 2017. *Recoding World Literature, Libraries. Print Culture and Germany's Pact with Books.* New York: Fordham University Press.

Nilsson, Camilla. 2011. "*I semesterparadisets bakgård*" [In the Backyard of the Vacation Paradise]. 12 October. *Nt*. Accessed August 24, 2020. https://nt.se/7156350.

Perera, Ylva. 2018. "Den Nya Akademiens litteraturpris är intressant som process och protest – men spelar det nån roll vem som får det?" [The Literary Prize of the New Academy is Interesting as a Process and Protest – but does it matter who gets it?] *Yle*. Accessed April 14, 2020. https://svenska.yle.fi/artikel/2018/10/04/den-nya-akademiens-litteraturpris-ar-intressant-somprocess-och-protest-men.

Sapiro, Gisèle (ed.). 2008. *Translatio. Le marché de la traduction en France à l'heure de la mondialisation.* Paris: CNRS Éditions.

Sapiro, Gisèle and Mauricio Bustamante . 2009. "Translation as a Measure of International Consecration Mapping the World Distribution of Bourdieu's Books in Translation". *Sociologica. Italian Journal of Sociology online*. 2–3. Società editrice il Mulino, Bologna. Accessed September 28, 2017. http://www.sociologica.mulino.it/doi/10.2383/31374.

Torgerson, Sten. 1982. *Översättningar till svenska av skönlitterär prosa 1866–1870. 1896–1900. 1926–1930.* Göteborg: Litteraturvetenskapliga institutionen, Göteborgs universitet.

Watts, Richard. 2005. *Packaging Post/Coloniality. The Manufacture of Literary Identity in the Francophone World.* New York/Toronto/Oxford: Lexington Books.

Werner, Michael and Bénédicte Zimmermann . 2003. "Penser l'histoire croisée: entre empirie et réflexivité". *Annales. Histoire, Sciences Sociales*, 58, 7–36. Accessed June 21, 2022. https://www.cairn.info/revue--2003-1-page-7.htm.

Werner, Michael and Bénédicte Zimmermann . 2006. "Beyond Comparison: Histoire croisée and the Challenge of Reflexivity". *History and Theory* 45 (1): 30–50.

Wrede, Hedvig. 2018. "Ingen skillnad på nobelpriset och det alternativa nobelpriset". *SVT nyheter*. December 10. Accessed April 14, 2020. https://www.svt.se/kultur/maryse-conde-ingen-skillnad-pa-nobelpriset-ochdet-alternativa-nobelpriset.

CHAPTER 9

# The role of literary agents in the international flow of texts
## A case study

Duygu Tekgül-Akın
Bahçeşehir University

This study investigates the role of international literary agents in the flow of texts and the network of relations of the global literary market. A major element of agents' work is interlingual translation, complemented by cultural and intersemiotic translation, as they act as brokers between authors, translators and publishers located in different national contexts. In the case of literary agents promoting lesser-known national literatures abroad, the role of cultural mediation also includes managing the image of nations and cultures. The study explores the acts of translation that international literary agents undertake and commission, as well as acts of image building through such translation. The analysis is based on a case study from Turkey: Kalem Agency, the largest literary agency in the country. The discussion draws on content and discourse analysis based on interviews with the co-founder, Nermin Mollaoğlu, as well as published news items and promotional material produced by Kalem.

**Keywords:** literary agents, cultural mediators, text flows, Turkish literature, Kalem

## Introduction

Literary agents represent authors and manage their relations with publishers and other institutions in the culture industry. International literary agents in particular help authors find publishers abroad and sell their rights to foreign agents and publishers on their behalf. Interlingual translation constitutes an integral part of such work, e.g. having readers' reports translated and providing sample translations in the pre-contract stage, and commissioning the translation of the entire book in the post-contract stage, not to mention the overall work of producing multilingual promotional material.

The work of international agents promoting their respective national literatures often entails elements of cultural translation as well, such as introducing authors to international publishers, explaining why they would fit in their lists, how individual books compare with the award-winning titles and bestsellers that are more visible, and how they can be set apart from similar products in the same category. To these ends, professionals working for such literary agencies undertake a considerable amount of marketing through various media: participation in international publishing events, pitching titles to publishers via e-mail, producing promotional material, and introducing books on social media, some of which could be considered instances of intersemiotic translation.

This study examines aspects of interlingual, intralingual, intersemiotic and cultural translation, and the concomitant cultural image building that literary agents undertake; it is based on a case study of the Kalem Agency, based in Istanbul, Turkey. The article attends to the multiple and overlapping roles (Roig-Sanz and Meylaerts 2018: 6) that literary agents play as cultural mediators, highlighting their role in the international flow of texts.

## Methodology

The research questions that the study aims to answer are: i) What types of translation do international literary agents undertake or commission? (ii) How are these related to the overall flow of texts? iii) What roles do these acts of translation play in transnational cultural intermediation? iv) How does the work of international literary agents fit into the broader network of the literary translation industry? The article seeks to address these questions through a case study of the Kalem Agency. The case study has been selected for its weight in the related field of cultural production, which endows it with the representativeness necessary to illustrate the research field. After an exposition of the case study, the article addresses a related research question in the discussion: v) How does TIS benefit from the inclusion of literary agents as transnational cultural mediators?

After a literature review in the disciplines of TIS and cultural studies, I collected data from the Kalem Agency website, read 17 news items about the Agency, including interviews with co-founder Nermin Mollaoğlu, and listened to four interviews with her available online. Additionally, I interviewed Mollaoğlu myself (Mollaoğlu 2019) for more focused questions. I also drew primary material from social media, namely Mollaoğlu's Instagram feed, which attests to the networked nature of transnational cultural intermediation. Primary data were then examined through content and discourse analysis. Such a methodology locates the chapter firmly within the literature on translation flows.

## Cultural intermediaries in translation research

This section draws a conceptual framework for the study by providing an overview of the relevant research on the topic. Translation flows have inspired a significant research tradition within the sociology of translation, as several scholars have explored the institutions and processes involved (see van Es and Heilbron 2015; Sapiro 2016, 2017; Heilbron and Sapiro 2018; Roig-Sanz and Meylaerts 2018; McMartin 2019; Heilbron 2020; Loogus and van Doorslaer 2021). However, the work of specifically literary agents has been underrepresented in this body of literature. This is a well-documented research field in the discipline of publishing studies (see Gillies 2007; Squires 2009; Cottenet 2017), but it is relatively new to TIS. For example, Milton and Bandia's influential 2009 collection on agents of translation do not take into account the work of literary agents, modern or in historical context, and there were not many attempts at linking the work of literary agents with translational activity until well into the 2010s (cf. Buzelin 2011). In 2016 Sapiro highlighted the role of literary agents in the circulation of world literature. In the introduction to their 2018 collection, Roig-Sanz and Meylaerts consider the activities of literary agents to be one of the key issues to be examined for a full understanding of literary translation (24), but the studies of examined literary agents from a TIS perspective remain haphazard and disparate.

The present study is theoretically underpinned by the notion of cultural intermediation (Smith Maguire and Matthews 2010, 2012), which refers to brokering between producers and consumers of cultural products. The concept is originally drawn from the work of Pierre Bourdieu, who defines the new cultural intermediaries as "all the occupations involving presentation and representation (sales, marketing, advertising, public relations, fashion, decoration and so forth) and in all the institutions providing symbolic goods and services" (1984: 359). How are the "new" cultural intermediaries different from "old" cultural intermediaries? According to Wright, "where intermediaries used to be arbiters of highbrow taste (boundary maintenance) their role is now the translation and evaluation of other cultures" (2005: 111). The use of the term "translation" transcends its metaphorical sense here, for mediation between professionals representing different literary markets requires "translation" not only in the way of explaining, contextualizing, comparing and contrasting, i.e. intersemiotic and cultural translation, but also in the interlingual sense.

According to the literature on cultural intermediation, these professionals generate value through "objective practices and subjective outlooks" (Smith Maguire and Matthews 2010: 411). Objective practices here refer to the material and practical manifestations of their work whereas subjective outlooks refer to their "dispositions, rationalities, motivations and aspirations" (ibid.). In

Bourdieusian terms (1984), each cultural intermediary has a certain position-taking, shaped by a certain habitus, which is acted out in a series of strategies. Cultural intermediation is intimately linked with cultural and social capital: professionals rely on personal taste and on connections as they undertake mediation work.

Having generated fruitful research in the social sciences, the notion of cultural mediation[1] has also been applied to translation research. Uslu (2012) has utilized it as a conceptual framework in her study of translations from Turkish into English. Contributions to the collection edited by Roig-Sanz and Meylaerts (2018) mentioned above examine various aspects of cultural mediation. In their introduction to the collection, Roig-Sanz and Meylaerts highlight the multifaceted work of cultural mediators:

> Their complex, partially overlapping roles, which transgress linguistic, artistic, and spatial boundaries, form important cultural practices, but are rarely acknowledged as such, nor studied at large, because they transcend the traditional binary concepts (source-target, original-translation, author-translator etc.) of disciplines like translation studies, transfer studies. The binary concepts prevent us from seeing the complexity of both the mediators' roles and their mediating practices.
>
> (2018: 13)

In effect, the study of cultural intermediaries, which can be said to inhabit an "in-between" space theoretically, requires a holistic approach that operationalizes "flows" and "networks," in line with the framework adopted for this volume and in which this chapter is embedded.

The idea of cultural mediation provides a convenient tool to study international literary agents. Claire Squires links the emergence of literary agents to the intensification of marketing practices and the growing professionalization of the publishing industry in the 19th and 20th centuries (2009: 35). The bulk of what they do professionally is to match individual authors and books with publishers, which requires an eye for aesthetic consistency (see McCracken 1988; Moor 2008). In order to accurately pitch the latest crime novel of a promising author, for example, they study the front and backlists of publishers abroad. During this process of trial and error, subjective outlooks are materialized into objective prac-

---

1. Scholarly work on cultural intermediation from the social sciences refers to the phenomenon as "cultural intermediation" whereas researchers from TIS have been using the term "intercultural mediation" or "cultural mediation" (see Katan 2013; Liddicoat 2016a, 2016b). The use of the term in social sciences is understood to refer to what is here called vertical mediation, while the TIS term is often used to mean horizontal; but since the case study here covers both activities, the terms will be used interchangeably for convenience.

tices that cover, among many other things, interlingual, cultural and intersemiotic translation. This is how literary agents add value to the flow of texts.

In the case of international literary agents promoting "peripheral" literatures, their work also has a pedagogical aspect (see Entwistle 2009: 715): they have to make sure that foreign publishers understand how a local author is positioned in the literary landscape and how the work would fit their list. This includes communicating a wide range of information about the author, from biographical details to prizes and comparisons with internationally known literary figures. The pedagogical work might be extended to national and cultural images (van Doorslaer 2012) as well, which might entail rectifying misconceptions and challenging the popularity of local themes that had previously brought success to other authors from the same national literature. Kuipers (2012) has coined the term "transnational" mediation, which is applicable to international literary agents as well: the gap that they are trying to bridge is a linguistic as well as a cultural gap, and therefore translation features prominently in their activities. International literary agents need to mediate both horizontally – between peers i.e. publishers and literary agents across the globe – and vertically – between producers and consumers, i.e. readers.

## Kalem Agency and Nermin Mollaoğlu

Founded in 2005, Kalem is the largest literary agency in Turkey. It represents international authors, translators, publishers and rights agencies within the country, and represents Turkish authors, translators and illustrators abroad. As of April 2023, it has signed 3,265 contracts to promote Turkish literature abroad, representing 147 Turkish authors and working with a list of 64 other languages, covering not only major European languages such as English and French, but also languages of limited diffusion such as Georgian and Danish. Several translation scholars laud the efforts of literary agents in boosting the visibility of Turkish literature internationally in the last decade (see Uslu 2012; Tekgül and Akbatur 2013: 49; Kıran 2020: 623) and Kalem deserves much of the credit.

The Agency was co-founded by Nermin Mollaoğlu and Mehmet Demirtaş. Mollaoğlu herself has been working in publishing since 2002, when she was hired by Yapı Kredi Publishing as Turkey's first copyright professional: prior to that, this job title was non-existent as acquisitions and commissioning editors handled copyright agreements on the side. She started visiting international book fairs representing Yapı Kredi and gained an insight into the work of a literary agent. In the early years of her career, she learned the trade of buying and selling copyright: how to present books, how to introduce authors, how to handle questions from publishing house representatives, and how much to engage in professionally-informed personal talk (Celâl 2021). Mollaoğlu has a degree in Teaching English as a Foreign Language, but while working for Yapı Kredi, she studied economic law at postgraduate level, focusing on copyright law. She researched legal loopholes in author and translator agreements for her dissertation. She set up Kalem Agency after resigning from Yapı Kredi in 2005. She and co-founder Mehmet Demirtaş initially planned on allocating 90% of their operations to bringing in international authors to Turkey and only 10% to promoting Turkish ones abroad. However, the following year, Orhan Pamuk became the first Turkish author to win the Nobel Prize in Literature and two years later in 2008 Turkey was the Guest of Honour at Frankfurt Book Fair, which increased the visibility of Turkish literature and provided opportunities for Turkish literary agencies. These events proved to be a turning point for Kalem Agency. Mollaoğlu's career path as it is delineated here demonstrates that she found herself in the position of being a trailblazer in the Turkish publishing industry. According to Sapiro, literary agents are involved in streamlining professional norms across national publishing industries (2016: 93). Considering the pioneering status of Nermin Mollaoğlu in the Turkish publishing industry, there would be no doubt that she has played a pivotal role in that respect.

Across the cultural and creative industries, matters of personal taste are of paramount importance (Kuipers 2012), but in the case of Kalem Agency, the way Nermin Mollaoğlu's professional persona manifests itself transcends mere expressions of personal taste. It would probably not be wrong to claim that her personal identity is very much blended with the corporate identity of the literary agency. She is a sociable person who enjoys the limelight and harnesses her personal attributes alongside her professional credentials to achieve success in this competitive business. The UK-based publishing industry magazine *Publishing Perspectives* described her as "perhaps the most visible advocate for Turkish publishing on the international scene" (Nawotka 2015). Her success was recognized by London Book Fair as well when she received the Literary Agency Award in 2017. According to one interview published in Turkish (kalem kahve klavye 2018), there have been cases in the history of Kalem where Turkish books sold better abroad in translation than they did in Turkey, which serves as proof to the value added by the literary agency.

Nermin Mollaoğlu uses her personal Instagram[2] account to promote the works of authors and translators that her Agency represents, which further illustrates how her personal identity and the corporate identity of the Agency are fused. Apart from book recommendations and snapshots from book fairs and

---

2. https://www.instagram.com/mollaoglunermin/

meetings with industry professionals, she shares pictures of the covers of books whose translation and publication processes her Agency saw through. The whole Instagram feed may be considered an intersemiotic translation of Kalem's promotional efforts – a "non-discursive transfer mode" (Roig-Sanz and Meylaerts 2018: 15) – bringing together text and image, the posts and stories condense the time and effort that must otherwise be invested in other marketing practices. In this context the Instagram account serves as a memorable reminder to the work of presentation and representation that Bourdieu (1984: 359) attributes to cultural intermediaries, and also a manifestation of the aesthetic consistency (McCracken 1988; Moor 2008) maintained across media.

On the other hand, in an interview with an Italian literary journalist (Perotti 2015), Mollaoğlu explains that her social media presence is a professional requirement, perhaps more so than it is for her European counterparts. She chooses to be active on social media to track and mirror the activity of the Turkish authors that her Agency represents. Authors, in turn, enjoy the greater freedom of expression that social media platforms afford compared to conventional media outlets. Through social media Mollaoğlu also reaches out to the eventual end users of the commodities that she markets: readers. The work of literary agents is often limited to business-to-business, that is, horizontal, mediation without direct contact with readers. However, Instagram gives Mollaoğlu the chance to interact with readers, often through book recommendations. Maintaining an active social media presence is arguably a means of accumulating social capital as well. Her Instagram activity also exemplifies the "objective practices and subjective outlooks" (Smith Maguire and Matthews 2010: 411) that cultural intermediaries engage in. Social media activity is eventually carried out from an individual perspective, inflected by personal choices and preferences, but from a professional point of view it can be considered as some of the material and practical devices that are outwardly visible.

Horizontal mediation requires an endorsement of cosmopolitanism as a political and aesthetic value (see Delanty 2009: 18–88) as part of the literary agent's habitus, (Bourdieu 1984). In her various statements, Mollaoğlu signals that she assumes equal distance in relation to all national literatures, no matter whether they are based on less- or more-widely spoken languages. If anything, she seems to champion promoting the literatures of Turkey's eastern and western neighbours, for example, Armenia, even if diplomatic relations have often been fraught.

That said, I have not come across any mention of the Kurdish language or Kurdish literature in her interviews, on the Kalem website or in any publicized Kalem activity. Kurdish constitutes the second largest linguistic community in

Turkey after Turkish, the official language, and using the language has for decades been marked with political tension. According to Bourdieu

> The space of *literary or artistic position-takings*, i.e. the structured set of the manifestations of the social agents involved in the field – literary or artistic works, of course, but also political acts or pronouncements, manifestos or polemics, etc. – is inseparable from the *space of literary or artistic positions* defined by possession of a determinate quantity of specific capital (recognition) and, at the same time, by occupation of a determinate position in the structure of the distribution of this specific capital. (2009 [1993]: 30, emphasis in the original)

In an industry where artistic position-taking cannot be separated from a political one, the inclusion or otherwise of the Kurdish language in a multilingual programme is highly indicative. The artistic/political nexus parallels the personal/professional one in this regard, and the choice may partly be explained by the need to access resources owned or controlled by the state (see discussion below).

Before proceeding further, a side note on Mollaoğlu's preferred job title in Turkish: she's a self-styled *edebiyat ajanı* [literary agent], an epithet in Turkish that comes as a surprise to the uninitiated. The term incorporates the word *ajan*, derived from the French word *agent*, used mostly in Turkish to mean "spy".[3] This bears resemblance to Roig-Sanz and Meylaerts' (2018) use of the word "smuggler" in the title of their book *Literary Translation and Cultural Mediators in 'Peripheral' Cultures: Customs Officers or Smugglers*. The authors justify the metaphor by defining cultural mediators as "agents who promote exchanges and often create their own norms, circuits, channels and forms" (2019;14; cf. Pym 2014 [1998]: 188). This is indeed an apt description for Mollaoğlu, who has in effect set new standards and whose work has therefore defied the established nomenclature in Turkey. In a televised interview, she states that the work of an *ajan* also entails building a network (Murat 2019), which is not unlike what one would expect from a spy.

## Networks

Building and maintaining networks is essential for the work of a literary agent, which necessitates the accumulation of social capital to be mobilized at a later stage. Kalem is credited with creating and sustaining a network of professionals –

---

3. A more conventional alternative would be *ajans* – *agence* in French – as most agencies e.g. "advertising agency", "casting agency" are called such in Turkish and the term is used to refer to individuals as well as institutions.

which is crucial for an industry such as literary translation that relies on freelancers (see Folaron and Buzelin 2007). In the early years, Kalem's biggest expense was incurred by mailing copies of books to contracted or prospective translators abroad. Mollaoğlu is still happy to post books to translators who prefer reading printed books and who would like to keep up-to-date with contemporary Turkish literature – she believes this is part of her unwritten job description (Celâl 2021).

While answering an interview question, Mollaoğlu explains that Kalem's efforts are geared towards the acceleration of Turkish authors' entry into international literary networks (Arkunlar 2011). This brings to mind the three-tiered circuit model that Heilbron (2020) has come up with for authors achieving recognition progressively from more restricted circles to international fame: initially, authors gain recognition in the first circuit, composed of transnational linguistic communities. In Heilbron's case study this represented Dutch-speaking enclaves outside of the Netherlands; for Turkish literature, this would mean the Turkish communities of Europe, including Northern Cyprus. The second circuit corresponds to fields of cultural production in receiving countries, which is what brings real commercial success. The TEDA project, the translation subvention programme funded by the Turkish Ministry of Culture and Tourism, has supported the publication of many books in Germany, for example (Alkan and Günay-Erkol 2021: 7). The third tier, finally, is that of international fame, reserved for Nobel laureates and runners-up (Heilbron 2020: 139–140). Mollaoğlu's networking circle is not limited to the world of publishing: she has contacts in academia as well, which has proven crucial in the case of lesser-spoken languages. She also acknowledges the work of Directorate General of Libraries and Publications at the Ministry of Culture and Tourism, without whose efforts Kalem Agency wouldn't be where it is today (Celâl, 2021). She mentions contacting the Turkish Consulate in Sofia, Bulgaria, seeking assistance from the Cultural Attaché to access their literary network (ibid.). This highlights how wide the net has been cast, with government officials, commercial establishments and freelance artists alike. She points out that relationships have been reciprocal as she has done her best to help others as she benefitted from their service (ibid.).

The web of relations is essential not only at the production stage – finding a publisher, commissioning a translator, etc. – but also at the marketing stage (Kopan 2020). This is in line with what Roig-Sanz and Meylaerts argue about cultural mediators being involved in "production, circulation, transformation, and reception of cultural products" (2018: 13). Events participation takes up a significant portion of Kalem's work – not only book fairs, where authors are introduced to editors and deals are struck, but also literary festivals, with a view to facilitating post-production promotion (Murat 2019). She recounts how, for four or five years, she went to Beijing Book Fair meeting publishers, trying to gauge their positions in the industry, making note of potential publishers and even venues where they could hold events if they were to launch a book. She describes these efforts as "building a net" which she can fall back on when needed (Kopan 2020).

## Transnational cultural mediation: Practices

The cultural mediation practices of Kalem can be discussed in terms of liaising between players in the global publishing industry and managing professional relations. All of those practices may be further divided into the categories of incoming and outgoing, depending on whether they are aimed at bringing international titles to Turkish publishers or introducing Turkish books abroad. The management of professional relations in the outgoing category also entails the construction and maintenance of national and cultural images (cf. Heilbron and Sapiro 2018: 194–202). Furthermore, Kalem's mediation work covers the horizontal as well as the vertical axes, as mentioned before. All in all, their work is "multi-layered," as Mollaoğlu herself concedes (Murat 2019). This section addresses activities aimed at horizontal transnational liaison.

Kalem acts as a bridge between authors and publishers, between authors and translators, and between translators and publishers, often far apart, physically and linguistically. "We sit in the middle of the table" (Murat 2019). When pitching outgoing books, she also has at the ready a list of possible translators, and in the case of pitching incoming books, information about funding opportunities from source language countries must be supplied at the outset, all of which she describes as "managing a network" (ibid.).

In the publishing business, a great deal of marketing takes place through word of mouth. International fairs and festivals are where recommendations are made. Mollaoğlu jokingly describes this as "professional gossip" (Murat 2019). In other words, position-taking is manifested in the informal spaces of discussion created by the professional network.

Knowledge of both the home market and international markets is essential. Kalem's work involves tipping international publishers about the potential sales of individual titles in the Turkish market. Mollaoğlu also advises foreign publishers to exercise caution when it comes to issues such as religion and other controversial topics (Nawotka 2015). Such warnings are in order considering the prevalence of censorship and the prosecution of translators in Turkey (see Tahir Gürçağlar 2009: 54–57; Üstünsöz 2015; Aktener 2019).

Gauging trends in foreign markets has helped make inroads in selling Turkish rights internationally. Mollaoğlu explains that when she is well versed in a national literature, she can better pitch Turkish authors to publishers located in that market. She gives the example of meeting a Norwegian publisher and being able to tell him that a particular Turkish author is "the Turkish Jo Nesbø" (Celâl 2021). This amounts to establishing cultural "equivalences," a kind of cultural translation.

Kalem organizes events bringing together publishers, authors, translators and readers. Since 2009 they have been holding the Istanbul International Literature Festival (ITEF), which kicks off with a glamorous opening ceremony and is the venue for talks and readings by authors and translators. According to the ITEF website, the event provides "a meeting point for authors, publishers, agencies, translators, journalists, literary fund managers, literary event coordinators and everyone else in the publishing industry."[4] As of 2023 ITEF has hosted 534 authors and 147 publishing professionals from 62 countries. The Kalem team envisages ITEF as an alternative method to promote Turkish literature abroad (Murat 2019): a "pull" mechanism to complement the "push" strategy. When the foreign publishers leave for their respective home countries, their knowledge about Turkey the country outweighs impressions to be gleaned from coverage in the politics pages of newspapers (Celâl 2021). The festival also serves to introduce promising international authors in Turkey. The Israeli novelist Etgar Keret, for example, rose to fame in Turkey thanks to his exposure in ITEF (Artjurnal, 2021).

As part of ITEF, Kalem runs the Publishing Fellowship programme, whereby they host for five days a team of 20 publishing industry professionals: translators, literary critics and events organizers who are interested in the Turkish literary market. The principal aim of the programme is to familiarize these professionals with Turkish literature and the local industry: from classical to contemporary authors, publishers from across the political spectrum, various book-marketing strategies, booksellers, publishing industry bodies, and the work of the Ministry of Culture and Tourism. Mollaoğlu refers editors from international publishers to her colleagues in Turkey when they inquire about authors Kalem doesn't represent. She remembers that it was through the fellowship that a Colombian publisher met a Norwegian editor and decided to take on a translation from the Nordic language (Murat 2019). Kalem's outreach efforts illustrate how international literary agents can be conceived of as nodes in a network of multiple lines of mediation.

McMartin explains that the Flemish Literary Fund, in promoting Flemish literature abroad, "tread[s] a fine line between matchmaking and deal-making and demonstrate[s] a highly professionalized intermediary role where learning and responding to the tastes of individual publishers is paired with cultivating direct interpersonal ties" (2019: 37). In a similar vein, Kalem operationalizes professional

---

4. https://www.itef.com.tr/

networks that they themselves initiate and/or sustain in order to mediate between their international clients.

In 2021, Kalem also opened KalemHouse, a literary house located in the Gacık village of Yalova province, to the south of Istanbul. Once it is ready, Kalem will be able to offer residencies for authors and translators there (cf. Heilbron and Sapiro 2018: 193). Such a residency will likely strengthen Kalem's network, but it also demonstrates their commitment to the literary culture of Turkey and their determination to elevate the image of Turkish literature internationally.

Heilbron and Sapiro point out how state-funded agencies working to promote lesser-known literatures abroad have state-sponsored infrastructures at their disposal (2018: 193). All things considered, Kalem's promotion efforts can be compared to the work of those official agencies in terms of efficiency. In contrast to what Loogus and van Doorslaer argue (2021: 176) about the Estonian state agents evolving towards literary agents, Kalem may be argued to be evolving towards the role of an all-round official agency. This fits in with the shifting relations between state and private agents pointed out by McMartin: the former have started to model the latter and the latter started to dominate markets (2019: 37). At the end of the day, though, Kalem does not have an official infrastructure at its disposal, so they must make up for that through their network. The situation is compounded by the fact that they must preserve their autonomy from the political field, while trying to maximize access to state-controlled resources since they are subject to the imperatives of commercial publishing (Heilbron and Sapiro 2018: 194, cf. Loogus and van Doorslaer 2021: 163).

## Translation and other textual-linguistic practices

When asked about her job, Mollaoğlu says that a literary agent is someone who "reads, and talks about her reading" (Murat 2019), which in a way sums up layers of translation – intralingual and interlingual – between the written and oral semiotic systems: Mollaoğlu spends a considerable amount of time perusing novels – both original and in translation – in her reading languages, and analysing and summarising these texts in the company of other publishing professionals.

When it comes to textual-linguistic practices on a more concrete level, Kalem Agency commissions a high volume of interlingual translation for the marketing of Turkish books abroad. Turkey follows the international norm in that literary translation processes are usually initiated after having secured a contract with a publisher, but at Kalem sometimes the process is flipped: they have the entire translation ready at hand at the pre-contract stage so that they can take advantage of this complete text to more effectively promote the book. In these cases, the target language is usually English, the *lingua franca* of the global book trade, which means that even if the eventual destination is another language market, the English version of the text is dispatched to publishers for an initial evaluation. The author often pays for the translation, in cases of what is often called source-initiated translation. At other times though, Kalem gets in touch with a translator post-contract (Mollaoğlu 2019). Such a break from established professional standards is proof that individuals engaged in cultural intermediation are willing to take the initiative in order to strategise more efficiently.

While trying to convince an international publisher to take on a Turkish book, Kalem sends them ample documentation about the title. For each outgoing book, they prepare a 5-page summary and a 1-page synopsis in English. These texts are first drafted in Turkish and then rendered into English by freelance literary translators (Mollaoğlu 2019).

The Agency sometimes makes available in English favourable reviews placed in Turkish literary magazines and the book supplements of Turkish newspapers. This strategy is understandably subject to selection and de-selection procedures (van Doorslaer 2010). Finally, they maintain multilingual promotional material, e.g. on their website and their catalogues. All in all, then, considering the volume of texts they commission to be translated, the literary agency acts like a translating institution (Mossop 1988, Koskinen 2011) whose primary function is to produce translated texts, much like a publishing house.

## National and cultural images

The construction and maintenance of national and cultural images is intertwined with Kalem's promotional activities and their management of professional relations. This is where the pedagogic aspect enters the picture. At the baseline Mollaoğlu has met editors at international book fairs who asked about the language(s) spoken in Turkey, which suggests that their knowledge of Turkish literature is close to nil. Mollaoğlu remembers a Japanese and a Mexican editor who hurt her professional pride with such questions (Arkunlar 2011; Tatlıpınar 2013, Çınar 2016). From that starting point, Mollaoğlu takes incremental steps to overcome the social obstacles to the circulation of texts (van Es and Heilbron 2015; Sapiro 2016: 88–92): setting up as many face-to-face meetings as necessary, and supplying relevant information by e-mail (Arkunlar 2011). During professional meetings at international book fairs, Mollaoğlu has apparently been receiving "ten questions about Turkish politics for every two literary questions" (Yıldırım 2016). Turkey has been making the headlines in the international press more for political crises and scandals than anything else and Mollaoğlu has more often than not found herself in a position of having to offer explanations.

International publishers have been known to go for books "with a Turkish flavour", as Orientalism still has considerable purchase in the literary scene (see Paker 2004, Tekgül and Akbatur 2013). Novels, written from a purportedly realist perspective, portraying Turkey as colourful and mysterious and Turkish society as traditional and spiritual, have an enduring appeal. The following quote from an article in *Publishing Perspectives* reveals that Mollaoğlu is committed to changing this:

> As for buying books from Turkey, Mollaoğlu encourages publishers to look beyond the "exotic" titles to those that also reflect the daily realities of life in Turkey, which is not dissimilar from that of anywhere else in Europe or throughout the developed world. But this, she acknowledges, demands education – a process she is fully committed to pushing forward. (Nawotka 2015)

In an interview five years later, she admitted that books that explore "stereotypical Turkish themes" sell much better than others (Kopan 2020). These would include domestic violence, breaches of women's and LGBT rights, and intergenerational conflict. This restricted thematic framework actually seems to motivate Mollaoğlu, especially given that her work has a pedagogical dimension. According to Gentile, Kovács and van der Watt (2021: 1), personal contacts are likely to make an impact on national and cultural images represented in translated literature, which means that Mollaoğlu is on the right track. The maintenance of national and cultural images is also couched in the value construction function of cultural mediation.

Not all ethnotypes related to Turkey have a negative impact, of course; certain national and cultural images actually do help with promotion. For instance, Kalem wishes to capitalize on the popularity of Turkish soap operas in South America (Kopan 2020, see Tali 2016). These TV shows portray a romanticized and glamorized Turkey set against an exotic backdrop imbued with nostalgia; however, they may open up spaces for parallel cultural consumption.

### Discussion

How does TIS benefit from the inclusion of literary agents as transnational cultural mediators? First of all, a focus on the translational activity of literary agents broadens the remit of translation (see Tymoczko 2007). The complex and multifaceted work of literary agents must be recognized as translation work and as such, this topic deserves more academic attention from TIS scholars. The study of the literary agent builds on agent-oriented research in TIS and helps better understand networks in the industry.

Furthermore, analysing the work of literary agents as engaged in transnational cultural intermediation will encourage more interdisciplinary interaction, which is likely to bring new perspectives. The concept of transnational cultural mediation may complement, or encourage, a reconsideration of the notion of patronage (Lefevere 1992) that has been instrumental in theorizing translation phenomena past and present. According to Lefevere, professionals in the publishing industry exert a regulatory force on the literary system. They perform a gatekeeping role, wielding power on behalf of the patrons who are located outside the system (1992: 14–15). Some of the assumptions underlying the idea of gatekeeping have become untenable in the light of new developments in the field of cultural production (see Kuipers 2012: 583–584). Not only have the categories of "high" and "low" literature almost become obsolete, notions previously considered to be more or less stable, such as "national literature," have also been destabilized. The relationship between producers and consumers has changed, and therefore expert status is challenged and continually negotiated (see Hewison 2014: 233). As we established earlier, "the new cultural intermediaries" are more concerned with evaluation than with boundary maintenance (Wright 2005: 111). In such a context, the professional persona of the publishing professional, e.g. the literary agent, can no longer be defined as the moral guardian of "high literature", or the "national canon." Scholarly work has defined cultural mediators and gatekeepers alike as arbiters of taste, but such arbitration today is not based upon notions of distinction, acquired through elite education, or exclusive access to resources. According to Squires, literary value today is created and maintained through collusion between publishers and other industry insiders: "it can also be circumvented, and made anew for both promotional and cultural effect" (2009: 93). New communication technologies have radically transformed value formation, which means, for example, that social media platforms have gained primacy over conventional promotional activities. In fact, Mollaoğlu explains that an author's presence on social media platforms sometimes overrides the consecration bestowed through a literary prize (Murat 2019). The framework of cultural mediation offers a more fine-grained analysis of the contemporary art world than that of manipulation and patronage (see Asimakoulas 2009: 242–244).

Finally, a focus on the "in-between" counteracts the methodological nationalism that has been axiomatic in TIS: a spill-over effect of zooming in on source texts/languages and target texts/languages (see Roig-Sanz and Meylaerts 2018: 30). In effect, as early as 1998, Pym outlined the concept of "interculture," (2014[1998]: 177–192) which had the potential to inspire a transnational methodological outlook. Pointing out that "intercultures methodologically precede monocultures" (2914:190), he challenged the notion that translators are located solely in target cultures (2001: 457). However, the study of translation agents who are, for the sake of convenience, presumed to be located within neatly-defined national, or at best regional, contexts took precedence (see e.g. Milton and Bandia 2009).

## Conclusion

This study investigated how various types of translation play out in the work of an international literary agent engaging in transnational cultural mediation. The case study demonstrates that not only interlingual but also intralingual, intersemiotic and cultural translation are indispensable to the international flow of texts. The paper highlights the relevance of the institution of the literary agency for TIS research, which has largely been overlooked. It builds on the existing literature with a case study involving an agent of translation in a less researched aspect of cultural mediation, and a language of low diffusion.

The article benefits from two methodological strategies: drawing on a theoretical framework that has originated in another discipline, namely cultural sociology, and factoring in data from social media, which is a pertinent source of insights into networks today. Moreover, it sheds light on a contemporary institution and a contemporary agent of translation, whereas agent research in translation has often featured historical figures (see Milton and Bandia 2009). It also represents a holistic approach tying together not only various modes of translation, but also production and promotion in the literary translation industry.

On the other hand, the contribution is eventually limited with one case study anchored in one national context. Future studies could explore the work of literary agents working with more widely spoken languages, e.g. Chinese or Russian, operating across transnational markets united by the same language, e.g. Spanish or Arabic, or in multilingual societies, e.g. Belgium, South Africa or India. In their 2014 study on cultural mediators in Antwerp in the late 19th century and early 20th century, Meylaerts and Gonne ask "Does translation studies offer appropriate concepts and methods to analyse these new literary cartographies, these new forms of writing and translating and new roles of authorship and translatorship?" (2014:133). The present study has offered a perspective on this methodological question by considering the work of international literary agents, but more studies are needed to unravel the complexities of transnational cultural intermediation.

## References

Aktener, Ilgın. 2019. "Censorship and Literary Translation: Translating Obscenity after The Soft Machine and Snuff Court Cases." *Neohelicon* 46 (1): 347–367.

Alkan, Burcu and Çimen Günay-Erkol. 2021. "Introduction: 'Turkish Literature as World Literature?' What is in a Preposition?" In *Turkish Literature as World Literature*, ed. by Burcu Alkan and Çimen Günay-Erkol, 1–16. New York: Bloomsbury Academic.

Arkunlar, Merve. 2011. "Nermin Mollaoğlu Röportajı [Interview with Nermin Mollaoğlu]." *TimeOut Istanbul*. Available from http://www.timeoutistanbul.com/kitap/makale/2391/Nermin-Mollaoglu-roportaji

Artjurnal. 2021. "'Edebiyat Ajanı' Nermin Mollaoğlu – Pencere B2 [Nermin Mollaoğlu, 'literary agent' – Window B2]." Available from https://www.youtube.com/watch?app=desktop&v=HZBI7mwHbQo

Asimakoulas, Dimitris. 2009. "Rewriting." In *Routledge Encyclopedia of Translation Studies, 2nd Edition*, ed. by Mona Baker and Gabriela Saldanha, 241–245. Abingdon: Routledge.

Bourdieu, Pierre. 1984. *Distinction: A Social Critique of the Judgement of Taste* (trans. Richard Nice). London: Routledge.

Bourdieu, Pierre. 2009 [1993]. *The Field of Cultural Production: Essays on Art and Literature*, Cambridge: Polity Press.

Buzelin, Hélène. 2011. "Agents of Translation." In *Handbook of Translation Studies*, Vol 2, ed. by Yves Gambier and Luc van Doorslaer, 6–12. Amsterdam/Philadelphia: John Benjamins.

Celâl, Metin. 2021. "Hayatımız Kitap – 27: Metin Celâl – Nermin Mollaoğlu Söyleşisi [Our Life is Books – 27: Metin Celâl's interview with Nermin Mollaoğlu]." https://www.youtube.com/watch?v=3-2IIiNfOn8

Çınar, Sayım. 2016. "Nermin Mollaoğlu: Son Hız Çalışmaya, Üretmeye Devam! [Nermin Mollaoğlu: I'll keep up with the hard work!]" *Gazeteciler*. http://www.gazeteciler.com/roportaj/nermin-mollaoglu-son-hiz-calismaya-uretmeye-devam-100282h.html

Cottenet, Cécile. 2017. *Literary Agents in the Transatlantic Book Trade: American Fiction, French Rights, and the Hoffman Agency*. New York: Routledge.

Delanty, Gerard. 2009. *The Cosmopolitan Imagination: The Renewal of Critical Social Theory*. Cambridge: Cambridge University Press.

Entwistle, Joanne. 2009. *The Aesthetic Economy: Markets and Values in Clothing and Modelling*. London: Berg.

Folaron, Deborah and Hélène Buzelin. 2007. *Special Issue on Translation and Network Studies*. Meta 52 (4).

Gentile, Paola, Fruzsina Kovács, and Marike van der Watt. 2021. "Introduction: Transnational Image Building: Linking up Translation Studies, Reception Studies and Imagology." *Translation Spaces* 10 (1): 1–4.

Gillies, Mary Ann. 2007. *The Professional Literary Agent in Britain, 1880–1920*. Toronto: University of Toronto Press.

Heilbron, Johan. 2020. "Obtaining World Fame from the Periphery." *Dutch Crossing* 44 (2): 136–144.

Heilbron, Johan and Gisèle Sapiro. 2018. "Politics of Translation: How States Shape Cultural Transfers." In *Literary Translation and Cultural Mediators in 'Peripheral' Cultures: Customs Officers or Smugglers?* ed. by Diana Roig-Sanz and Reine Meylaerts. 183–208. London: Palgrave Macmillan.

Hewison, Robert. 2014. *Cultural Capital: The Rise and Fall of Creative Britain*. London/New York: Verso.

kalem kahve klavye. 2018. "Yabancı Okur Çoğunlukla 'Türkiye Kokan' Romanlara İlgi Gösteriyor [International readers mostly seek Turkish novels with local colour]." http://kalemkahveklavye.com/2018/10/nermin-mollaoglu-kalem-ajans-roportaj-yazar-yayinci-okur-iliskisi.html

Katan, David. 2013. "Intercultural Mediation." In *Handbook of Translation Studies*, Vol 3, ed. by Yves Gambier and Luc van Doorslaer, 84–92. Amsterdam/Philadelphia: John Benjamins.

Kıran, Aysun. 2020. "Recontextualising Ece Temelkuran in the UK: A Paratextual Look at the English Translations of her Works." *Litera: Journal of Language, Literature and Culture Studies* 30 (2): 621–643.

Kopan, Yekta. 2020. "Yekta Kopan'la Yazar Söyleşileri – Nermin Mollaoğlu [Author interviews with Yekta Kopan – Nermin Mollaoğlu]." https://www.youtube.com/watch?v=4VGaTaULuJs

Koskinen, Kaisa. 2011. "Institutional Translation." In *Handbook of Translation Studies Vol 2*, ed. by Yves Gambier and Luc van Doorslaer, 54–60. Amsterdam and Philadelphia: John Benjamins.

Kuipers, Giselinde. 2012. "The Cosmopolitan Tribe of Television Buyers: Professional Ethos, Personal Taste and Cosmopolitan Capital in Transnational Cultural Mediation." *European Journal of Cultural Studies* 15 (5): 581–603.

Lefevere, André. 1992. *Translation, Rewriting, and the Manipulation of Literary Fame*. London/New York: Routledge.

Liddicoat, Anthony J. 2016a. "Translation as Intercultural Mediation: Setting the Scene." *Perspectives*, 24 (3): 347–353.

Liddicoat, Anthony J. 2016b. "Intercultural Mediation, Intercultural Communication and Translation." *Perspectives*, 24 (3): 354–364.

Loogus, Terje and Luc van Doorslaer. 2021. "Assisting Translations in Border Crossing: An Analysis of the Traducta Translation Grants in Estonia." *Translation Spaces* 10 (1): 161–180.

McCracken, Grant. 1988. *Culture and Consumption: New Approaches to the Symbolic Character of Consumer Goods and Activities*. Bloomington: Indiana University Press.

McMartin, Jack. 2019. "'Our Catalogue is our National Literature': State Agents and Target(ed) Publisher Outreach in the World Market for Book Translations" In *Translation in and for Society: Sociological and Cultural Approaches in Translation*, ed. by Beatriz Martínez Ojeda and María Luisa Rodríguez Muñoz, 23–40. Córdoba: UCO Press.

Meylaerts, Reine and Maud Gonne. 2014. "Transferring the City – Transgressing Borders: Cultural Mediators in Antwerp (1850–1930)." *Translation Studies* 7 (2):133–151.

Milton, John and Paul Bandia. 2009. *Agents of Translation*. Amsterdam/Philadelphia: John Benjamins.

Mollaoğlu, Nermin. 2019. Interview with the Author, 29 August.

Moor, Liz. 2008. "Branding Consultants as Cultural Intermediaries." *The Sociological Review* 56: 408–428.

Mossop, Brian. 1988. "Translating Institutions: A Missing Factor in Translation Theory." *TTR* 1 (2): 65–71.

Murat, Ahmet. 2019. "Edebiyat Söyleşileri / Nermin Mollaoğlu / 29. Bölüm [Literature talks / Nermin Mollaoğlu / Episode 29]." https://www.youtube.com/watch?v=303UzLtp-5U

Nawotka, Edward. 2015. "Turkey Wants You and Your Translations, Says Agent Nermin Mollaoğlu." *Publishing Perspectives*. http://publishingperspectives.com/2015/09/turkey-wants-you-and-your-translations-says-agent-nermin-mollaoglu/

Paker, Saliha. 2004. "Reading Turkish Novelists and Poets in English Translation: 2000–2004." *Translation Review* 68: 6–18.

Perotti, Simone. 2015. "Cultural Meetings in Istanbul: Nermin Mollaoglu, or about the Turkish Literature." *Progetto Mediterranea: A Sailing Cultural Scientific Expedition*. http://www.progettomediterranea.com/Travelog/nermin-mollaoglu-en.html

Pym, Anthony. 2014 [1998]. *Method in Translation History*. London/New York: Routledge.

Pym, Anthony. 2001. "Alternatives to Borders in Translation Theory." *Athanor* 12, Nuova serie: Lo stesso altro, ed. by Susan Petrilli, 172–182.

Roig-Sanz, Diana and Reine Meylaerts. 2018. "General Introduction. Literary Translation and Cultural Mediators. Toward an Agent and Process-OrientedApproach." In *Literary Translation and Cultural Mediators in 'Peripheral' Cultures: Customs Officers or Smugglers?* ed. by Diana Roig-Sanz and Reine Meylaerts, 1–37. London: Palgrave Macmillan.

Sapiro, Gisèle. 2016. "How Do Literary Works Cross Borders (or Not)? A Sociological Approach to World Literature." *Journal of World Literature* 1: 81–96.

Sapiro, Gisèle. 2017. "The Role of Publishers in the Making of World Literature: The Case of Gallimard." *Letteratura e letterature* 11: 81–93.

Smith Maguire, Jennifer and Julian Matthews. 2010. "Cultural Intermediaries and the Media." *Sociology Compass* 4 (7): 405–416.

Smith Maguire, Jennifer and Julian Matthews. 2012. "Are we all Cultural Intermediaries Now? An Introduction to Cultural Intermediaries in Context." *European Journal of Cultural Studies* 15 (5): 551–562.

Squires, Claire. 2009. *Marketing Literature: The Making of Contemporary Writing in Britain*. Basingstoke: Palgrave Macmillan.

Tahir Gürçağlar, Şehnaz. 2009. "Translation, Presumed Innocent: Translation and Ideology in Turkey." *The Translator* 15 (1): 37–64.

Tali, Didem, 2016. "An Unlikely Story: Why do South Americans Love Turkish TV? *BBC News*, 8 September. https://www.bbc.com/news/business-37284938

Tatlıpınar, Eyüp. 2013. "Moda, Yabancı Dile Çevrilen Yazar Olmak [The fashion is now to be translated into foreign languages]." *Akşam*, 28 April. http://www.aksam.com.tr/ekler/moda-yabanci-dile-cevrilen-yazar-olmak/haber-200222

Tekgül, Duygu and Arzu Akbatur. 2013. "Literary Translation from Turkish into English in the United Kingdom and Ireland: 1990–2010." *Literature Across Frontiers*. http://www.lit-across-frontiers.org/wp-content/uploads/2013/03/Literary-Translation-from-Turkish-into-English-in-the-UK-and-Ireland-NEW-UPDATE-final.pdf

Tymoczko, Maria. 2007. *Enlarging Translation, Empowering Translators*. Manchester: St Jerome.

Uslu, Muazzez. 2012. "Representation of the Turkish Literature in English: Translations of Short Stories as a Case." *İ.Ü. Çeviribilim Dergisi* 5 (1): 1–38.

Üstünsöz, İrem. 2015. "Censorship of 'Obscene' Literary Translations in Turkey: An Analysis of Two Specific Cases." In *Tradition, Tension and Translation in Turkey*, ed. by Şehnaz Tahir Gürçağlar, Saliha Paker and John Milton, 219–232. Amsterdam/Philadelphia: John Benjamins.

van Dooslaer, Luc. 2010. "The Double Extension of Translation in the Journalistic Field." *Across Languages and Cultures* 11 (2): 175–188.

van Dooslaer, Luc. 2012. "National and Cultural Images." In *Handbook of Translation Studies*, Vol 3, ed. by Yves Gambier and Luc van Doorslaer, 122–127. Amsterdam/Philadelphia: John Benjamins.

van Es, Nicky and Johan Heilbron. 2015. "Fiction from the Periphery: How Dutch Writers Enter the Field of English-Language Literature." *Cultural Sociology* 9 (3): 296–319.

Wright, David. 2005. "Mediating Production and Consumption: Cultural Capital and 'Cultural Workers.'" *British Journal of Sociology* 56 (1): 105–121.

Yıldırım, Nermin. 2016. "Nermin Nermin'e Karşı" [Nermin vs. Nermin] *Artful Living*. http://www.artfulliving.com.tr/edebiyat/nermin-nermine-karsi-i-8529

CHAPTER 10

# Flowing to the reception side
## A trade-off model of translation acceptance

Bei Hu
National University of Singapore

The empirical line of reception studies has staked out new research questions regarding the effects of translation on actual readers. Nevertheless, the underlying mechanisms of how the translated text flows towards and is received by the target reader remain elusive, notably with respect to attempts to rationalise the individual reader's decision-making in compromising situations. Drawing on empirical evidence from a quasi-experiment in which a group of 22 readers in Australia responded to various translations of Chinese foreign affairs discourses, this chapter illustrates how a nonlinear trade-off model serves to explain the reader's ultimate judgements in which linguistic and ethical considerations are weighed against each other. It is found that a pair of two incompatible but desirable expectations is (un)consciously calculated by the reader. The extent to which the translation can be accepted is susceptible to the degree to which the reader trusts the translator.

Keywords: translation reception, reader expectations, trust, trade-off model, translated Chinese foreign affairs discourse

# Introduction

The empowerment of readers on the reception side has haunted modern translation studies for decades. Consider Skopos theory, in which readers are viewed as creating a necessity for loyalty on the translator's part (Nord 1997/2018). Descriptivists have made use of readers to generate norm-oriented behaviour (Toury 2012). Using a discourse analysis of reviews, a strong tradition of reception studies deals with literary translation (McAuley 2015; McMartin and Gentile 2020; Xu and Yu 2019), paratexts (Ross 2021) and editorial choices (Todorova 2021). With a thrust beyond descriptivism into the "social turn" (Enríquez-Aranda and García Luque 2018), and strongly supported by cognitive research (Kruger and Kruger

2017), especially within the realm of audio-visual translation (Zheng and Xie 2018), empirical investigations of the nature of reception are steadily coming to the fore in translation studies (Di Giovanni and Gambier 2018). Recent scholarship (Gentile, Kovács and Van der Watt 2021) has also paid particular attention to the dynamism of cultural images in translation across time and space, highlighting the cross-pollination between imagology and translation studies.

Nevertheless, reception-specific models *sui generis* have only recently been put on the research agenda (Tuominen 2018), often without rigorous theoretical back-up directly tested against empirical evidence (Kruger and Kruger 2017). Despite a frequent emphasis on the complicated nature of flows of translational communication, the conceptual underpinnings of translation reception tend to be simplified as an either/or choice of acceptance or rejection in a general sense (e.g. Lefevere 1992/2017). Most previous reception research has privileged the reader's textually-based comprehension (Di Giovanni and Gambier 2018), in which prominence is usually given to the acceptance of the traditional dichotomy of strategies (e.g. foreignisation and domestication), without devoting too much attention to extralinguistic criteria. In addition, with few exceptions focusing on the individual reader's behaviour patterns and the reasons behind the reasons (e.g. Enríquez-Aranda and García Luque 2018), numerous previous studies have tended to focus on the holistic reception of translated work, usually suggesting that text type is the main conditioning factor that makes a translation acceptable for a given readership (Arzık-Erzurumlu and Yilmaz 2022; Kurz 2001). This is perhaps partly because the nature of target readerships is, as Athique (2016, 6) put it, "notoriously elusive". Reader expectations are considered less clear-cut, discrete or sometimes mutually exclusive, making them difficult to define, let alone address via appropriate translation strategies. Reader (and user) expectations are conventionally constructed on the basis of top-down-designed survey-based research (Wehrmeyer 2015; Zwischenberger and Pöchhacker 2010), which until recently had been vigorously contested by experimental-empirical studies (Kruger and Kruger 2017) which suggested that the reader's reception could be conditional, with postulated fuzzy boundaries between various textual and extra-textual expectations.

Against this background, this chapter sets out to focus on the underlying mechanism of the actual reader's decision-making, with an emphasis on investigating the potential negotiations between conflicting reader expectations. Based on the thematic analysis of how 22 readers in Australia responded to various translations of Chinese foreign-affairs texts into English in a quasi-experimental setting and on the empirical examination of the recurring patterns of the reader's *in situ* expectations, a trade-off model as a tentative analytical framework of translation reception is envisaged. It is found that when evaluating a translation, readers are often confronted with a trade-off between seemingly mutually contradictory expectations, sometimes unconsciously. More specifically, three pairs of reader expectations are identified and categorised as follows: faithfulness vs fluency, explicitation vs implicitation, and distance vs proximity. In each pair, two clear manifestations are found at either end of their scales, and each manifestation is considered important for the reader's reception of translation. It is worth noting that different pairs of reader expectations may share overlapping commonalities. For instance, implicitation might also indicate the reader's desire for linguistic faithfulness. Nevertheless, different pairs of expectations underline the reader's different considerations when evaluating various translations, which will be discussed in more precise detail in Section 4.

The outline of this chapter is as follows. An initial section starts with a critical review of three of the main conceptual frameworks (i.e. binary thinking, continuum and fuzzy logic) of translation as prototypical realisations of a model of translation reception with an explicitly contrastive focus; this leads to a proposal for a trade-off model of translation reception in which the three pairs of expectations can be accommodated. I will proceed to illustrate how the tentative analytical framework can be realised by the empirical-experimental data under study. Trust as the necessary linchpin for reconciling the initially opposed expectations will serve as a basis for a concluding discussion of its role in promoting successful intercultural communication.

## Moving beyond linear progression towards a trade-off model

In view of Toury's (2012: 65) remarks on translation, "[c]onstraints on any kind of behavior can be described along a scalable continuum anchored between two extremes." It is somewhat paradoxical that many of the theoretical reflections on translation reception have historically been bound to binary propositions, which might to some extent result in a rather reductionist, polarising view of translation acceptance. For instance, in discussing the ways in which literary texts can be manipulated, Lefevere (1992/2017) examined what factors decisively contribute to the acceptance or rejection of literary products (Gambier 2018). In this sense, the reader's choice seems to be either/or; the nature of the reception is rather absolute. Previous translation reception studies (e.g. Kershaw 2013; Kruger 2012) also tended to examine the reader's responses to static translation strategies with binary orientations (e.g. foreignisation vs domestication). However, one might suggest that some traditionally binary oppositions of translation strategies are reversible and commonly "hybridised" (Kruger 2016: 21). Koskinen's (2000: 61) study of European Union institutional translation found that the "excessive" use of domestication may cause a "comical foreignizing effect". For example, when Finnish translations resort to using native variants to translate loanwords, the "translatedness" of the texts, paradoxically, becomes visible. Here the attempts to "domesticate" the text, on the one hand, have nevertheless "foreignised" it, on the other. Therefore, it is unreasonable to place the reception of translation on a binary scale of translation strategies.

The perpetuation of the traditional bivalent paradigm in translation studies has been seriously challenged by subsequent proposals (e.g. Marais 2019; Toury 2012). For instance, following Toury's (2012) idea of continuum anchored between two extremes, by the same token translation reception can be viewed as a scalable continuum spanning different kinds of communicative situations, ranging from those in which a translation is definitely refused to those in which a text is accepted without hesitation or doubt. A continuum is therefore precisely considered "appealing as an antidote to bivalent logic" (Blumczyński and Hassani 2019: 336), as it allows spaces between the extremes within which more nuanced translation decisions have been studied among a range of intermediate options while preserving two basic orientations in thinking of translation (e.g. Colina 2008; Henitiuk 2008; Meylaerts and Gonne 2014).

Nevertheless, although the dangers of strict bivalence are relatively alleviated by the continuum proposal, the explanatory power of the continuum is relatively weak when applied to translation acceptance. Some typologies of translation strategies are not linear at all (e.g. Koller 1995; Pym 2016), muddying their reception and resulting in a substantial degree of uncertainty among readers. Despite ambivalence and indeterminacy being given attention, the idea of continuum seems to suggest that translation (and hence its reception) is anchored in a narrative of linear progress and is still strongly "unidimensional" (Blumczyński and Hassani 2019: 340), moving from one direction to the other.

Another theoretical framework that may shed some light on translation reception starts from a more nuanced measurement of fuzzy logic, a notion that was first proposed in computer science (Zadeh 1965) and later applied to language encounters (e.g., Adamczyk 2015; O'Brien 2008). More specifically, Pym (2014: 103) postulated fuzzy logic as "partial set membership" in the sense that "an element can be a member of two different sets but to different degrees". For example, a translation strategy "might be 80 percent foreignizing and 20 percent domesticating" (Pym 2014: 103). In a similar vein, Tymoczko (1999/2014: 140) argued that fuzzy logic should govern translation studies because "in cultural matters such as translation one cannot generalize from classical logic". However, as Blumczyński and Hassani (2019) pointed out, categorising membership in terms of percentages suggests that the respective membership values should add up to the whole (i.e. the mathematical value of 100%). Consequently, the model implies a kind of zero-sum thinking in the sense that someone's gain is at the expense of another's loss, as a variable moving away from one side inevitably moves towards the other, which is hardly applicable to translation reception. Different expectations may be equally demanding and may form a hybridity of reception, rather than meeting distinct needs. For instance, in reading a literary translation, the reader's expectations of form ("signifier") may be interwoven with function ("signified"). Similar to a continuum, under the fuzzy logic framework of hypothetical distributions, we are still invited to divide a certain envisaged shape of pie into various sizes (Blumczyński and Hassani 2019). The problem is that the pie itself is all we have – no more, no less. The application of a framework of fuzzy logic to translation reception would nevertheless suggest that translation acceptance is a fixed range that cannot be enlarged, leaving no room for creating new readerships.

With the aforementioned in mind, based on the empirical data generated from the study with actual readers' expectations in a bottom-up manner, a trade-off model of reception is envisaged, which it is hoped will gain a degree of formalisation that would enable us to test it with complex, real-world data and justify empirical facts.

The idea of a trade-off is not new in language planning (e.g. Grin et al. 2014; Rossi et al. 2004; Weimer and Vining 2005). There have been some attempts to explicitly apply the notion to translation (Becher 2010; Scarpa 2020); for instance, Kotze's (2019: 353) discussion of the translator's "cognitive processing trade-off" between providing contextual information and minimising cognitive effort. More specifically, Becher (2010) pointed out that when communicating, the speaker sometimes has to determine where a favourable trade-off exists along the explicitness-implicitness scale. The trade-off reception model tentatively proposed in this study is especially indebted to the analysis of language policy in Grin et al. (2014), in which they visualised how policies of multilingualism across the European Union could simultaneously favour both mobility and social inclusion. Here, based on the analysis of the empirical data (see Section 4), I refer to the notion of a trade-off by presenting an emulated model combining two contrasts of translation expectations to identify situations in which the two values are balanced to maximise desired outcomes. In the model, the indifference curves symbolise the realm of translation acceptance. While Figure 1 is designed to be visualised as a diagram that exemplifies faithfulness in the horizontal dimension, the vertical arrangement of the dimension suggests fluency. The other two pairings of reader expectations under study (explicitation vs implicitation and distance vs proximity) are also argued to be applied to the theoretical model: "explicitation" and "proximity" can be reflected in the horizontal axis, respectively, corresponding to "implicitation" and "distance" on the vertical axis, the rationale of which will be discussed in Section 4.

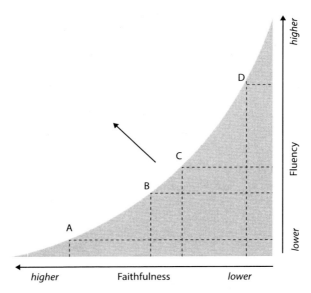

**Figure 1.** Trade-off model for translation reception (faithfulness vs fluency)

The underlying logic is that the reader's acceptance of a translation is measured by the realm circumscribed by the individual's two incompatible but desired expectations. Take the pair of faithfulness and fluency as an example. If the reader's expectations can be compromised at point B or C, the realm of translation acceptance is larger than that of points A (e.g. an extremely literal translation) and D (e.g. a radical rewriting). The trade-off model also suggests that translation acceptance is not a fixed point, since points B and C are both fairly acceptable (the circumscribed realms are similar in area) and regarded as "adequate" translations. The arrow in black denotes the direction of relaxing the curve to expand the realm of acceptance. By increasing the compatibility between the two seemingly conflicting expectations and relaxing the constraints, we can expand the possible realm of acceptance and heighten the communicative effect in translation flows. In this sense, the acceptance of translation might be neither binary nor linear, but accumulative.

## This study

This chapter reports a quasi-experiment in which 22 readers in Australia were asked to rank different translations of Chinese foreign-affairs discourses, with a focus on investigating the changing nature of reader expectations and identifying indicators that may have affected the reader's acceptance of the text. Reader expectations have posed a myriad of problems in reception studies that can be considered a set of constraints in which values are different in kind and are not all mutual opposites. Our point of departure is that it is through the lens of the reader's expectations that translation acceptance is quintessentially realised, and it is in the analyses of the interplays between the reader's all-pervasive expectations that the conditioning factors for translation reception are possibly mapped out. Three research questions are proposed as follows:

1. To what extent are reader expectations (in)compatible or characterised by different ranges of application in different situations?
2. How does the target reader make a decision in terms of different, seemingly exclusive expectations when comparing different translations?
3. Under what circumstances do readers dismiss a translation as unacceptable?

Instrument

In this study, 22 readers were asked to evaluate translations in four tasks. In each task, one Chinese foreign-affairs text was presented with three different English translations that represented different degrees of translator intervention. Follow-up semi-structured interviews were conducted to explore the underlying reasons for their perceptions of the translated texts. Seven focus-group interviews and four individual interviews with 22 interviewees were conducted between June and December 2018 in Melbourne, Australia.

Foreign-affairs discourse is used as translation material because this type of discourse, as a country's authoritative narrative on its ideological, political and social agendas produced for both domestic and international readership, is regarded as maximally embodying national identity, cultural knowledge and ideological conventions that may trigger different expectations among target readers. In this study, the four source texts (STs), published between 2016 and 2017, were excerpts selected from the Chinese government's official discourse, including a government report (coded as M-ST1), a state media report on premier Li Keqiang's visit to Australia (M-ST2), a speech by President Xi Jinping on the Belt and Road Initiative (M-ST3) and an introduction to the China-Australia Free Trade Agreement published on the Chinese government's website.

Translator intervention was taken as an umbrella concept that denotes a wide range of translator options, from word-for-word translation (i.e. low-level intervention) to radical adaptation (i.e. high-level intervention). For example, a word-for-word translation of a Chinese policy was regarded as a low-degree translator intervention. Any attempt to explicitate or reformulate culture-specific items in the source was considered a higher degree of intervention. In other words, in each task, the degree of intervention was measured and compared by the semantic and cultural-ideological distance from a close rendering of the source text (i.e. the lowest intervention among the three texts in the same task was coded as -INT). The second version was the medium-intervention translation (coded as +INT), and the third version was the highest-intervention translation (++INT). In each task, the +INT and ++INT were distinguished based on within-group comparison according to the degree of semantic distance and the scope of the interventions: +INT may represent an explicit version of -INT, in terms of information density; compared to +INT, ++INT may further tailor cultural and ideological elements to address the target-culture readerships. For instance, in Task 4, when describing the implementation of the China – Australia Free Trade Agreement (ChAFTA), the -INT text literally translated the source text as "ChAFTA is an important decision of the Party Central Committee and the State Council to implement the strategy of opening up to the outside world". In contrast, the ++INT version largely downscaled the Chinese Communist ideological components, summarising the Chinese government's effort and institutional endorsement of the ChAFTA as indicative of the fact that "the Chinese government believes in the benefits of free trade". All translations were designed and translated by the researcher and proofread by two English first-language speakers, who were instructed to further improve the texts in line with the research purpose.

In the experiment, the readers were not given information about how the translations had been designed and were not aware which translation might carry higher levels of "intervention". Rather, they were instructed to evaluate the translations based on their own preferences and were encouraged to share their rationale during the interview session, which it was hoped would shed light on the criteria the reader resorted to when comparing and contrasting the various translations. The purpose of using invented translations with varying levels of intervention was because the purpose of this study was not to attempt to assess linguistic qualities in authentic translations or pinpoint instances of mistranslations. Instead, I sought to understand how readers compare different translator interventions in culturally and ideologically charged discourses and make potential compromises within different constraints.

## Participants and sampling

Following area sampling, snowball sampling and convenience sampling, 22 selected subjects were invited to participate in the quasi-experiment. Fourteen of the participants were studying at different levels of university programmes (BA, MA and PhD) in Australia when the interviews were conducted, and the rest were invited by convenience sampling; they were Australians with different levels of engagement with China. To further enrich the data, two participants in a specific "expert" group with over 20 years' professional experience in Chinese-Australian political affairs were deliberately selected and approached through convenience sampling.

Of the 22 interviewees, six were male. Their ages ranged from 19 to 52 years, with an average age of 26 years. The interviewees had a high level of education, as all had (or were studying for) a bachelor's degree, seven had a master's degree and four had a PhD. After analysing the multifactorial quantitative data of the subjects, they were categorised into six groups in terms of their profile, engagement with China and familiarity with Chinese foreign-affairs discourse. The interviewees were coded in accordance with sequence and type of the interviews, demographic information (i.e. gender and age) and engagement with China. For example, a 25-year-old female subject who participated in the third individual interview in the group "Have been to China for less than three months" was coded as IN3F25L3 (third individual interview, female, aged 25, less than three months). This coding is designed, to some extent, to illustrate the potential link between the subject's sociolinguistic identity and the individual's responses to translations in the Discussion section.

| Subjects who do not know Chinese | | Subjects who know Chinese | | |
|---|---|---|---|---|
| Never been to China | Have been to China but for less than three months | Have been to China for more than three months | Chinese overseas students in Australia | China-Australia foreign affairs experts |

**Figure 2.** Types of readers interviewed in the quasi-experiment

Semi-structured interviews were used in the study to capture the potentially differentiated understanding of translation and the various expectations of translation that the readers might assume and to determine the level of interaction (cf. Márquez Reiter 2018).

In the interview trajectory, open-ended questions were used with some flexibility to allow variation in the order and the ways in which the questions were formulated. The interview questions were designed and categorised into four groups: (1) the readers' general evaluation of the various translations; (2) their comprehension of given textual choices in the translations; (3) their assumption of what good translations are like; and (4) their perceptions of the image of China presented in the translations and their view of China in general (see Appendix for a sample set of the interview questions).

All subjects gave their permission and informed consent to voluntarily participate in the study in accordance with the requirements of the local ethics committee of the institution where the study was conducted. With the participants' written permission, all the spoken parts of the experiment sessions were audio-recorded. The participants completed the interviews in their preferred language: all did so in English, except for IN2F51EX and the four subjects in the "students from mainland China" category, who preferred to be interviewed in Chinese. The recorded materials were then fully transcribed by Xunfei Tingjian, an online transcription service. The transcript quoted and analysed in this chapter was translated into English by us.

## Discussion

The quantitative ranking results of this study were reported elsewhere (Hu 2022: 207) and will not be elaborated on in this chapter due to space limitations. The major finding is that there are no linear, static links between the level of intervention and the reader's acceptance of a translation, as in three out of the four tasks the translations with medium-level interventions were ranked as the most accepted texts. This suggests that adjustment to the level of translator intervention is not a causal factor in enhancing translation acceptance underlying the potential dynamics of the reception of translated Chinese foreign-affairs discourse.

This chapter thus adopts an exploratory approach to examine the role that reader expectations play in affecting translation reception. By using an exploratory and inductive approach to analyse the readers' qualitative responses to various translations, this study utilises a thematic analysis of the interview data to investigate how conflicts between various expectations can be reconciled. Three pairs of reader expectations of translated Chinese foreign-affairs discourses are hence identified based on recurrence and repetition; they are formulated as follows: (1) faithfulness vs fluency, (2) explicitation vs implicitation, and (3) distance vs proximity. The first pairing hinges on the textual profile of the translations, the second refers to reading experience and the final concerns emotional reactions.

Drawing on Butterworth's (1980) notion of mental organisation, it can be argued that the first two pairs of expectations make manifest the reader's evaluation of the translator's global and local translation strategies on textual levels, and the third pair of expectations concerns the reader's extralinguistic evaluation of the stretches of text. Here, global translation strategies refer to those that affect the translator's decisions about translating the text as a whole, while local strategies denote those that deal with particular textual units (Chesterman 2005).

## Faithfulness vs fluency

This study identified a point that was made clear by many readers: they wanted to read a "faithful" translation, namely a text that would be considered an exact representation of the original. This echoes what Chesterman (1998) called the "*de re* effect" of a translation, referring to the effect of the message itself. Nevertheless, the readers in the experiment also paid attention to the *de dicto* effects of the text – that is, the readability of the message. The two expectations might not readily be able to coexist, if "faithful" was loosely understood by the readers as "literal". What interests us here is exploring how readers prioritise one over the other.

One important question pertaining to faithfulness is the matter of degree. When asked whether the Chinese premier's words in Task 3 should be rendered literally, IN3F25M3 suggested that rather than seeking formal equivalence, faithfulness to the message was a more decisive aspect of good translation; therefore, some linguistic adjustments to the original version would be acceptable. Similarly, IN2F18L3 argued that an "accurate translation" in the sense of a word-for-word translation in the literal sense might turn out to be inadequate or simply inappropriate.

Another point made by the readers was that a bad translation would easily arouse negative affective reactions and naturally undermine their trust in the translator's competence. If a world-for-word translation turned out to be "weird" (IN3F25L3) or "awkward" (IN2F26M3), or was suspected of being illogical, while still being linguistically faithful to the original, the readers would pause and wonder whether they could still trust the translator as having the status of a "professional":

IN3F25L3   The last line is not accurate English. I'm a bit jarred by that. I mean the translator didn't take it seriously. I would say they didn't even check their work.

Commenting on fluency, on the one hand, FG1M22D admitted that compared to the word-word M1-INT version, a more explicit ++INT version in Task 1 that provided explanations for Chinese political jargon would be easier to follow. On the other hand, adding "extra stuff" would still be "unforgivable" for the reader (FG1M22D). Here, favouring the strict sense of faithfulness would suggest that equal value was expected to be achieved on one level or another, which, *prima facie*, entails the notion of accuracy. This might be an unsurprising observation, as examples abound in the early literature on translation studies. Newmark (1997:77), for instance, emphatically concluded that "translation is a noble, truth-seeking activity, and that it should normally be accurate". Likewise, although ++INT in Task 4 was considered a more fluent translation compared to other alternatives and recognised as "the easiest to read" by IN1F34D, the reader still believed that $M_4$-INT – the most literal rendering of the three alternatives – should be accepted as the most "accurate".

This consideration may stem from the translation ethics of representation. It is widely acknowledged that the ethical imperative for a good translator is to represent the original text "accurately, without adding, omitting or changing anything" (Chesterman 2001: 139); otherwise, the text would be perceived as a distorted, biased and unethical rendering. This would explain why, although IN1F24M3 regarded M1++INT as "certainly the most positive" translation, she disliked it the most because the text was considered to inaccurately represent the original. Similarly, IN1M41EX's reservation had to do with the ethical status of translators as intermediaries of their particular role. In his view, the translator does not have the right to change the original text for whatever purpose:

IN1M41EX   But that is not what the original texts say. You know, as a translator, you don't make the judgment, right? You don't change the content for the audience.

Nevertheless, what IN1M41EX, a foreign affairs expert, stressed was not the relatively subsidiary status of translators to authors; what was more at stake was the reader's own interests and particular purpose for reading Chinese value-rich foreign-affairs texts. Translators may tend to adapt culture-bound items to dilute ideological differences for fear that receivers will not be able to cope with them. However, as IN1M41EX suggested, what he expected to find was exactly the traces of alterity. The reader's dismissal of fluency seems to endorse the enduring hypothesis of resistance in translation that foreignness should be privileged in the text (Venuti 1995), albeit at a less discernible level.

Interestingly, an insistence on linguistic sameness was sometimes stronger for the readers without source language proficiency. Although neither FG1F19N-a nor IN2F18L3 spoke Chinese, they could still sense that a text with a high level of translator intervention was "unfaithful". One possible reason for their doubts is that high-intervention translations conform to target norms, not only linguistically but also culturally, which in turn leads to the suspicion that the text might be altered and the readers had been manipulated. As IN1F34D commented on M3++INT, the domesticating translation with the highest level of translator intervention in Task 3 was "rubbish" because it could not be "true" and hence it was untrusted.

To understand why faithfulness is given so much attention, even when it can involve sacrificing readability, drawing on Pym's (2015) risk analysis, we can model the trade-off within a risk-aversion framework: faithfulness is tacitly considered valid by virtue of its presumed elimination of risky distortions. Because a faithful translation may come close to the original message, the readers can "be very clear that [the original text] said this or not," (FG1F19N-a), making a translation more "truthlike" (IN2F26M3). At the bottom, it is a play-safe option; for some target readers in this study, if the translator was considered to belong to a different ideological-cultural camp, and hence was not entirely trusted, fluency would be side-lined since any radical adaption as an indication of translator intervention would seem too dangerous to accept. Disputes in the trade-off between faithfulness and fluency boil down to the degree to which the reader can trust the translator's intervention.

Explicitation vs implicitation

In terms of expectations of the length of the translation, contradictions and inconsistencies were constantly demonstrated in the readers' answers. On the one hand, many readers stated clearly that they preferred a "concise" (FG2F19N), "succinct" or "dense" (IN1F19L3) translated text rather than a longer one, as it would be easy to digest. As IN2F34D recounted, translators generally tend to explain source information, albeit unnecessarily. This seems to echo the "explicitation hypothesis" (see Blum-Kulka 1986; Pápai 2004), one of the assumed universals of translation, which argues that translators are more likely to make implicit relations explicit by providing extra information.

Nevertheless, when evaluating the various translations in the four tasks, readers frequently expressed a similar desire for explicitation, making the translator's effort worthwhile, since they argued that they preferred more "informative" (FG1F20D) or "elaborate" (FG1F19N-a) translations. For some readers, the ethics of sameness gave way to explicitation because the reader considered extra information to be an "added value" (IN2F26M3), making the text "an enhanced translation" (IN2F26M3) even at the cost of not being faithful to the original:

IN2F26M3     [M1+INT] adds information, so it's not a direct translation. It's an enhanced translation. Not very faithful [hesitation], but I think it's the best one for readers.

For these readers, an adequate explicitation increased their understanding of the whole picture of the text by providing contextual information and thus enhanced the readability and fluency of translation in a general sense, whereas implicitation may affect the degree to which the reader can enjoy and understand the translation. Indeed, this study found that a lack of context was among the most common complaints made by readers who had no previously acquired knowledge of the original text:

IN1F19L3   I really had very little context for [M1-INT].

IN3F25M3   The term "five-sphere integrated plan" [in the -INT vesion of Task 1] is strange. If it had explained what that was afterwards, it would have been much better.

A fair justification for the -INT version would be that the translation is a word-for-word rendering of the source text without explicitation. However, when target-language readers, especially those without linguistic access to the original, evaluated the translation, they were more likely to shift the onus of blame onto the translator. The implicitation here was not only blamed for comprehension challenges but also obviously jeopardised the credibility of the translation. For IN1F19L3, implicitation was certainly unconvincing:

IN1F19L3   This reads like someone has given you the information but none of the context. So it doesn't support what the text says.

Such implicitation may make target-culture readers feel confused, alienated or unmotivated. The demand for explicitation is partly explained by a reader's psychologically precarious state. Without explicit information, the readers in this study typically felt that the translation was "annoying" (IN1M19N).

The emphasis on explicitation contradicts the expectation of a concise, implicit translation, suggesting that there is always a trade-off of effort. The readers might be fearful of losing potentially important information and would ask for more explicitation, but if the less important text was too long, the readers would lose focus and feel bored.

Nevertheless, there was a certain discrepancy in comprehension among different readers, largely due to the fact that they had differing relationships with the text, with different interests and levels of understanding of the source culture. Although explicitation provides contextual knowledge to save readers cognitive processing effort, it is not the antidote to every translation problem. Infelicitous explicitation can be risky; as IN1M31EX pointed out, the more you explain, the more unknown effects there may be upon readers due to the possibility of cultural relativity: "I don't think it's translated wrong. It's just that we understand the meaning differently." That is, whether the English translation can carry exactly the same contextual meaning as the Chinese translation remains unclear. IN2F26M3 similarly argued that the explicitation of socialism in M1++INT might cause a communicative risk for the Western reader:

IN2F26M3   It means something different for a Chinese person than for a Western person. If I think of socialism, I don't think of what exists in China, even though that's what Chinese people call socialism.

In a preliminary study on the production side that we reported in a separate article elsewhere (Hu 2020:114f), a Chinese institutional translator had proposed a similar argument against excessive explicitation: "The more you try to say, the less the readers understand." What is at stake here is an acknowledgement of the risk-generating factors that may affect the trade-off between explicitation and implicitation – a point we will return to in the Summary section.

Distance vs proximity

The third pairing of expectations is bound to the reader's extralinguistic reaction to the translation. Cultural distance seemed to make the general readers under investigation who had little knowledge of the context "very uncomfortable", since they would feel "alienated" (IN2F18L3) and excluded from the communication. In that case, readers appear to have grave doubts about whether they could be intended as the target audience of the translated text if they cannot associate with the text. An archetypal example is that, according to FG2M52N, as soon as he saw phrases such as "the Third and Fourth Plenary Sessions of the 18th CPC Central Committee", he suspected the text was written for a Chinese audience rather than for Australian readers like him. Readers might question the value of reading the translation as a whole if they feel excluded from the translational activity and are not direct addressees (cf. Pym 1992/2010).

The expectation of proximity denotes the tendency for translations to adapt to target-language norms, making the target reader feel more culturally and ideologically close to the text. The premise of proximity is that the target reader can correctly understand the foreign elements in the text; we like things we can understand. However, the study found that some readers who preferred cultural distance did not fully comprehend the content. When asked how FG1F19N-a understood the literal translation of the Chinese idiom "peaches and plums do not speak, but they are so attractive that a path is created below the trees", which she had ranked as her "favourite", the reader hesitated for a brief moment and said, "I don't know." This idiom was used by Chinese President Xi Jinping to express his gratitude for the support that the Belt and Road Initiative received worldwide. A couple of Australian readers who ranked the literal, foreignising translation as their first choice gave some interesting interpretations. For FG1F22N, peach and plum trees are so beautiful that people approach them not only for their beauty and fresh fruit but also "for the shade" they provide. Despite not being entirely faithful to the original, this creative interpretation at some point echoes the Chinese president's intention in using the idiom to imply the role of Belt and Road Initiative in balancing and protecting the interests of the participating countries. For FG1F19-a, the desire for cultural distance can be attributed to a greater propensity for cultural diversity. She suggested that "if you think about it enough" and relate the unknown to the known, a foreignising translation could work. This study found that if the readers had a strong interest in exploring foreign elements and trusted that a translation has a pedagogical value to help them explore new worlds, they might show a propensity to invest extra cognitive effort in decoding an obscure text.

Nevertheless, for the more general readership, whether the foreignising translation is "making sense" is often construed as a basic question. As FG2F19N argued, the cost of cognitive effort and the pleasure of exposure to a foreign culture should be carefully calculated. Here, a trade-off enters the picture: the effort to understand a foreignising translation should not exceed the positive values generated by exoticism. As FG2F19N contended, readers might find an exotic text appealing if foreignness is maintained at a reasonable level. This refers to the kinds of "internal goods" earned on the reception side (cf. Chesterman 2006): the reader's "aha!" experience of learning something new and the enjoyment of decoding a tricky term.

The next question is how to define the fuzzy boundary between distance and proximity. IN2F24N proposed a solution to this: the more common ground a target reader can find in a distance translation, the more possible it is for them to accept the text. For FG2M52N, she liked the fact that in the last sentence of M2-INT, namely the conventional expression "fruitful results", referred back to the unfamiliar "peaches and plums" idiom, enabling the reader to seek something new while not being completely excluded from the source culture and ending up as an outsider. What makes the reader accept the literal, foreignising translation is not the exoticism shown in the text or the resistance to target stylistic norms, but the fact that readers can strike a balance between proximity and the pleasure of learning new things.

Another reason for accepting cultural distance is pedagogical. As IN1M19N suggested, a foreignising translation would be accepted because the reader believed that the translation helped promote intercultural understanding. One may suggest that to accept a foreign element, readers would need to trust that the distance benefited them, pedagogically or practically.

With respect to proximity in a domesticating translation, many of the readers under scrutiny here appreciated it when the translator conformed to their target-culture conventions. One main reason is that a proximity translation that exhibits idiomatic English that captures the gist without missing nuances, "sounds familiar" to target readers, making the message easier for them to digest and imbuing readers with confidence in the translator's language proficiency. Cultural familiarity is in line with the virtue of predictability in Chesterman's "norm-based ethics" (2001: 141): if a translation is done in norm-obeying ways, it has a certain degree of predictability, which suggests the good faith of the translator's consistent and stable behaviour and hence enhances the credibility of the text.

However, there always remains a degree of doubt if the reader is not sanguine about the translatability of culturally specific items. When asked whether IN1F24M3 would prefer an original Chinese idiom being replaced by an established English proverb, the interviewee's answer was "not really".

As IN1F19L3 argued, a domesticating, norm-obeying translation entailed "someone putting the Australian language into [the Chinese premier's] mouth". The ways in which the readers negatively commented on domesticating translation was not consistent. Similarly, for IN2F24N, seeing Australian slang in a foreign politician's speech was "weird", "odd" and "insincere", and the translator should "stop trying so hard". One possible reason for the reader's disdain for the translator's use of a "very Aussie" term is that the use of unique items (Tirkkonen-Condit 2004) within the text may suggests that a translation is apocryphal and untrustworthy. For Australian readers, if the Chinese premier's message sounded too native, it would show traces of intervention, making them suspect that the premier's initial message had been distorted. If the reader interpreted the intervention of narrowing down cultural distance as a sort of manipulation, the possibility of accepting the text would be even lower. Here, what the reader distrusts is not only the translation but also the image of the translator.

## Summary and interpretation of findings

The analyses of the three pairs of reader expectations side by side attempt to demonstrate the extent to which such expectations do not merely reflect a list of possibilities or directives but a dynamic trade-off process; expectations are not static but are always in a state of flux, depending on the extent to which the translation is trusted by the readers to function in their best interests. I do not wish to disregard the divergence in the twin sets of expectations in favour of conflating them; my contention is that the relationship between two incompatible expectations can be seen in terms of basic mutual dependency.

In the first pair – faithfulness vs fluency – the study shows that the readers required the translation to be faithful to its nature of being a reliable reference, whereas fluency was usually considered a measure of the extent to which a translation could actually be used. These relationships might be complicated by the reader's familiarity with the source culture, but mutual dependence remains. The reader's trade-off decision is conditioned by cognitive considerations. Despite the reader's knee-jerk resistance to "unfaithfulness" and their negative comments on overt domestication, linguistic sameness might be overruled by the pragmatic use of the criterion of readability. In this sense, translation can be conceptualised as a transaction cost (Pym 1995); ideally, the costs of investing in translational communication should not exceed the mutual benefits achieved.

In the second pair – between explicitation and implicitation – the readers in the study naturally preferred more concise texts, but if they felt "unsafe" and suspected that important information was being hidden, they were motivated to spend more processing effort digesting explicated translations. It seems that the readers struck a balance between excessive explicitation and a complete lack of it. One possible reason for this is the asymmetrical knowledge of information between the production and reception sides (cf. Pym 2014), in that translators are generally presumed to know more about the source text than their readers do. Readers thus need to trust the translator not to bend the truth to mitigate the risk of being distorted or misled.

Taking the above logic one step further, we reached the point of viewing translation reception as an exercise in compromising the risk of distrust. In the third category, proximity in norm-conforming translations and cultural distance in foreignising translations could both be resisted, in that the reader loses trust in the translation when they suspect they are being manipulated. The ethical dimension deserves serious attention because it underpins the way in which a trade-off can be reached. It is plausible to argue that the more trust the translator gains, the more open the reader is going to be to accept a wider range of translator interventions. This suggests the significance of ongoing translational communication; after all, trust itself can be cumulative, which exists both at the individual reader level and at the aggregate societal level.

## Conclusion

Based on the qualitative thematic analysis of how actual readers responded to various translations of Chinese foreign affairs discourses, three pairs of reader expectations (faithfulness vs fluency, explicitation vs implicitation, and distance vs proximity) from textual, emotional and ethical perspectives were identified and categorised. In the space of the reception, the reader's judgements of the asymmetry in a series of values tended to be in tandem: there was always a pair of two incompatible but desirable expectations, which were (un)consciously calculated by readers, in which both linguistic and ethical considerations were weighed against each other.

In this study, we conceptualised that the actual reader can activate an underlying mechanism of optimal trade-offs when engaging in translations with different levels of translator intervention, roughly weighing the benefits and losses in such a way that at least two positive expectations are sought simultaneously as a double solution. Thus, translational trade-offs underpin translation acceptance; at some point, readers attempt to realise more than one positive expectation at the cost of a certain degree of risk-taking in order to reach a compromise. For instance, the degree of literalism within the translated narrative that aims to be faithful and accurate to the source text should not make the cognitive burden needed to comprehend the text outweigh the reader's desire to continue reading. An optimal balance should be sought between the readerly effort invested and the benefits gained. Note that the idea of compromise as a result of reception does not necessarily denote the classic notion of translation as a *loss* but is more closely related to Pareto optimality, in which the maximum desired effects are yielded for minimum risks, with more attention being given to the former than the latter.

This study also found that trust, as a value *sui generis* in intercultural communication, serves as a promising pathway towards expanding translation acceptance. It is understandable that the reader's trust in the translator's competence and credibility becomes eroded if the textual quality of a translation is deemed subpar. Perhaps more interestingly, if the reader believes that there has been dialogical infighting in the translated text, or if a sense of cultural proximity is suspected to be fabricated, no matter how fluent the text is, it is less likely to be accepted or trusted. Conversely, if the translator's intervention in the text is perceived as well-intentioned and trustworthy, a wider range of translation strategies might be more bearable and, therefore, accepted at reception.

As actual agents negotiating different degrees of translator interventions, the varying profiles of readers, including their cultural location, personal ideologies and familiarity with the source language, together with their purposes in reading the translation, affect how the trade-offs can be ultimately enacted and the extent to which trust can be established. To increase the compatibility of potentially exclusive expectations is to increase mutual trust linguistically and culturally in intercultural communication, a situation in which cooperation can somehow be attained.

Obviously, the complexity of translation reception necessitates analysis that goes well beyond the three pairs of expectations that have been crystallised here. The two-dimensional modelling of values might seem simplistic, but there should be value in an attempt to gain a degree of formalisation by simplifying complex situations. It would also be interesting to investigate whether trade-offs always need to be theoretically reduced to just two values. As also shown in this study, multiple variables overlap; occasionally, there is even causation involved (e.g. fluency ensures cultural proximity), oftentimes creating the difficulty of defining the actual virtues in question. More variables of reader expectations need to be factored in to offer a theorised empiricism that helps us gain a more acute awareness of how translational flows operate and are received in a profoundly multilingual world.

## References

Adamczyk, Magdalena. 2015. Do hedges always hedge? On non-canonical multifunctionality of jakby in polish. *Pragmatics* 25 (3): 321–344.

Arzık-Erzurumlu, Özüm and Gamze Yilmaz. 2022. From remote control to tweets. How viewers' use of Twitter shapes quality criteria in interpreting the Oscars. *Interpreting*.

Athique, Adrian. 2016. *Transnational Audiences: Media Reception on a Global Scale*. Cambridge: Polity Press.

Becher, Viktor (2010). "Abandoning the notion of "translation-inherent" explicitation. Against a dogma of translation studies". *Across Languages and Cultures* 11 (1): 1–28.

Blumczyński, Piotr and Ghodrat Hassani. 2019. "Towards a Meta-theoretical Model for Translation. A Multidimensional Approach." *Target* 31 (3): 328–351.

Blum-Kulka, Shoshana. 1986. "Shifts of Cohesion and Coherence in Translation." In *Interlingual and Intercultural Communication: Discourse and Cognition in Translation and Second Language Acquisition Studies*, eds. by Juliane House, and Shoshana Blum-Kulka 17–35. Tübingen: Narr.

Butterworth, Brian. 1980. "Evidence from Pauses in Speech." In *Language Production. Volume 1: Speech and Talk*, ed. by Brian Butterworth, 155–176. London: Academic Press.

Chesterman, Andrew. 1998. "Causes, Translations, Effects." *Target* 10 (2): 201–230.

Chesterman, Andrew. 2001. "Proposal for a Hieronymic Oath." *The Translator* 7 (2): 139–154.

Chesterman, Andrew. 2005. Problems with strategies. In *New Trends in Translation Studies. In Honour of Kinga Klaudy*. (17–28), Krisztina Károly and Ágota Fóris (eds). Budapest: Akadémiai Kiadó.

Chesterman, Andrew. 2006. "Questions in the Sociology of Translation." In *Translation Studies at the Interface of Disciplines*, eds. by João Ferreira Duarte, Alexandra Assis Rosa, and Teresa Seruya, 9–27. Amsterdam: John Benjamins.

Colina, Sonia. 2008. "Translation Quality Evaluation: Empirical Evidence for a Functionalist Approach." *The Translator* 14 (1): 97–134.

Di Giovanni, Elena and Yves Gambier 2018 (eds). *Reception Studies and Audiovisual Translation*. Amsterdam: John Benjamins.

Enríquez-Aranda, Mercedes, and Francisca García Luque. 2018. "The Reception of Subtitled Films from a Sociological Perspective. An Empirical Case Study." *Babel* 64 (3): 464–489.

Gambier, Yves. 2018. Translation studies, audiovisual translation and reception. In *Reception Studies and Audiovisual Translation*, edited by Elena Di Giovanni and Yves Gambier (pp. 43–66). John Benjamins.

Gentile, Paola, Fruzsina Kovács, and Marike van der Watt (eds). 2021. Transnational Image Building: Linking up Translation Studies, Reception Studies and Imagology, *Special Issue of Translation Spaces* 10 (1).

Grin, François, László Marácz, Nike K. Pokorn, and Peter A. Kraus. 2014. Mobility and Inclusion in Multilingual Europe: A Position Paper on the MIME Project. University of Geneva. Access: https://www.mime-project.org/resources/MIME-POSITION-PAPER-V4.pdf

Henitiuk, Valerie. 2008. "'Easyfree Translation?' How the Modern West Knows Sei Shônagon's Pillow Book." *Translation Studies* 1 (1): 2–17.

Hu, Bei. 2020. "How are translation norms negotiated? A case study of risk management in Chinese institutional translation." *Target* 32 (1): 83–122.

Hu, Bei. 2022. "Feeling foreign: A trust-based compromise model of translation reception." *Translation Studies* 15(2): 202–220.

Kershaw, Angela. 2013. Complexity and Unpredictability in Cultural Flows: Two French Holocaust Novels in English Translation. *Translation Studies* 7 (1): 34–49.

Koller, Werner. 1995. "The Concept of Equivalence and the Object of Translation Studies." *Target* 7 (2): 191–222.

Koskinen, Kaisa. 2000. "Institutional Illusions." *The Translator* 6 (1): 49–65.

Kotze, Haidee. 2019. "Converging What and How to Find Out Why. An Outlook on Empirical Translation Studies." *In New Empirical Perspectives on Translation and Interpreting*, eds. by Lore Vandevoorde, Joke Daems and Bart Defrancq, 333–371. London: Routledge.

Kruger (Kotze), Haidee. 2012. Postcolonial Polysystems. *The Production and Reception of Translated Children's Literature in South Africa*. Amsterdam: John Benjamins.

Kruger (Kotze), Haidee. 2016. Fluency/resistancy and Domestication/foreignisation: A Cognitive Perspective. *Target* 28 (1): 4–41.

Kruger (Kotze), Haidee, and Jan-Louis Kruger. 2017. "Cognition and Reception." In *The Handbook of Translation and Cognition*, eds, by John Schwieter, and Aline Ferreira, 71–89. Hoboken: John Wiley and Sons.

Kurz, Ingrid. 2001. Conference interpreting: Quality in the ears of the user. *Meta* 46 (2): 394–409.

Lefevere, André. 1992/2017. *Translation, Rewriting and the Manipulation of Literary Fame*. London: Routledge.

Marais, Kobus. 2019. *A (Bio)Semiotic Theory of Translation: The Emergence of Socio-cultural Reality*. London: Routledge.

Márquez Reiter, Rosina. 2018. "Interviews as sites of ideological work". *Spanish in Context* 15 (1): 54–76.

McAuley, Thomas E. 2015. "Audience Attitude and Translation Reception. The Case of Genji Monogatari." *Babel* 61 (2): 219–241.

McMartin, Jack, and Paola Gentile. 2020. "The Transnational Production and Reception of 'A Future Classic': Stefan Hertmans's War and Turpentine in Thirty Languages." *Translation Studies* 13 (3): 271–290.

Meylaerts, Reine and Maud Gonne. 2014. "Transferring the City – Transgressing Borders: Cultural Mediators in Antwerp (1850–1930)." *Translation Studies* 7 (2): 133–151.

Newmark, Peter. 1997. "The Customer as King." *Current Issues in Language and Society* 4 (1): 75–77.

Nord, Christiane. 1997/2018. *Translating as a Purposeful Activity*. Manchester: St. Jerome Publishing.

O'Brien, Sharon. 2008. "Processing fuzzy matches in translation memory tools: An eye-tracking analysis." In *Looking at eyes: Eye-Tracking studies of reading and translation processing*, Susanne Göpferich, Arnt L. Jakobsen and Inge Mees (eds.), 79–102. Frederiksberg: Samfundslitteratur.

Pápai, Vilma. 2004. "Explicitation: A Universal of Translated Text?" In *Translation Universals. Do They Exist?*, eds. by Anna Mauranen, and Pekka Kujamäki, 143–164. Amsterdam: John Benjamins.

Pym, Anthony. 1992/2010. *Translation and Text Transfer: An Essay on the Principles of Intercultural Communication*. Frankfurt am Main: Peter Lang.

Pym, Anthony. 1995. "Translation as a Transaction Cost." *Meta* 40 (4):594–605.

Pym, Anthony. 2014. *Exploring Translation Theories* (2nd edition). London: Routledge.

Pym, Anthony. 2015. Translation as Risk Management. *Journal of Pragmatics* 85: 67–80.

Pym, Anthony. 2016. *Translation Solutions for Many Languages: Histories of A Flawed Dream*. London and New York: Bloomsbury.

Ross, Dolores. 2021. "'My Language Has an Immense Potential.' A Review of Cees Nooteboom's National and Transnational Circulation." In *Transnational Image Building: Linking up Translation Studies, Reception Studies and Imagology*, eds. by Paola Gentile, Fruzsina Kovács and Marike van der Watt, Special Issue of Translation Spaces 10 (1): 70–93.

Rossi, Peter H., Mark W. Lipsey, and Howard E. Freeman. 2004. *Evaluation: A Systematic Approach* (7th ed.). Thousand Oaks, London: Sage.

Scarpa, Federica 2020. *Research and Professional Practice in Specialised Translation. Palgrave Studies in Translating and Interpreting*. Palgrave Macmillan.

Tirkkonen-Condit, Sonja. 2004. "Unique Items – Over- or Under-represented in Translated Language?" In *Translation Universals. Do They Exist?*, eds. by Anna Mauranen, and Pekka Kujamäki, 177–184. Amsterdam: John Benjamins.

Todorova, Marija. 2021. "The Western Balkans in Translated Children's Literature Location-dependent Images of (Self)representation." In *Transnational Image Building: Linking up Translation Studies, Reception Studies and Imagology*, eds. by Paola Gentile, Fruzsina Kovács and Marike van der Watt, the special issue of Translation Spaces 10 (1): 94–114.

Toury, Gideon. 2012. *Descriptive Translation Studies and Beyond*. Amsterdam: John Benjamins.

Tuominen, Tiina. 2018. "Multi-method Research. Reception in Context." In *Reception Studies and Audiovisual Translation*, eds. by Elena Di Giovanni, and Yves Gambier, 69–90. Amsterdam: John Benjamins.

Tymoczko, Maria. 1999/2014. *Translation in a Postcolonial Context*. Manchester: St. Jerome.

Venuti, Lawrence. 1995. *The Translator's Invisibility: A History of Translation*. London and New York: Routledge.

Wehrmeyer, Ella. 2015. "Comprehension of Television News Signed Language Interpreters: A South African Perspective." *Interpreting* 17 (2): 195–225.

Weimer, David L. and Aidan R. Vining. 2005. *Policy Analysis: Concepts and Practice* (4th ed.). Englewood Cliffs: Prentice-Hall.

Xu, Minhui, and Jing Yu. 2019. "Sociological Formation and Reception of Translation. The Case of Kinkley's Translation of Biancheng." *Translation and Interpreting Studies* 14 (3): 333–350.

Zadeh, Lotfi. A. 1965. "Fuzzy Sets". *Information and Control* 8, 338–353.

Zheng Binghan, and Mingqing Xie 2018. "The Effect of Explanatory Captions on the Reception of Foreign Audiovisual Products. A Study Drawing on Eyetracking Data and Retrospective Interviews." *Translation, Cognition and Behavior* 1(1): 119–146.

Zwischenberger, Cornelia, and Franz Pöchhacker. 2010. "Survey on Quality and Role: Conference Interpreters' Expectations and Self-perceptions". *Communicate!* Spring 2010. Accessed January 25, 2011. http://www.aiic.net/ViewPage.cfm/article2510.htm.

# Appendix. Sample semi-structured interview questions

## Demographic questions for readers

Age
Education
The reader's strongest language
The reader's potential proficiency in the Chinese language
Engagement with China

## Part 1. Reader's general evaluation of the various translations

For each task, could you please rank the three translations in the order in which you prefer them most and explain your reasons?

For each translation, what makes you like or dislike the text?

## Part 2. Reader's comprehension of given textual choices in the translations

How do you understand the 'Four-Pronged Comprehensive Strategy' in M1-INT?

How do you understand that 'Peaches and plums do not speak, but they are so attractive that a path is formed below the trees' in M2-INT?

In Task 3, how do you understand that the Chinese premier insisted on wearing two scarves together?

How do you understand terms such as 'the Party Central Committee and the State Council' and 'the Third and Fourth Plenary Sessions of the 18th CPC Central Committee'?

## Part 3. Reader's assumption of what good translations are like

How important is it to read a fluent translation of Chinese foreign-affairs discourse?

How important is it to read a faithful translation of Chinese foreign-affairs discourse?

What do you think are the important criteria for translating China's foreign-affairs texts?

Do you like to read a longer translated text or a shorter one? Why?

What will not be accepted by you when reading translated China's foreign-affairs texts?

In your opinion, what constitutes a 'faithful' translation?

In your opinion, what constitutes an 'accurate' translation?

What expectations do you have when reading a translation? Do you think translations of other text types could differ from translations of China's foreign-affairs texts?

Who do you think will be the translator of the translation?

Could you give any suggestions on how to translate Chinese foreign-affairs discourse?

## Part 4. Readers' perceptions of the image of China presented in translations and their views of China in general

What words would you use to describe the image of the Chinese premier?

Do you think your impression of the premier might change according to the different translations you read?

What is your opinion of China?

CHAPTER 11

# The tidalectics of translation
## On the necessity of rethinking translation flows from the Caribbean

Laëtitia Saint-Loubert
University College Dublin

This chapter aims to contribute to debates on non-market-centric, more equitable, sustainable routes of transnational literary circulation, particularly for those literatures originally produced, translated, disseminated and distributed in fragilized ecosystems. To this end, it proposes an epistemological move away from traditional core-periphery, Global North-Global South paradigms. Rather than adopting a market-oriented approach, it aims to rethink Translation Studies from the perspective of the complex, varied and fragile ecosystems of the Caribbean. In relation to flows from and beyond the Caribbean, it will concentrate on Kamau Brathwaite's 'tidalectics' (or 'tidal dialectic[s]') to envisage more sustainable flows of transnational literary circulation and rethink acts and processes of translation within their 'natural', vulnerable contexts of emergence (Brathwaite, 1983).

**Keywords:** tidalectics, translation flows, circle culture, solidarity, Caribbean literary ecosystem, circular economy, Kamau Brathwaite, South-South connections, episteme-shifting

## Introduction

Translation is a market that manifests complex circulation flows. When examining the global circulation of translated literature from a Western perspective, gravitational models have emerged as the dominant paradigm. Such models consist in dividing up literary markets into systems composed of unequal literary spaces, so-called "centers" and "peripheries", that remain largely regulated by the asymmetrical forces of globalization and the politics of neocolonial imperatives. More and more, though, centers and peripheries are further subdivided into semi-centers and semi-peripheries, as well as identified as part of pluri-centric and multiscalar systems, depending on the focus of attention and the linguistic areas under study (Edfeldt et al. 2022; Lindqvist 2016: 174–187; Sievers and Levitt, 2020: 467–480). Multiscalar approaches, in particular, aim to further complicate the Global North-Global South divide by bringing to the fore the points of intersection between centers and peripheries; yet the angle from which translation is approached remains chiefly addressed in vertical and terrestrial terms. In their introduction to a special issue of the *Journal of World Literature* dedicated to scale shifting, for instance, Wiebke Sievers and Peggy Levitt argue the following:

> The contributors to this special volume map the political, economic, and cultural factors that affect scale shifting by building upon earlier analyses that began to spell out the aesthetic and sociological factors that enabled outsiders to be recognised and travel (Casanova; Bourdieu). Our contributors move these conversations forward by focusing on how peripheralised writers scale up to gain global visibility in multiscalar literary fields and the ways in which this scale shifting transforms the national, regional and global levels of these fields.
>
> (2020: 468–469)

Scale shifting therefore designates an upward or downward movement, from a micro to a macro level, or vice versa, that remains inscribed within vertical logics of transnational literary circulation (see Casanova 2007, 2015; D'haen 2012; Sapiro 2008, 2016) as well as within literary "fields" (Bourdieu 1992) or "actor-networks" (Latour 2005; Folaron and Buzelin 2007). In other words, as Angela Kershaw put it, "[r]esearch on translation flows approaches literary exchanges from the point of view of a hierarchized world system in which concepts such as capital and consecration, derived from Bourdieu, are deployed to describe the unequal nature of translation exchanges" (2019: 446). Yet, as this chapter is going to argue, those approaches not only prove insufficient to produce relevant insights into the actual circulation of literary works and translation flows in complex literary ecologies such as the Caribbean literary ecosystem, they also contribute to make even more invisible those literary works whose production and circulation, including in translation, already fall outside the purview of mainstream analyses. The aim of this contribution will therefore be two-fold: by focusing on contemporary cultural and literary initiatives that promote solidarity and a circular economy in the Caribbean, the chapter will show (1) how these ongoing efforts not only work towards a more integrated Caribbean literary ecosystem, despite a context of economic fragility, structural (inter)dependencies and fragmentation in the region, but also (2) how they can offer a much-needed alternative analytical model for Translation Studies, beyond the Caribbean region, that can help us rethink dominant paradigms and a disciplinary bias towards vertical, terrestrial and anthropocentric perspectives. In short, this contribution will argue that the Caribbean literary ecosystem and Caribbean Studies as a discipline are absolutely central to a decolonial approach to translation and literary circulation.

## Methodology and material

To do that, translation flows will be analyzed as tidal movements, with the primary focus of study literary (non-)circulation within the insular Caribbean. Kamau Brathwaite's "tidalectics" – and some of its academic and artistic readings – will serve as the main theoretical framework to envisage Translation Studies from the angle of Caribbean Studies. In doing so, the chapter will study translation flows in terms of the intermittent, varying tidal rhythm of the sea to explore, on the one hand, "alter/native" modes of circulation based on fluidity and "circle culture" (Brathwaite 1983: 38–39), and, on the other, the potential benefits of (trans)oceanic, ex-centric epistemologies for Translation Studies, particularly when thinking the discipline within and beyond the Anthropocene. The concept of tidalectics will be applied, on the one hand, to infrastructures such as public libraries, which echo Brathwaite's "circle culture" and contribute to the "submarine unity" of the Caribbean (Brathwaite 1982) by acting as community nodes that provide access to regional literature through non-centric, pan-Caribbean translation flows, and, on the other, to literary initiatives that foster pan-Caribbean solidarity and a (more) circular economy – as opposed to a top-down, market approach based on accumulation and consecration.

As this contribution is part of a wider research project, at this point it is worth providing the reader with some background information about our research methodology.[1] Adopting a comparative approach, the research project aim to analyze the contemporary Caribbean literary ecosystem. It focuses on Puerto Rico,[2] Martinique, Guadeloupe,[3] and Trinidad and Tobago,[4] and studies more partic-

---

[1]. The research project is a two-year project entitled "Rethinking Translation Studies from Caribbean Meridians: Towards an Ecosystemic Approach" that is funded by the Irish Research Council.

[2]. In Spanish the status of Puerto Rico is described as "Estado Libre Asociado". It is a non-incorporated US territory, which means that Puerto Rico is not a US state, although it is subject to US laws.

[3]. Martinique and Guadeloupe are DROMs (Départements et Régions d'Outre-Mer), that is French overseas territories that have the official status of a department and a region. They are fully part of France and subject to French laws.

[4]. Trinidad and Tobago gained independence from the UK in 1962, before the territory became a Republic in 1976. It is part of the Commonwealth of Nations.

ularly how the (post)colonial condition of each territory impacts on their literary ecosystem, while examining transversal, pan-Caribbean cultural and literary initiatives that work towards greater regional integration and sustainability. Our approach is mainly qualitative and entails conducting archival work and interviews with various actors across the Caribbean book sector, from the production side (book creation and publication process) to the reception end (distribution, diffusion and access).

The material that has been analyzed thus far as part of this project has primarily covered 20th- and 21st-century works of fiction and non-fiction, with a focus on books and texts (some of which were published in Caribbean journals and anthologies) that have been translated and circulated within the region, including in Caribbean indigenous languages. As such, children's literature available in either print, audio or digital format and transmitted orally has, where relevant, been taken into consideration.[5] Schoolbooks and educational materials, however, fall outside the scope of the study.

## On the origins and subsequent readings of "tidalectics"

Kamau Brathwaite's neologism, "tidalectics", has been used as a methodological tool and a guiding principle in several theoretical works and artistic projects since the Bajan poet coined the term in the 1980s. Before examining such readings of his tidalectics and their relevance for Translation Studies, this chapter will return to the poet's original definition of the concept, as well as to its context of publication.

In his contribution to a volume entitled *Missile and Capsule*, published in Bremen, Germany, in 1983, following a one-week festival organized on the Caribbean,[6] which Brathwaite attended, he defined tidalectics as follows:

---

5. In the context of Martinique and Guadeloupe, for example, publications originally written or translated in Creole usually deal with children's literature, although some translations of (French) classics and original texts in Creole can also be found in the catalogues of local publishers, often specialized in Caribbean fiction and non-fiction for adults, such as Neg Mawon, K Éditions or CaraïbEditions.

6. The introduction to the conference proceedings, by Jürgen Martini, is interesting inasmuch as it places Brathwaite's tidalectics within a creative process whose fluidity is hinted at by the editor, as he explains that many contributions, among which Brathwaite's, were elaborated, revised "and brought into a coherent form" by the authors themselves in the printed version. (Martini 1983: 5–6). This suggests that the spontaneous, oral/aural impetus of Brathwaite's tidalectics, which could not be reproduced on the printed page, should nevertheless be included in analyses of his concept.

> 'success' of dialectics: synthesis. For dialectics is another gun: a missile: a way of making progress:
> farward
> but in the culture of the circle 'success' moves outward from the centre to circumference and back again: a tidal dialectic: an ital dialectic: continuum across the peristyle (Brathwaite 1983: 42)

In the appendix provided at the end of his contribution, Brathwaite further explains a number of "prosewords" he coined, among which "tidal dialectics", which he uses interchangeably with "tidalectics", and sums up as "our native version (less optimistic, perhaps) of Eurodialectics" (1983: 54). Based on this initial definition, tidalectics can be identified as a cyclical movement that not only wishes to distance itself from a Eurocentric, teleological dialectics, but also as a circular continuum that aims to challenge the Hegelian ideal of synthesis. Although Brathwaite does not expand on the oceanic trope of the tide here, more recent readings of his tidalectics have emphasized this specificity. This is the case, in particular, of Stefanie Hessler's contribution to *Tidalectics: Imagining an Oceanic Worldview through Art and Science*, a volume that is comprised of visual art and text, published in 2017 as part of an exhibition held at the Thyssen-Bornemisza Art Contemporary-Augarten, in Vienna, in which she argues that Brathwaite's "*tidalectics* formulates an oceanic worldview, a different way of engaging with the oceans and the world we inhabit. Dissolving purportedly terrestrial modes of thinking and living, it attempts to coalesce steady land with the rhythmic fluidity of water and the incessant swelling and receding of the tides" (Hessler 2018: 31). Echoing this reasoning, the volume offers a transoceanic dialogue between visual art, science and literature originating, for the most part, in the Caribbean and the Pacific, and places the ocean as a dynamic, unifying element. In her introduction to *Routes and Roots*, Elizabeth De Loughrey similarly argues for an epistemological shift that would move from landscape to seascape as a way of deconstructing Eurocentric, colonial paradigms:

> One of the central but unacknowledged ways in which European colonialism has constructed the trope of the isolated island is by mystifying the importance of the sea and the migrations across its expanse. In order to recuperate the centrality of the ocean in island discourse, I turn to Kamau Brathwaite's theory of "tidalectics," a methodological tool that foregrounds how a dynamic model of geography can elucidate island history and cultural production, providing the framework for exploring the complex and shifting entanglement between sea and land, diaspora and indigeneity, and routes and roots. (DeLoughrey 2007: 2)

The last point raised by DeLoughrey here on the history of islands and cultural production is of particular relevance considering that translation and the flows of literary circulation within the insular Caribbean as movement from one territory or island to the next remain largely regulated and restricted by legal and (geo)political frameworks that are based on criteria of terrestrial continuity or exclusion.[7] In that regard, investigating translation from a tidalectic perspective will allow us not only to interrogate the complex circuitry of transnational literary (non)circulation from a cyclical, non-gravitational approach, but it will further allow us to look at translation as a dynamic, fluid process that defies conventional readings of translation as a linear movement from source to target scripted (hi)stories.

## "Circle culture" and "alter/native" flows of literary circulation

When examining translation flows, especially between so-called dominant and peripheralized or minority languages, directionality is often used as a yardstick by which to measure asymmetrical tendencies. Thus, as the European Council of Literary Translators' Association has observed, cultural diversity remains an issue in the European book industry, where the dearth of translations into English, concomitant with a plethora of translations from English – "especially in smaller countries, where the number of translations from English can reach an incredible 80% of all translations"[8] – coincides with very few translations from one minor language to another, although that point ought to be qualified.[9] To our knowledge, in the context of the Caribbean, there are no similar reports on regional translation flows and literary circulation.[10] Our current research has in fact revealed that, in the context of the insular Caribbean, adopting a gravitational model when looking at translation flows and literary circulation in the region often leads to the conclusion that literature produced in a given island or territory seldom reaches the shores of its closest neighbor, unless both entities are part of the same (for-

---

7. This is especially true of distribution and diffusion in the book industry, as will be further discussed below.
8. See the European Council of Literary Translators' Association: https://www.ceatl.eu/current-situation/translation-statistics. Accessed January 2, 2022.
9. On that point, see the 2020 "Diversity Report" by Wischenbart et al., which highlights the exportation of Nordic (crime) fiction into European markets for a decade, but which further argues that "languages other than those from Western Europe seem, by and large, to be excluded from gaining similar substantial traction with international audiences, with the occasional Chinese or Japanese author as the only exceptions" (p. 28).
See https://www.dropbox.com/s/t9em3m8h36qsah8/2020_final_final_opt.pdf?dl=0. Accessed January 2, 2022.
10. See Saint-Loubert (2021: 71–72).

mer) imperial jurisdiction or share a common – often European – linguistic and cultural heritage. As such, within the logics of (neo)colonial continental continuity, it could be argued that fragmentation and literary non-circulation are the rule in the Caribbean, especially when examining infra-regional translation flows, and that inter-island, transversal connections are the exception.[11] In Brathwaite's terminology, such an approach would be equated to the culture of the "missile",[12] which he opposes to "circle culture" and the image of the "capsule": "Space capsule/is the image this phenomenon/how circle culture travels keeps miraculous intact despite the/ intense outside heat/ of the oppressor" (Brathwaite 1983: 39; phrases underlined in the original). In the glossary he provides as an appendix to his contribution to *Missile and Capsule*, Brathwaite further defines "space capsule" as an "image trying to explain how culture(s) can be transported/transplanted" (54) and, interestingly, he also provides another entry for "circle culture", under the indigenous term "oomanayana", which he further defines as follows:

> ikon of culture of the circle (qv); name of circular Amerindian ceremonial structure made of wood and thatch (native material), used here as indicative of a word/concept central to what I am trying to say (and do); the idea of the circle: cycle: continuum with man/nam (qv) at its atomic centre. (*Ibid.*, 53)

When examining infra-regional literary circulation in the Caribbean, adopting a theoretical framework that similarly proposes a shift of epistemology articulated around circularity and indigenous beliefs and practices seems particularly apt to give more visibility to transversal, minor (and often oral/aural) flows that are otherwise regarded as absent from larger routes of exchange and reduced to non-existence. This is especially true of small, independent publishing ventures, particularly those where writers publish at their own expense and self-distribute their books, which is quite common in the Caribbean, and whose role often goes unnoticed on a larger scale as the status of those publishers is usually deemed less legitimate than more traditional publishing outlets. Yet recent forms of literary "consecration", which include the famous Prix Carbet de la Caraïbe et du Tout-Monde 2021, prove that Caribbean writers do not need to be published in

---

[11] See previous work conducted on South-South connections in the Caribbean (Saint-Loubert 2020a).

[12] This is how Brathwaite presents European missile culture: "The thing about Europe in the Caribbean, in the New World, imperial over/sees and seas: the reason why that occidental (far from accidental) culture formed itself into a missile (seek explore destroy); it is because an alteration of consciousness (as already stated) took place from the moment when Christopher Columbus successfully crossed Atlantic Ocean: bringing with him them no Boticelli no Beethoven no no Michelangelo Da Vinci Descartes Newton La Fontaine. In fact no body but those guns his faith. And Mammon." (Brathwaite 1983: 37; terms underlined in the original)

a "literary centre" (Casanova) to gain international recognition.[13] Similarly, when browsing the shelves of local bookstores and public libraries as well as the catalogues of Caribbean university libraries, alternative flows of circulation emerge. In Martinique and Guadeloupe, for instance, our research has shown that a number of titles available both in French translation and in their original language of production can be found. The presence of those titles is often due to individual initiatives and book donations that could hardly be described as constituting a systemic mode of circulation, but that nevertheless reveal alternative flows within the market of literary circulation. Visits to local public and university libraries, independent bookshops and access to private book collections have, for instance, confirmed that non-vertical flows of circulation do exist in Guadeloupe and Martinique, beyond the core-periphery model, although they remain largely unaccounted for and little known, even sometimes to local readers.[14] At the Médiathèque Ernest J. Pépin located in Le Lamentin, in Guadeloupe, for example, a special collection featuring the works of Ernest Pépin includes several translations (in Dutch, Russian and Spanish) of his works. Some of those translations were originally published and circulated in the Caribbean, as a copy of the Cuban translation of *L'Écran rouge* by Lourdes Arencibia shows. Similar examples of pan-Caribbean translation flows have been observed during work conducted in other public and university libraries in Martinique, Guadeloupe and Puerto Rico, suggesting that "alter/native" initiatives that aim to constitute a culture of the circle for the Caribbean literary ecosystem – inasmuch as they promote transversal,

---

13. Loran Kristian's first collection of poems, *Les Mots de silence*, published by K. Éditions, received the Prix Carbet de la Caraïbe et du Tout-Monde 2021. This recognition is all the more noteworthy as K. Éditions is a small, Martinican self-publishing structure founded in 2003 by Jean-Marc Rosier that aims to promote local authors of French and/or Creole expression and to help them publish their own books. See https://www.keditions.com/edition_marche.php. Accessed January 9, 2022.

14. I especially wish to thank Professor Lambert-Félix Prudent, based in Le Gosier, Guadeloupe, for his generosity and for giving me access to his private book collection. My warmest thanks extend to Louis-Guy Florisse, bookstore owner at Point-Lire, in Le Moule, Guadeloupe, Gwenaëlle Guenguant, Director of the Médiathèque Yvon Leborgne, in Port-Louis, Guadeloupe, Alexandra Citadelle, Director of the Médiathèque Ernest Pépin, in Le Lamentin, Guadeloupe, Sabrina Tanda, Director of the Bibliothèque municipale in Le François, Martinique, Frédéric Vigouroux, Curator of the Caribbean book collection at the Bibliothèque Universitaire de Schoelcher, Martinique, Ernest Yerro, from the Bibliothèque Schoelcher, Fort-de France, Martinique, and Jean-Claude Malaud, bookstore owner of Kazabul, Fort-de-France, Martinique, for welcoming me in their respective structures and for agreeing to be interviewed as part of the IRC-funded research project mentioned above.

inter-island circulation – are available to readers. It remains to be seen, however, whether library-goers actually consult, borrow and read those books.[15]

Going back to Brathwaite's "circle culture" and the "oomanayana", some public infrastructures, among which the Médiathèque Yvon Leborgne, located in Port-Louis, Guadeloupe, work at preserving the region's linguistic and cultural diversity, while promoting a tidalectic model that privileges "an alter/native historiography [over] linear models of colonial progress" (DeLoughrey 2018). Although the library's Caribbean literature section for adults and children, in particular, can be seen as relatively modest when compared with other public libraries located in the French Antilles, its architecture and spatial organization are particularly illuminating when thinking alongside Brathwaite and his circle culture.

**Figure 1.** Carbet du conte, Médiathèque Yvon Leborgne, Port-Louis, Guadeloupe ©Saint-Loubert, January 2022

---

**15.** We especially wish to thank Alexandra Citadelle and her colleagues from the Médiathèque Ernest J. Pépin in Le Lamentin, Guadeloupe, who generously shared some bibliometrics as part of our research project.

**Figure 2.** The carbet du conte seen from above, Médiathèque Yvon Leborgne, Port-Louis, Guadeloupe ©Saint-Loubert, January 2022

As Figures 1 and 2 show, the Carbet du Conte, a children's kiosk dedicated to oral culture and storytelling, is a semi-open circular structure built inside the public library (a former girl's school), surrounded by plants and a small garden patch, indicating that nature and culture are meant to coexist within the Caribbean ecosystem. This is further evidenced by initiatives taken by the library staff who are growing local root vegetables in the yard of the Médiathèque, showing the potential of gardening as a tool to promote agricultural work and social cohesion.[16] As Figure 2 further shows, the roof of the kiosk also serves as an exhibition space for art work created by local school children and the inner space of the kiosk was designed with built-in seats all around the structure, while the center of the kiosk remains vacant for the storyteller to come and invest the space. Implanted in a town with fewer than 6,000 inhabitants, the Médiathèque Yvon Leborgne is located near the water front in Port-Louis and benefits from a nearby skatepark as well as from (aquatic) murals painted by local street artists, which further contributes to connecting the library with various modes of cultural expression in the municipality and potentially makes it all the more attractive to young readers (see Figures 3 and 4).

**Figure 3.** Street art and parking space next to the Médiathèque Yvon Leborgne, Port-Louis, Guadeloupe ©Saint-Loubert, January 2022

Other initiatives, both on an institutional and individual level, are taken in Guadeloupe and Martinique to further stress alter/native connections between oral and written Caribbean cultures. This is the case, for example, of a workshop

---

**16.** See their Facebook page and their post from 24 February 2021: < https://www.facebook.com/M%C3%A9diath%C3%A8que-de-Port-Louis-343066152503742/ >. Accessed January 12, 2022.

**Figure 4.** Mural at the entrance of the Médiathèque Yvon Leborgne, Port-Louis, Guadeloupe ©Saint-Loubert, January 2022

co-run by Creole specialist Hector Poullet and a guest speaker who meet on a weekly basis at the Mémorial Acte in Pointe-à-Pitre, Guadeloupe, to discuss the specificities of *kréyòl gwadloupéyen* and, at a more advanced stage, the translation of Caribbean texts of French expression into Creole. In Martinique, incentives to encourage young people of French and Creole expression to write fiction are similarly promoted by public libraries and publishers specialized in children's books.[17] If, on the whole, those "local" incentives continue to fall under the radar of continental frameworks of literary circulation, they nevertheless prove that more circular, non-centric cultural and translation flows, perhaps more in tune with Caribbean ecosystems, exist.

---

17. See, for instance, the call for short stories published by the Médiathèque du Lamentin and sponsored by the Éditions du Sucrier: < https://mediatheque-lelamentin.fr/cms/articleview/id/284>. Accessed January 10, 2022.

## Episteme-shifting: On the submarine flows of translation

In *Caribbean Discourse*, Édouard Glissant observed the following in relation to what he called "national literatures":

> Where the absence of a preexisting cultural hinterland does not allow a people to take cover in a cultural underground and where an autonomous system of production has no longer been maintained, the tragedy begins. The maternal oral language is repressed or crushed by the official language, even and especially when the latter tends to become the natural language. That is a case of what I call a "cornered" community. (Glissant 1992: 103)

If, on the surface, Caribbean literature seems to circulate "back" to the region only once it has gone through major literary hubs located, for the most part, in continental Europe and America, particularly where processes of translation and non-indigenous languages are concerned, as has been observed, submarine flows of circulation can nevertheless be observed in the region.[18] Insofar as those flows continue to be limited and do not constitute an "autonomous system of production", the Caribbean literary ecosystem can still be regarded as a fragmented "cultural underground", all the more so as issues of diffusion and distribution continue to hinder access to and circulation of books in the region.[19] That said, within this complex and fragile literary ecosystem, submarine[20] flows could be described as defying the logics of cultural imperialism exemplified by the homogenizing tendencies of global book conglomerates. In the context of the intensified predatory practices of capitalistic ventures – including in the book sector – that have been taking place in Puerto Rico in the wake of "natural" disasters – such as hurricane María in 2017, the series of earthquakes that hit the South of the main island of the archipelago and the outbreak of Covid-19;[21] it is interesting to note, in fact, that

---

18. See Saint-Loubert 2017 and 2020b for South-South circulations within the Hispanophone Caribbean and between the Caribbean and the Indian Ocean, especially.

19. Since the outbreak of Covid-19, various interlocutors across the local book industry, among whom booksellers, publishers and librarians, have confirmed that they experienced significant setbacks and delays in the delivery of books they had commissioned or ordered, as a number of commercial flights were canceled because of the pandemic. In November and December 2021, the situation was made worse by social protests and unrest in Guadeloupe and Martinique which blocked access to local freight ports and shipments.

20. In reference to Brathwaite's oft-quoted phrase according to which Caribbean "unity is submarine" (as cited by Glissant in *Poétique de la relation*, 1990).

21. The closure of independent bookstores such as Libros AC in Santurce and La Tertulia in Río Piedras, in San Juan, marked the arrival of several Bookmark bookstores in the metro area, which mostly sell classics and bestsellers, a majority of which can be found in English

other forms of literary circulation have emerged in the US territory, some of which reflect a (more) circular approach to the book economy and, to a relative extent, the translation market. Our research project has shown, for instance, that some literary initiatives consist of restoring and giving a second life to existing printed materials, thereby favoring a circular economy which can be opposed to an extractive, linear market economy that centers on affluence and a high-yield production system. *El Post Antillano*, a media outlet created in 2011, based in the metro area of San Juan that fosters "critical thinking, solidarity, justice, literature and social responsibility"[22] therefore runs a regular "mercado de bienestar recíproco" through which they sell second-hand books (most of which are Spanish and English originals, but some of which are also Spanish translations) without any speculative value. The media outlet has also created several free online and face-to-face cultural events to give more visibility to marginalized Caribbean voices, whilst broadcasting their activities on YouTube and local radio stations (Radio Raíces, WLRP, 1460 AM, in San Sebastián). Some of those events, which are all streamed live, include a "Club de lectores", which meets on a weekly basis and discusses locally published books, the "Funche caribeño", which aims to bring together various interlocutors from the Caribbean to discuss various topics with music in the background, and a cultural program called "Cultura 7D". But incentives promoting popular reading and flows of literary circulation based on alter/native models have also appeared, interestingly, outside the metropolis and, in some instances, before María. This is the case, for example, of the McHondo book kiosk that can be found in the town square of San Sebastián, a town located in the West of Puerto Rico, or, more recently, of the Casa del Cuento y de la Historia Cayeyana, the headquarters of Cooplibri, a book cooperative located in Cayey, South of San Juan, which opened in December 2021 and aims to offer a different model for the (local) book sector by "facilitating individual, collective, communitarian and corporative literary incentives", whilst offering "a new editorial perspective based on collaboration, accessibility and justice".[23]

If such initiatives remain on the margins of the global book market and its main highways (and gateways) of circulation, they nonetheless constitute

---

(and some in Spanish), where independent bookstores like Libros AC and La Tertulia (Río Piedras) used to sell a more diverse range of locally (self-)published authors. For the role of local bookstores in the circulation of Caribbean literature in Puerto Rico, see Saint-Loubert, 2020a, pp. 205–209.

22. See http://www.elpostantillano.net/. Accessed January 10, 2022.
23. See Natalia Ortiz-Cotto's interview, co-founder and co-director of Cooplibri, in *El diario de Puerto Rico*, 8 December 2021. < http://diariodepuertorico.com/2021/12/08/cayey-abre-las-puertas-a-la-cultura-literaria-con-cooplibri-primera-cooperativa-editorial-de-puerto-rico-en-colaboracion-del-municipio/ >. Accessed January 15, 2022.

attempts to anchor and connect the local literary ecosystem with the larger Caribbean community within and beyond the region. That said, it must be noted that those initiatives rarely connect their attempts to foster greater access to Caribbean literature and culture with the crucial role that translation plays in such endeavors. In that regard, we believe that more pan-Caribbean translation flows are urgently needed to create a truly integrated, sustainable regional literary ecosystem.

When thinking beyond the Caribbean region, the tidalectic movement of the ebb and flow of literary circulation can also help shed more light on the uneven, intermittent nature of translation flows in other (post)colonial insular spaces. The unequal nature of those flows seems all the more revelatory when looking at (post)colonial insular spaces in relation to the wider Anthropocene. When we think, for instance, about the potentially destructive force of the ocean, its episodic crushing tidal waves and their impact on Caribbean literature, it is worth remembering that Brathwaite's home and archives in Irish Town, Jamaica, were completely destroyed by hurricane Gilbert in 1988, as the poet reminds us in *DS (2): dreamstories* (Brathwaite 2007). As such, examining literary circulation from a tidalectic perspective sheds light on the fact that seascapes further help reveal the more-than-human asymmetrical forces at play in translation flows. This is especially apparent in indigenous cosmologies that have traditionally revealed an understanding of the relationship between human beings and the world they are a part of. Michael Cronin has made a salient point in that regard, arguing that indigenous and minority languages are not a "legacy in peril", but represent communities deeply connected with present and future concerns, particularly where a more sustainable, more-than-human ecology is concerned: "It is indigenous groups living in sacrifice zones, however, who have an understanding of the relationship of the human to the non-human world which becomes especially valuable in an era of environmental degradation." (Cronin 2019: 15–16) In a similar vein, when envisaging Translation Studies from the perspective of Caribbean epistemologies, it becomes apparent that scale shifting is an important step in better apprehending the discipline from ex-centric, plural perspectives, but this does not, in and of itself, constitute a solution to issues of continental and anthropocentric bias. That would require a shift of epistemes – a shift from missile to capsule culture.

## Conclusion

This chapter has argued that the study of translation flows in the complex, fragmented and vulnerable Caribbean literary ecosystem indicates that existing models of analysis for the transnational circulation of literature are not adapted for the region, all the more so as they largely reproduce the immutable, linear logics of (neo)colonial agendas. Drawing instead on the concept of "tidalectics" imagined by Kamau Brathwaite, the purpose of this contribution was twofold: it aimed to analyze, on the one hand, literary circulation in the region from a more fluid, decentered perspective in order to reveal transversal, submarine (translation) flows, and on the other, to link Caribbean and Translation Studies to propose an epistemological shift that is more attentive to indigenous cosmologies and more-than-human approaches to literary circulation. If, through the case studies examined in this contribution, individual and community-based initiatives manifest solidarity and resourcefulness that resist mainstream and vertical circulation flows, it nevertheless remains true that a more integrated, inter-connected approach, within and beyond Caribbean ecologies, is urgently needed to address issues of bibliodiversity (diversity in the book industry) and epistemological justice. This shift requires nothing less than decolonizing the mainstream book market, together with the theory and praxis of translation. That would not only entail devoting more careful attention to flows that have been made invisible yet do exist, but also – and crucially – a complete rethinking of systemic approaches.

## References

Bourdieu, Pierre. 1992. *Les Règles de l'art. Genèse et structure du champ littéraire*. Paris: Seuil.
Brathwaite, Edward Kamau. 1982. *Sun Poem*. Oxford: Oxford University Press.
Brathwaite, Edward Kamau. 1983. "Caribbean Culture – Two Paradigms." In *Missile and Capsule*, ed. by Jürgen Martini, 9–54. Bremen: Universität Bremen.
Brathwaite, Edward Kamau. 2007. *DS(2): dreamstories*. New York: New Directions.
Casanova, Pascale. 2007. *The World Republic of Letters*, trans. by M. B. Debevoise. Cambridge, MA/London: Harvard University Press.
Casanova, Pascale. 2015. *La langue mondiale. Traduction et domination*. Paris: Seuil.
Cronin, Michael. 2019. *Irish and Ecology/An Ghaeilge agus an Éiceolaíocht*. Baile Átha Cliath (Co. Dublin): Foilseacháin Ábhair Spioradálta.
DeLoughrey, Elizabeth M. 2007. *Routes and Roots: Navigating Caribbean and Pacific Island Literatures*. Honolulu: University of Hawai'i Press.
DeLoughrey, Elizabeth M. 2018. "Revisiting Tidalectics: Irma/José/Maria 2017". In *Tidalectics: Imagining an Oceanic Worldview through Art and Science*, ed. by Stefanie Hessler, 93–102.
D'haen, Theo (ed.). 2012. *The Routledge Concise History of World Literature*. Abingdon/New York: Routledge.
Edfeldt, Chatarina, Erik Falk, Andreas Hedberg, Yvonne Lindqvist, Cecilia Schwartz and Paul Tenngart (eds). 2022. *Northern Crossings: Translation, Circulation and the Literary Semi-Periphery*. New York: Bloomsbury Academic.

Folaron, Deborah and Hélène Buzelin. 2007. "Introduction: Connecting Translation and Network Studies". In *Meta*, 52 (4), 605–642.

Glissant, Édouard. 1990. *Poétique de la relation*. Paris: Gallimard.

Glissant, Édouard. 1992. *Caribbean Discourse: Selected Essays*, 2nd edn, trans. and ed. by J. Michael Dash. Charlottesville: University of Virginia Press.

Hessler, Stefanie. 1998. "Tidalectics: Imagining an Oceanic Worldview through Art and Science". In *Tidalectics: Imagining an Oceanic Worldview through Art and Science*, ed. by Stefanie Hessler, 31–81. Cambridge: MIT Press.

Kershaw, Angela. 2019. "Publishing Landscapes". In *Routledge Encyclopedia of Translation Studies*, ed. by Mona Baker and Gabriela Saldanha, 3rd ed., 445–449. London/New York: Routledge.

Kristian, Loran. 2021. *Les mots de silence*. Ducos: K. Éditions.

Latour, Bruno. 2005. *Reassembling the Social. An Introduction to Actor-Network Theory*. Oxford: Oxford University Press.

Lindqvist, Yvonne. 2016. "The Scandinavian Literary Translation Field from a Global Point of View: a Peripheral (Sub)Field?" In *Institutions of World Literature: Writing, Translation, Markets*, ed. by Stefan Helgesson and Peter Vermeulen. London/New York: Routledge, 174–187.

Martini, Jürgen. 1983. "Introduction". In *Missile and Capsule*, ed. by Jürgen Martini, 9–54. Bremen: Universität Bremen, 5–6.

Saint-Loubert, Laëtitia. 2017. "Publishing against the tide: Isla Negra Editores, an example of pan-Caribbean transL/National solidarity." In *Mutatis Mutandis: La traducción literaria en el Gran Caribe*, 10, 1, 46–69.

Saint-Loubert, Laëtitia. 2020a. *The Caribbean in Translation: Remapping Thresholds of Dislocation*. Oxford: Peter Lang.

Saint-Loubert, Laëtitia. 2020b. "(Trans-)Archipelagic Modes of Publishing Indian Ocean and Caribbean Multilingual Ecologies." In *Borders and Ecotones in the Indian Ocean: Cultural and Literary Perspectives*, ed. by Markus Arnold, Corinne Duboin and Judith Misrahi-Barak. Montpellier: Presses universitaires de la Méditerranée, 273–288.

Saint-Loubert, Laëtitia. 2021. "Penser un écosystème littéraire durable pour et à partir de la Caraïbe: de la nécessité d'une écologie décoloniale du livre." In *Les alternatives – Ecologie, économie sociale et solidaire*. Paris: Alliance des éditeurs indépendants and Double ponctuation, 66–84.

Sapiro, Gisèle. 2008. "Normes de traduction et contraintes sociales." In *Beyond Descriptive Translation Studies*, ed. by Anthony Pym et al. Amsterdam/Philadelphia: John Benjamins, 199–208.

Sapiro, Gisèle. 2016. "Strategies of Importation of Foreign Literature in France in the Twentieth Century: The Case of Gallimard or the Making of an International Publisher." In *Institutions of World Literature: Writing, Translation, Markets*, ed. by Stefan Helgesson and Pieter Vermeulen. London/New York: Routledge, 143–159.

Sievers, Wiebke, and Levitt, Peggy (eds). 2020. "Scale Shifting: New Insights into Global Literary Circulation – Introduction." In *Journal of World Literature*, 5, 467–480.

Wischenbart, Rüdiger, Miha Kovač and Michaela Anna Fleischhacker. 2020. "Diversity Report. Trends in Literary Translation in Europe." Verein für kulturelle Transfers, CulturalTransfers.org and Rüdiger Wischenbart Content and Consulting. https://www.dropbox.com/s/t9em3m8h36qsah8/2020_final_final_opt.pdf?dl=0

CHAPTER 12

# Combining translation policy and imagology
The case of Dutch literature in Italy

Paola Gentile
University of Trieste

This chapter establishes a connection between the fields of translation policy and imagology to scrutinize the strategies employed by governmental organizations in their support of literary translations. It aims to investigate the role of these strategies in facilitating cultural transfers and shaping evolving perceptions of a country internationally. An overview of the policy by the Dutch Foundation for Literature in transnational events will be followed by an examination of promotional strategies employed by the Italian publisher Iperborea. The similarities between the advertising material employed by the DFL and the images used by Iperborea to promote Dutch literature in Italy will be illustrated by means of paratexts[1] and a series of interviews with relevant stakeholders.

**Keywords:** Dutch Foundation for Literature, literary transfer, Iperborea, Italy, translation policy, imagology

## Introduction[2]

This chapter aims to combine two research topics that have rarely been studied together in Translation Studies: translation policy and imagology. In this context,

---

1. According to Genette (1997), there is a distinction within the category of paratexts, which comprises two other subcategories, namely peritexts and epitexts. Peritexts are all those elements around (and in) the text supplied by the publisher (title, preface, epilogue, chapter titles, footnotes, etc.). The term 'epitexts', on the other hand, denotes all those elements that relate to the text, but are external to it and therefore are not part of the book (diaries, interviews, reviews, advertising material, etc.). I am aware that this distinction exists, but for the sake of convenience I will use the general term 'paratexts'.
2. This chapter contains quotes from official policy documents originally written in Dutch. Unless indicated otherwise, all translations from Dutch are mine.

translation policy will be analysed within the framework of literary circulation, which is new, taking into account that previous studies have mainly focused on this topic in the legal, administrative and political spheres (Meylaerts 2011; González Núñez and Meylaerts 2017; González Núñez 2019; Bourguignon, Nouws and van Gerwen 2021). The main objective is therefore to understand why institutional agents make certain choices in the selection and reception of translated literature, and which cultural images transpire from these processes.[3] The need to fill this knowledge gap was already expressed by Toury, who underlined the importance of studying "the factors that govern the choice of text types; or even of individual texts, to be imported through translation into a particular culture/language at a particular point in time" (1995: 58). The recent publication of a special issue of *Perspectives* entitled "Translation Support Policies vs. Book Industry Practice in Non-English Settings" testifies to the increasing interest in exploring translation policy in peripheral literatures (Hedberg and Vimr 2022).

The case of Dutch literature is worth studying, since it is the perfect example of how the links between the various actors involved in the translation processes and a well-implemented translation policy can positively influence the translation flows between two peripheries, not only quantitatively (the number of works translated from Dutch into Italian has skyrocketed in the past 20 years), but also in terms of a change of image of the Netherlands in Italy. Previous studies (Bielsa 2013; Gentile 2021) have shown that the processes of selection and reception are intertwined with image building and that, in contrast to more central languages, literature serves as the primary medium in which images of the Netherlands circulate in Italy. Drawing on previous studies in the field of the sociology of translation (Heilbron and Sapiro 2018; McMartin 2019b), this chapter will add an imagological perspective to an examination of transnational literature circulation through a qualitative analysis combining the results of interviews with the Dutch Foundation for Literature (DFL), the Italian publisher Iperborea and translators. The interviews were carried out between 2018 and 2021. Furthermore, concrete examples of image building will be illustrated in relation to the strategies used by the DFL to promote Dutch literature at international book fairs and in Italy. To that end, a (para)textual analysis will be carried out to show that the books published by Iperborea have contributed to challenging the old stereotypes associated with the Netherlands while simultaneously constructing a multifaceted literary and cultural image of this country in the *Bel Paese*.

---

3. The use of the term 'institutional agents' is not new in studies of the reception of translations in the Dutch-language context: Broomans had already carried out one of the first such studies in 2006 thorough analyses of the role of the Dutch Foundation for Literature in literary transfer.

## Bringing together translation policy and imagology

In order to examine the role of institutional agents in the selection and reception of translated titles, translation policy needs to be framed within the theoretical realm of cultural policy, which is understood as "the exchange of ideas, information, art, and other aspects of culture among nations and their peoples in order to foster mutual understanding" (Cummings 2003:1). Mechanisms of cultural policy are used when states or state-funded institutions use their soft power to promote their culture abroad through "the strategic channeling of cultural and media flow composed of texts created within the cultural industries" (Kang 2013:1). Attempts to connect translation policy with cultural policy have been made by von Flotow, who pointed out that

> The connections between the production of literary translations, the export of literature in translation as a cultural product, and so-called cultural diplomacy, have not been studied extensively, although literary histories do sometimes take account of the effects of translations as literary imports [...]. (2007:188)

Two important premises apply when analysing the link between translation and cultural policy. The first is that translation policy undergoes changes based on, among others, the political situation of a country: states where censorship is practised will import and export translations with an ideological agenda, whereas liberal democracies aim to "create interest, empathy and understanding" (von Flotow 2018:194). The second premise is that cultural policy transcends centre-periphery dynamics among cultures and languages. The branding theorist Simon Anholt (2002) points out that A-nations, with a strong international reputation, and B-nations, that do not have the same status as the A-nations, engage in a competitive race to stand out and capture the attention of foreign audiences with their cultural products such as books, films, and music. In this competition, "having a bad reputation or none at all is a serious handicap for a state seeking to remain competitive in the international arena" (van Ham 2001:2). To that end, all countries, from major world powers such as the United States (von Flotow 2018) and China (Jiang 2021) to peripheral countries such as Belgium (McMartin 2020), use forms of cultural policy to exert their cultural influence abroad. The only difference between these 'central' and 'peripheral' fields is the ways and modes by means of which cultural diplomacy is enacted; while the United States does not need to fund publishers to secure translations of American books, peripheral cultures rely on investments made by state-sponsored organizations to translate and promote literatures that would otherwise remain largely unnoticed on the international stage. This is the case of Dutch-speaking territories, which have set up institutions such as the DFL and Flanders Literature (FL) to promote literary translation from Dutch.[4] The same strategy is adopted by other "(semi-)peripheral"[5] countries including Estonia,[6] Sweden,[7] Denmark,[8] Norway[9] and Israel.[10] All these foundations have the same objectives: they finance translations, organize promotional events, offer scholarships to translators and seek to mediate between the interests of national and foreign publishing houses during the acquisition of titles. According to several scholars (Wilterdink 2015; van Es and Heilbron 2015; McMartin 2019a, 2019b), the intervention of these state agents is fundamental for the diversification of the publishing market, as their objective is to correct a market trend oriented almost exclusively towards profit and translations from and into the most central languages (English, French and German).

In addition to these compelling reasons, there is another driving force behind the "export" of literary works. In the ever-increasing complexity of the relations among the agents involved in the circulation of translated literature, cultural policy can also exert an influence in "shaping national identities and foreign perceptions" (Kang 2003:1). As Loogus and van Doorslaer point out in their analysis of the literary transfer of Estonian titles, "… when translation flows are analysed and presented in (comparative) terms of nation A and B or language A and B as main elements of the framework of analysis and interpretation, such a categorization will more easily generate national or cultural images as explanatory factors" (2021:177). Estonia is indeed an apt example of a country that has successfully shed the image of being a post-communist region and positioned itself as a technology-savvy, quasi Scandinavian country (Pawłusz and Polese 2017) through several cultural policy strategies, among which we find the massive investment in translations from Estonian (ibid.).

---

4. In particular, the DFL was set up at the beginning of the 1990s, whereas FL was established in 1999. For a comprehensive overview of the history of these two institutions, see McMartin (2020).

5. Drawing on Sapiro (2014), Schwartz and Eldfeldt (2021) state that Italy and Sweden can be regarded as semi-peripheral cultures, since they account for 1–3 percent of translations worldwide, at least according to recent research.

6. ELIC, Estonian literature, <http://estlit.ee/> (Accessed December 6, 2021).

7. Swedish literature exchange, <https://www.kulturradet.se/en/swedishliterature/> (Accessed December 6, 2021). The Swedish institute was founded in 1945 to promote Swedish culture and literature. Later the Kulturrådet, founded in 1974, took over its literary activities.

8. Danish art foundation, <https://www.kunst.dk/english/art-forms/literature> (Accessed December 7, 2021).

9. Norwegian literature abroad, <https://norla.no/en/pages> (Accessed December 8, 2021).

10. The institute for the translation of Hebrew literature, <http://www.ithl.org.il/> (Accessed December 8, 2021). For more information on the Israeli literature foundation, see Heilbron and Sapiro (2018).

When states intervene in the transnational circulation of literature, the selection and reception of translated titles are influenced not only by economic and symbolic factors (sales, prizes), but also by subjective evaluations that eventually shape cultural images in target cultures. The example provided by von Flotow (2007) further highlights the interconnections between translation policy and imagology. In 2006, the former First Lady Barbara Bush launched the *Global Cultural Initiative*, which aimed, among other things, to promote literary exchange through the sponsoring of translations. This much-welcome focus on translated literature in the American cultural policy was supported by an imagological reason. The document entitled *Cultural Diplomacy: the Linchpin of Public Diplomacy* published by the US State Department in 2005 concludes that military actions in Afghanistan and Iraq and the prison scandals of Guantánamo tarnished the international reputation of the USA. Therefore, it suggests that "literature (and culture, more generally) must be mobilized as one of the most important forces with which to repair the world's view of the United States" (von Flotow 2007: 190).

As for the Netherlands, the report on cultural diplomacy 2021–2024 issued by the Ministry of Foreign Affairs and the Ministry of Education, Culture and Science states that one of the main strengths of the Dutch political system is a strong cultural policy, which acts as a driving force not only for the international visibility of cultural sector, but also for the economy of the country.[11] Interestingly, this report establishes a link between soft power, cultural policy and the cultural image of the Netherlands:

> Culture is 'soft power'. Through culture, a country strengthens its ability to make friends and wield influence. In a world of increasing international contacts and conflicts, culture can contribute to positive images of the Netherlands and foster debate. […]. International cultural policy is beneficial for the Netherlands' *image* abroad. We seek to present ourselves as an open and creative country, a country that is appealing as a partner. This image is also important for other sectors – like tourism – and strengthens our international relations.
> (Dutch Ministry of Foreign Affairs 2021: 5, my italics)

This statement suggests that exporting a dynamic and creative image of the Netherlands is an integral part of the Dutch cultural policy and an organization and the DFL is among the key entities responsible for implementing this strategy (ibid: 13). Also clearly expressed in the DFL's strategic plan 2021–2024 is one of the

---

**11.** The Dutch cultural policy plan stems from the collaboration between the Minister of Foreign Affairs, the Minister for Foreign Trade and Development Cooperation and the Minister of Education, Culture and Science.

main goals of this institution: "the DFL will work with creators and talent development organizations to show a more complete, broader, diverse and richer image of our country's literature abroad" (DFL 2020a: 11, my translation).

These examples show that there is a close link between cultural policy and imagology, which is defined as "the study of cultural representation, myths of cultural identity and cultural stereotypes" (Beller and Leerssen 2007:xv). Initially developed within the framework of comparative literature (Leerssen 2000), the imagological approach to the study of the circulation of cultural products has been used in recent years to identify and interpret the cultural/national images disseminated by the media (van Doorslaer 2012), by cultural products such as films, TV series (Lankenau 2018) and, of course, by translated literature (Ross and Gentile 2020; Gentile, Kovács and van der Watt 2021). The ground-breaking volume *Interconnecting Translation Studies and Imagology* (van Doorslaer, Flynn and Leerssen 2016) has clearly shown that the choices and strategies adopted by the agents implementing translation policy can result in image formation. Particularly interesting are the results obtained by Jansen (2016), who studied the reception of Italian cultural products in Denmark and came to the conclusion that some features of the titles translated from Italian into Danish "aimed at meeting the 'common' Danish readers' preconceived notions about Italian culture, lifestyle and society" (ibid: 174). The results by Gentile on the images of the Low Countries in Dutch-language novels translated into Italian (2021) are even more intertwined with institutional policymaking: the interviews with the DFL showed that they sometimes resort to cultural images of the Netherlands and Flanders when selecting and promoting the books to translate. Therefore, the study of the translation policy adopted in the literary transfer between two cultural peripheries (the Netherlands and Italy) is particularly interesting. Not only have the two literature foundations implemented the Dutch cultural policy by diversifying supply and demand mechanisms in a book market of translations overcrowded by 'central' languages, but they have also shaped an interesting image of themselves in a country where the Netherlands was associated, until not so long ago, with certain controversial political and religious matters (Gentile 2020).

## The Netherlands as an example of a successful translation (and image-building) policy environment

Before illustrating the reasons why Italy is a success story of the Dutch translation policy, a few examples will provide a clearer idea of the role of the literature foundations in spreading and promoting Dutch-language literature abroad. As stated above, one of the objectives of cultural policy is to display a positive national/

cultural image and translation is one of the means to this end. However, how does the Dutch cultural policy materialize in concrete terms? And how does the Netherlands construct its self-image? Two strategies will be illustrated to show how translation policy leads to the creation of cultural images.

The first is deployed in international book fairs. In Frankfurt, which hosts the world's most important book fair, the Low Countries[12] were guests of honour in 1993 and 2016. On both occasions, the organizers and sponsors of the promotional campaign (including the two literature foundations) adopted a very clear image-building strategy. The promotional slogan of the 1993 guest of honourship was *Flandern und die Niederlande: Weltoffen* [Flanders and the Netherlands: Open to the World]. The campaign poster featured a blue background with an abstract drawing reminiscent of a sail with a book page beside it. It thus contains a clear reference to the sea as a symbol of the openness of the Netherlands. This self-representation is also mentioned in the brochure presented at the book fair:

> Some of Europe's most important rivers flow into the sea in the Netherlands and Flanders, which makes this delta area predestined for a strong international role. This also shapes science and culture. International contacts have always been the daily bread of the Netherlands and Flanders. These countries are open to the world.
> (DFL 1993: 3, my translation)

The 1993 *Buchmesse* was the first occasion in which not only the literature, but also an image of the Low Countries was presented to the world. The impact of such a representation still reverberates today in the reception of Dutch-language literature. For example, in Germany this international spirit of the Low Countries has been reflected in a vast number of reviews: "This cosmopolitan image naturally fits in well with the image of Dutch society as the most tolerant of all, an image that has been firmly anchored in Germany for many years [...]" (Missinne 2018: 17, my translation).

Interestingly, during the 2016 Frankfurt Book Fair, the Netherlands and Flanders presented themselves in a very similar way, by projecting a joint image through the slogan "This is what we share", with an emphasis on their shared history (Van der Schaeghe 2016: 3). The first aspect that stands out is the almost total absence of national symbols:

> The branding materials and pavilion are just as striking for what they do not contain: no callouts to specific marquee authors, no claims of excellence, prestige, or singularity, and most striking of all, no national markers. There is no orange for the Netherlands, no yellow and black for Flanders. No windmills or recreated

---

12. For reasons of space, this chapter will focus only on the cultural and translation policy adopted by the Netherlands, even though in book fairs this is shared with Flanders Literature.

> red-light districts. No poppies or pastorals. Be it on the guest of honour website, the programming on the pavilion stage, or the membership of the official delegation, authors' Dutch or Flemish status is never outwardly advertised.
>
> (McMartin 2021: 287)

In line with this strategy, the prevailing colours were blue and beige, which evoke images of the sea and sand. They were also present in the promotional posters, coloured with several shades of blue and foregrounding the faces of the most famous Dutch-language writers. Moreover, the open spaces where the public presentations were held were surrounded by panels projecting images of the North Sea. The literature foundations played a major role in the creation of these pavilions by choosing The Cloud Collective studio for the project, in which they displayed "The horizon, the central theme that recalls the space and tranquillity of the North Sea coast; over this, verses of poems were accompanied by the rhythm of the tide" (DFL 2016: 47, my translation).

Their openness to the world, the neutral colours, the North Sea and their common cultural characteristics were the images selected to promote their culture in other book fairs as well. The slogan coined by the Low Countries at the 2003 Paris book fair was *Les Phares du Nord* [the Northern Lighthouses], and the same slogan was chosen for a literary campaign organized by the literature foundations in 2018 and 2019, in which Dutch-speaking writers were invited to several book festivals in France. The promotional leaflets of this campaign read:

> for many of you, our countries come across as being exotic. And yet they are so close. The Dutch-language region is characterized by a remarkable diversity of political, social and cultural views. This variety and richness are reflected in the contemporary literature of the Netherlands and Flanders.
>
> (Dijkgraaf and Pauw 2018: 1)

This remark inevitably suggests that the 'northernness' of these territories makes Dutch writers 'exotic' in the eyes of their French neighbours and, once again, the image of the (North) sea is predominant both in promotional campaigns and in the pavilions.[13] The image of the Netherlands as an 'open' country was repurposed on the occasion of the Beijing Book Fair in 2011 (DFL 2011). The slogan of the campaign country programme "Open landscape – Open book", associated the Dutch flat landscape with an open book. In this specific case, however, the concept of openness carried a political overtone. The opening speech by the former State Secretary for Education, Culture and Science Halbe Zijlstra, who stressed that tolerance is one of the main pillars of the Dutch society (Ham 2021: 320),

---

13. Some images of the pavilions can be found at this link: http://www.letterenfonds.nl/events/salon/images_stand.htm

sparked controversy about the participation of Dutch writers in a book fair organized by a country where fundamental freedoms are repressed. On the other side of the world, during the 39th Buenos Aires book fair in 2013, the representation of the Netherlands was somewhat different. On that occasion, Dutch literature was showcased thanks to the DFL's programme, entitled "Café Amsterdam", and was housed in a reserved pavilion built entirely of cork with orange outlines representing the national colour of the Netherlands. This minimalist design of the pavilion had a specific purpose, namely to shun "the stereotypes of bridges, canals, lanterns and all the traditional iconography associated with Amsterdam" (DFL 2013). Another aspect worth emphasizing is that in Buenos Aires Dutch literature was not presented as 'Nordic', but as coming from "the heart of Europe" (ibid). These promotional strategies show that images can be interpreted differently based on the country and the socio-political context of the receiving culture. According to Lindskog and Stougaard-Nielsen, the concept of North "transcends geography and has become an 'enviable' idea, even an imaginary social utopia, fashioned by foreign stereotypes and the image-making or nation branding of the Nordic countries themselves" (2020: 3) This suggests that the cardinal points – in this case the North – far from being fixed categories, are highly subjective mental schemata imbued with cultural features which change according to the beholder's perspective (Gentile and van Doorslaer 2019; Boulogne and van Doorslaer 2020).

The second cultural policy tool that creates images of the Netherlands is the DFL's promotional brochures. These leaflets include a selection of seven new fiction titles, a graphic novel, a classic and a thriller, and are usually published in spring (before the London Book Fair) and autumn (before the Frankfurt Book Fair). The selection of these ten titles is made according to precise quality standards. As a staff member of the DFL says: "We select the books according to three criteria: the literary quality, the good reviews and the potential interest for foreign publishers. The book must have gained visibility in the Netherlands: it must have obtained good reviews and/or literary awards" (my interview, 2019). On the first page of the leaflets another criterion is explained:

> We want to showcase the best fiction from the Netherlands. Most titles have been published recently and have done very well in terms of reviews, sales and awards or nominations. Equally important is the question: 'Does it travel?' An advisory panel gives us advice and input on new fiction. The final selection is made by the Dutch Foundation for Literature. (DFL 2021:1)

In order to appeal to non-Dutch readers, the book's themes must not be "too Dutch", that is to say, they must contain universal, generalisable stories that can resonate with anyone, such as "family, love, crime stories, historical novels, travel chronicles, etc." (my interview with the DFL, 2018). The Dutchness of the selected titles hardly transpires from the description of the books contained in the brochures – with the exception of Stefan Enter's *Pastorale*, containing "quintessentially Dutch themes" (DFL 2020b: 6) – but can be easily found in the covers of the brochures:

**Figure 1.** Covers of the brochures published by the DFL (from 2014 to 2021)

Even though the selection of the titles is not intentionally made to promote a specific image of the Low Countries, the visual elements chosen to represent this literature abroad are consistent with those used in the book fair pavilions that evoke a Nordic image of the Netherlands: the countryside, the culture of cycling and reading, the cold climate and, of course, water, which forms an integral part of the culture of the Low Countries. In the transnational circulation of Dutch literature, it is not only the books that travel through translation, but also the images used to promote them. This transnational image building will now be examined in one of the countries in which Dutch literature has attracted growing interest over the last ten years: Italy.

## The publisher Iperborea: A 'Nordic' image of the Low Countries in Italy

Let us now turn to Italy. While it would be inaccurate to state that there has never been interest in Dutch literature in Italy, it was only after the setting up of the DFL that the visibility of this literature started to increase. The fact that Italy ranks 7th in this list of prioritized countries in the official Cultural Policy Plan 2021–2024 means that, in the next few years, Italy and the Netherlands will cooperate closely in the cultural field. This will lead to the translation of a higher number of Dutch literary works in the *Bel Paese* (Dutch Ministry for Foreign Affairs 2019). In Italy alone, the DFL database reports 177 translations from 1990 to 1999 and 680 from 2000 to 2021 (all genres, reprints included), with 83 translations in preparation.[14] The two main peaks were recorded in the years preceding and following the two guests of honourship at the Frankfurt Book Fair: in 1993 and 2016, which account for 56 titles for the 1991–1994 period and for 126 for the 2014–2017 period. For a more comprehensive view of the investment made in Italy in terms of translation policy, a comparison can be made between the number of translated titles before and after the establishment of the DFL:

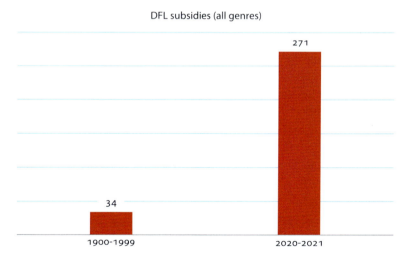

Graph 1. Number of subsidized translations in the periods 1900–1999 and 2000–2021

The most subsidized genres in Italy are:
The graphs clearly show the surge of funding for translations since the 2000s. Since the most widely funded genre is fiction, data were collected on which Italian

---

14. Last access: January 2022.

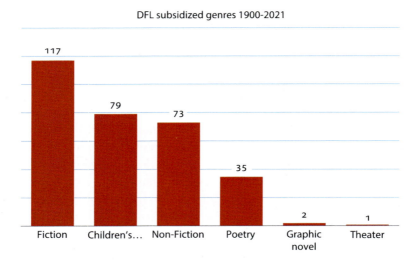

Graph 2. Most subsidized translation genres in Italy (including reprints)

publishers receive the highest number of translation grants from the DFL. Iperborea tops the list with 19 translations, followed by Marsilio (10) and Fazi (9). Iperborea is an interesting case study for two reasons: (1) it was the publisher that gave the most visibility to Dutch literature in Italy; (2) its marketing strategy has a significant imagological component.

The first Dutch book published by Iperborea is Cees Nooteboom's *A Song of Truth and Semblance* [*Il canto dell'essere e dell'apparire*][15] in 1991. This author was discovered by chance: Emilia Lodigiani, the publisher's founder, read this novel in its French translation and, as one of Iperborea's editors points out, "she immediately fell in love with this book. From that moment on, we became more and more interested in Dutch authors" (my interview with Iperborea, 2018). An important aspect to bear in mind is that Iperborea is the only Italian publisher specializing in Northern European literature: Sweden, Norway, Denmark, Finland, the Netherlands, Iceland, Belgium (Flanders), Estonia and Lithuania are the countries included in its catalogue. As can be seen below, the images Iperborea attributes to Nordic cultures are associated with modernity, open-mindedness and far-sightedness:

> Nordic writers have a great narrative capability (they are storytellers), they are not navel-gazers, they have a very broad horizon, they try to understand the world, to understand society, the problems of the world and they try to give

---

15. The original Dutch title is *Een lied van schijn en wezen* (first published in 1981).

Chapter 12. Combining translation policy and imagology 237

>  answers (From an interview with the executive editor Pietro Biancardi, published by Elisa Barbini et al. 2020)

In the article that accompanies the interview, Barbini et al. further describe the characteristics of Nordic literature that transpire from the publisher's catalogue:

> The harmony between man and nature and the broad perspective through which the world is investigated are the inspirational foundations of Iperborea, whose catalogue is dedicated exclusively to authors from northern Europe: not only cold and snow, but also a lot of humour can be found in these books [...] and topics treated with the sensitivity that is typical of this literary tradition.     (ibid.)

This interdependence between man and nature emerges (albeit in different ways) in almost all the Dutch novels published by Iperborea, from the descriptions of the endless Dutch plains in Gerbrand Bakker's novels to those of unspoiled Indonesian nature illustrated by Hella Haasse. Many of these natural elements can also be found on the book covers, where the blue colour and images of water and the sea recur very often:

**Figure 2.** Book covers of some Dutch authors published by Iperborea

The theme of nature was also the focus of the 2001 Turin Book Fair, where Dutch literature was chosen as guest of honour with the following motivation: "the Dutch culture has always reflected on the relationship between man and nature [...] and in particular on the ethical problems of the exploitation of the environment and its resources" (Vita Magazine 2001). References to nature can be found in another editorial project carried out by Iperborea: in 2018 this publisher launched a new series of travel guides entitled *The Passenger*, presented as "a collection of surveys, literary reports and narrative essays that form a portrait of contemporary life in a country and its inhabitants" (Iperborea 2018, my translation). The second issue was dedicated entirely to the Netherlands and received financial support from the DFL. The peculiarity of this volume is that it can be regarded as an inexhaustible source of cultural images, as can be seen from the book cover:

**Figure 3.** Book cover of *The Passenger – Olanda*

With this cover showing the Dutch countryside – with green meadows, ditches and canals – Iperborea provides Italian readers with a new image of the Netherlands. Interviews conducted with the Iperborea staff revealed that:

> there are a few similar guides in Italy, but they often focus on the stereotypes of a country from the perspective of a single writer. This is exactly what the book series avoids doing: it is evident that one of the main objectives of The Passenger is to challenge the old stereotypes about the Netherlands.[16]

One of the translators also confirms that the aim of this volume was to surprise the reader, who "expects to find essays about Dutch tolerance on cannabis, windmills, the use of bicycles, the tulip trade. But in *The Passenger – Olanda* we took a different approach and refused to publish essays about such predictable images" (my interview, 2019). The promotional campaign on social media confirms this image-building strategy:

---

16. One of the promotional tweets reads as follows: "Are you sure you know everything about the Netherlands? In the second edition of #ThePassenger we will try to debunk some #FalseMyths regarding this country. This time, #BenCoates deals with some clichés about the Netherlands: the Dutch are environmentalists, the Dutch are nonconformist and drugs are legal in the Netherlands".

## Chapter 12. Combining translation policy and imagology 239

Figure 4. Promotional posts on Facebook

As for the content, *The Passenger – Olanda* devotes four out of eleven reportages partly or entirely to environmental aspects (the waterworks, the extinction of the wood pigeon, the natural gas reserves, and the making of in vitro meat) and this attention to environmental issues is, according to one translator, "in line the publisher's editorial choices". Thanks to the isomorphic dynamics whereby the images used by the DFL were re-interpreted by Iperborea, this publisher has revolutionized the image that Italian readers have of the Netherlands. As one translator put it, "up until the early 2000s, this country was still associated with completely different images, like cannabis and window prostitution. Now we can finally see a side of this country that no one – apart from Dutch Studies scholars – knew before" (my interview, 2019). A member of the DFL adds: "Iperborea does an amazing job in translating and promoting Dutch titles. We have been working together for years and we know their editorial line, so it is very easy for us to decide if a book could be suitable for them" (my interview, 2020). This was confirmed by an editor at Iperborea: "The DFL is well organized and always makes targeted proposals. Thanks to its staff, but also thanks to our trusted translators, we have been able to translate authors like Kader Abdolah, Jan Brokken and Cees Nooteboom, who now have an established reputation in Italy" (my interview, 2020).

It is precisely this network of agents that has contributed to strengthening translation policy in the field of literary circulation. In the specific case of Dutch-language literature, it was the creation of an image by the DFL that caught the attention of Iperborea, which adapted it and used it to brand its translated titles. While the effects of this transnational image building would need to be studied more thoroughly with regard to other peripheral languages, the potential of the combination of translation policy and imagology can no longer be ignored.

## Conclusion

This study aims to follow up on previous studies on translation and cultural policy (von Flotow 2007; Loogus and van Doorslaer 2021) by conducting a more in-depth investigation into the relationship between translation policy and imagology. The case study on literary circulation between the Netherlands and Italy was particularly suitable for this purpose, not only because it analysed the translation flows between two peripheral cultures, but also because the policy adopted by the DFL has had a clear impact on the reception and image of Dutch culture and literature in Italy. Thanks to the mediation of large transnational events such as book fairs, the agents involved in literary circulation inspire each other in choosing certain marketing strategies for the promotion of titles in different markets. In the case of the Netherlands and Italy, it is clear that the "Nordic" image of Dutch literature, which was repeatedly displayed by the DFL at several book fairs, was used by the Italian publisher Iperborea to promote this literature on the Italian market.

This cross-field interaction can be witnessed in the similarity of the promotional material used at bookfairs and Iperborea's book covers, which confirms the results obtained by McMartin and Gentile concerning the transnational influence (and appropriation) of visual elements in the reception of Stefan Hertmans's novel *War and Turpentine* (2020).

Iperborea's strategy has thus far proven fruitful: Dutch literature has received much attention in Italy in recent years and some authors – like Kader Abdolah and Jan Brokken – have sold well.[17] According to one translator, this would have been unthinkable twenty years ago, when this literature had been suffering "from an inconsistent editorial policy and did not receive much attention from any publisher which, after releasing a couple of titles, dismissed the authors if they did not achieve the hoped-for success" (my interview, 2019). This link between the Netherlands and the Nordic countries has succeeded in giving a "frame" to a literature that had previously failed to find a place on the Italian editorial market. One could further discuss the parameters that define what is meant by "success". One important aspect to consider is that the symbolic capital of this literature has grown over the last few years, as can be seen from the exponential increase in the number of reviews written by authoritative journals (see Gentile 2021: 114). Moreover, Dutch authors are invited more often to book fairs, and cultural activities are frequently organised by the six Dutch university departments (Trieste, Padua, Milan, Bologna, Rome and Naples) with the financial support of the Dutch Embassy.

At imagological level, however, the translation policy implemented by Iperborea raises unanswered questions about what is really meant by the "North" and how this image can influence the readers' expectations. If Dutch literature is promoted as "Nordic" in Frankfurt and Turin, as "open" in Beijing and as "Western European" in Buenos Aires, it is worth wondering why these images change according to the part of the world where they are promoted and whether they are used by local publishers and translators to promote Dutch literature in these corners of the world. This dynamic seems to be confirmed in Italy, where Dutch literature has gained the status of "Scandinavian". However, in order to prevent this literature from being relegated to the confines of the "Scandinavian" themes, the editorial proposals would need to be differentiated in a much more nuanced way so as to offer Italian readers an increasingly varied spectrum of themes. Translation policy should therefore be redesigned from an imagological perspective.

---

17. Information provided by Iperborea during the interviews I conducted for this study.

## References

Anholt, Simon. 2002. *Brand New Justice.* Amsterdam: Elsevier.

Barbini, Elisa, Martina Mascitelli, Barlassina Cristiana, and Giorgia Chiumenti. 2020. "Il mondo visto dagli autori del Nord. Pietro Biancardi racconta Iperborea". *Master professione editoria – Università Cattolica del Sacro Cuore.* Accessed October 12, 2021. https://mastereditoria.unicatt.it/testimonianze/mondo-visto-dagli-autori-del-nord-pietro-biancardi-racconta-iperborea/.

Beller, Manfred and Joep Leerssen (eds). 2007. *Imagology: The Cultural Construction and Literary Representation of National Characters: A Critical Survey.* Amsterdam: Rodopi.

Bielsa, Esperança. 2013. "Translation and the International Circulation of Literature. A Comparative Analysis of the Reception of Roberto Bolaño's Work in Spanish and English". *The Translator* 19 (2): 157–181.

Boulogne, Pieter, and Luc van Doorslaer. 2020. "Russian bears on the move, or how national images are transferred". In *Transfer Thinking in Translation Studies. Playing with the Black Box of Cultural Transfer*, ed. by Maud Gonne, Klaartje Merrigan, Reine Meylaerts, and Heleen van Gerwen, 133–156. Leuven: Leuven University Press.

Bourguignon, Marie, Bieke Nouws, and Heleen van Gerwen. (eds) 2021. *Translation Policies in Legal and Institutional Settings.* Leuven: Leuven University Press.

Broomans, Petra. 2006. "Martha Muusens en de drie M's. Over de studie naar cultuurbemiddeling". In *Object: Nederlandse literatuur in het buitenland: Methode: onbekend: Vormen van onderzoek naar de receptie van literatuur uit het Nederlandse taalgebied*, ed. by Petra Broomans, Stella Linn, Marianne Vogel, Sandra van Vorst, Anders Bay, 57–71. Groningen: Barkhuis.

Cummings, M.C. 2003. Cultural Diplomacy and the United States Government: A Survey. Center for arts and culture. Accessed November 14, 2021. https://www.americansforthearts.org/sites/default/files/MCCpaper.pdf.

Dijkgraaf, Margot, and Bas Pauw. 2018. "Les Phares du Nord – Littérature des Pays-Bas et de la Flandre en France". Accessed November 15, 2021. https://www.lespharesdunord.nl/presse/.

Dutch Literature Foundation. 1993. "Buchmesse, Programmbroschüre – Schwerpunkt van de 45". Amsterdam.

Dutch Literature Foundation. 2011. "Auteurs, illustratoren en uitgevers over hun ervaringen op de Beijing International Book Fair 2011". Accessed December 12, 2021. http://www.letterenfonds.nl/nl/entry/67/beijing-internationalbook-fair-2011-bijzonder-succes.

Dutch Literature Foundation. 2013. "Café Amsterdam-Buenos Aires 2013". Accessed January 18, 2021. http://www.letterenfonds.nl/events/buenos-aires/cafe.php.

Dutch Literature Foundation. 2016. "*Dit is wat we delen. Nederland en Vlaanderen eregast van de Frankfurter Buchmesse. Verslag 2013–2016*". Accessed December 12, 2021. http://www.letterenfonds.nl/images/issue_download/FBM16-verslag.pdf.

Dutch Literature Foundation. 2020a. "*Beleidsplan 2021–2024*". Accessed January 20, 2022. http://www.letterenfonds.nl/images/issue_download/Beleidsplan-Nederlands-Letterenfonds-2021-2024.pdf.

Dutch Literature Foundation. 2020b. "New Dutch Fiction". Accessed January 21, 2022. http://www.letterenfonds.nl/images/issue_download/New-Dutch-Fiction-Spring-2020.pdf.

Dutch Literature Foundation 2021. "Autumn 2021 Dutch Foundation for Literature". *Nederlands Letterenfonds.* http://www.letterenfonds.nl/images/issue_download/New-Dutch-Fiction-Autumn-2021.pdf

Dutch Ministry of Foreign Affairs – Ministry of Education, Culture and Science of the Netherlands. 2021. "*International Cultural Policy 2021-2024*". Accessed January 15, 2022. https://www.government.nl/topics/international-cultural-cooperation/documents/parliamentary-documents/2020/02/20/international-cultural-policy-2021-2024.

Dutch Ministry of Foreign Affairs. 2019. "Priorities of the Netherlands' International Cultural Policy". Accessed January 25, 2022. https://www.government.nl/topics/international-cultural-cooperation/international-cultural-policy/priorities-international-cultural-policy.

Genette, Gerard. 1997. *Paratexts: Thresholds of Interpretation.* Cambridge: Cambridge University Press.

Gentile, Paola. 2020. "Religious Images of the Netherlands in Italy: An Analysis of Press Articles and Novel Translations". *Dutch Crossing* 44 (1): 81–101.

Gentile, Paola. 2021. *De beelden van de Lage Landen in Italiaanse literaire vertaling. Selectie, receptie en beeldvorming (2000–2020).* Trieste: EUT Edizioni Università di Trieste.

Gentile, Paola, and Luc van Doorslaer. 2019. "Translating the North-South imagological feature in a movie: Bienvenue chez les Ch'tis and its Italian versions". *Perspectives. Studies in Translation Theory and Practice* 27 (6): 797–814.

Gentile, Paola, Fruzsina Kovács, and Marike van der Watt. 2021 (eds). "Transnational Image Building: Linking up Translation Studies, Reception Studies and Imagology". *Translation Spaces* 10 (1): 1–4.

González Núñez, Gabriel. 2019. "Law and translation at the U.S. – Mexico border: Translation policy in a diglossic setting". In *Translation and Public Policy: Interdisciplinary Perspectives and Case,* ed. by Reine Meylaerts and Gabriel González Núñez, 152–170. London/New York: Routledge.

González Núñez, Gabriel, and Reine Meylaerts. 2017. (eds). *Translation and Public Policy. Interdisciplinary Perspectives and Case Studies.* London/New York: Routledge.

Ham, Laurens. 2021. "Branding the Open-minded Nation. Dutch Authors at the 2011 Beijing Book Fair". In *Branding Books Across the Ages. Strategies and Key Concepts in Literary Branding,* ed. by Helleke van den Braber, Jeroen Dera, Jos Joosten, en Maarten Steenmeijer, 313–334. Amsterdam: Amsterdam University Press.

Hedberg, Andreas, and Ondřej Vimr. 2022. "Translation Support Policies vs Book Industry Practice in Non-English Settings." *Perspectives* 30 (5): 753–759.

Heilbron, Johan, and Gisèle Sapiro. 2018. "Politics of Translation: How States Shape Cultural Transfers". In *Literary Translation and Cultural Mediators in 'Peripheral' Cultures,* ed. by Reine Meylaerts and Diana Roig-Sanz, 183–210. London: Palgrave Macmillan.

Iperborea. 2018. "*The Passenger – Per esploratori del mondo*". Accessed January 2, 2022. https://thepassenger.iperborea.com/.

Jansen, Hanne. 2016. "Bel Paese o Spaghetti Noir? The image of Italy in contemporary Italian fiction translated into Danish". In *Interconnecting Translation Studies and Imagology,* ed. by Luc van Doorslaer, Peter Flynn, and Joep Leerssen, 163–180. Amsterdam/Philadelphia: John Benjamins.

Jiang, Mengying. 2021. "Translation as cultural diplomacy: a Chinese perspective". *International Journal of Cultural Policy* 27 (7): 892–904.

Kang, Hyungseok. 2013. "Reframing Cultural Diplomacy: International Cultural Politics of Soft Power and the Creative Economy". Culturaldiplomacy.org. Accessed December 20, 2021. http://culturaldiplomacy.org/academy/content/pdf/participant-papers/2011-08-loam/Reframing-Cultural-Diplomacy-International-Cultural-Politics-of-Soft-Power-and-the-Creative-Economy-Hyungseok-Kang.pdf.

Lankenau, Regina. 2018. "Does Netflix's Narcos Challenge or Perpetuate Stereotypes?" *Regina Lankenau blog*. Accessed December 17, 2021. https://medium.com/regina-lankenau/does-netflixs-narcos-challenge-or-perpetuate-stereotypes-a8e9cb5d35bc.

Leerssen, Joep. 2000. "The Rhetoric of National Character: Introduction". *Poetics Today* 21 (2): 267–292.

Loogus, Terje, and Luc van Doorslaer. 2021. "Assisting translations in border crossing". *Translation Spaces* 10 (1): 161–180.

McMartin, Jack. 2019a. "Boek to Book. Flanders in the Transnational Literary Field". Unpublished dissertation. Leuven: KU Leuven.

McMartin, Jack. 2019b. "A Small, Stateless Nation in the World Market for Book Translations: The Politics and Policies of the Flemish Literature Fund". *TTR: traduction, terminologie, rédaction* 32 (1): 145–75.

McMartin, Jack. 2020. "Dutch Literature in Translation: A Global View". *Dutch Crossing* 44 (2): 145–64.

McMartin, Jack. 2021. "'This is what we share': Co-branding Dutch literature at the 2016 Frankfurt Book Fair". In *Branding Books Across the Ages. Strategies and Key Concepts in Literary Branding*, ed. by Helleke van der Braber, Jeroen Dera, Jos Joosten, and Maarten Steenmeijer, 273–292. Amsterdam: Amsterdam University Press.

McMartin, Jack, and Paola Gentile. 2020. "The transnational production and reception of 'a future classic': Stefan Hertmans' War and Turpentine in 30 languages". *Translation Studies* 13 (3): 271–290.

Meylaerts, Reine. 2011. "Translation policy". In *Handbook of Translation Studies* – volume 1, ed. by Yves Gambier and Luc van Doorslaer, 163–168. Amsterdam/Philadelphia: John Benjamins.

Missinne, Lut. 2018. "Van 1993 tot 2016. Nederlandstalige literatuur in Duitse vertaling tussen de twee Buchmessen". In *Tussen twee stoelen, tussen twee vuren. Nederlandse literatuur op weg naar de buitenlandse lezer*, ed. by Lut Missinne and Jaap Grave, 11–33. Gent: Academia Press.

Pawłusz, Emilia, and Abel Polese. 2017. "Scandinavia's best-kept secret. Tourism promotion, nation-branding, and identity construction in Estonia (with a free guided tour of Tallinn Airport)". *Papers, Nationalities Ethnicity, The Journal of Nationalism and Ethnicity* 45 (5): 873–892.

Ross, Dolores and Paola Gentile. 2020. "Grensverleggende Beelden. Literaire Transfer uit de Lage Landen naar Zuid-Europa". In *Grensverleggende Beelden. Literaire Transfer uit de Lage Landen naar Zuid-Europa*, ed. by Paola Gentile and Dolores Ross, 1–23. Gent: Academia Press.

Sapiro, Gisèle. 2014. *La Sociologie de La Littérature*. Paris: La Découverte.

Schwartz, Cecilia, and Chatarina Edfeldt. 2021. "Supporting Inter-Peripheral Literary Circulation the Impact of Institutional Funders of Italian and Portuguese Language Literatures in Sweden." *Perspectives* 30 (5): 811–27.

Toury, Gideon. 1995. *Descriptive Translation Studies and Beyond*. Amsterdam/Philadelphia: John Benjamins.

Van der Schaeghe, Koen. 2016. "Dit is wat we delen". *Vlamingen in de wereld*, april 2016. https://adoc.pub/vlamingen-met-job-en-al-de-liefde-achterna-semigreren-eigen-.html.

van Doorslaer, Luc. 2012. "Translating, Narrating and Constructing Images in Journalism with a Test Case on Representation in Flemish TV News". *Meta: Translators' Journal* 57 (4): 1046–1059.

van Doorslaer, Luc, Peter Flynn, and Joep Leerssen. (eds) 2016. *Interconnecting Translation Studies and Imagology*. Amsterdam/Philadelphia: John Benjamins.

van Es, Nicky, and Johan Heilbron. 2015. "Fiction from the Periphery: How Dutch Writers Enter the Field of English-Language Literature". *Cultural Sociology* 9 (3): 296–319.

van Ham, Peter. 2001. "The Rise of the Brand State. The Postmodern Politics of Image and Reputation". *Foreign Affairs* 80 (5): 2–6.

Vita Magazine. 2001. "La fondazione SFB sbarca a Torino", Accessed 13 January 2022. http://www.vita.it/it/article/2001/05/11/la-fondazione-sfb-a-torino/1828/.

von Flotow, Luise. 2007. "Revealing the 'soul of which nation?' Translated literature as cultural diplomacy". In *In Translation – Reflections, Refractions, Transformations*, ed. by Paul St-Pierre and Prafulla C. Kar, 187–200. Amsterdam/Philadelphia: John Benjamins.

von Flotow, Luise. 2018. "Translation and cultural diplomacy". In *The Routledge Handbook of Translation and Politics*, ed. by Jonathan Evans and Fruela Fernandez, 193–203. London/New York: Routledge.

Wilterdink, Nico. 2015. "De receptie van Nederlandse literatuur in het buitenland: aandacht, interpretatie, waardering". In *Nederlandse kunst in de wereld. Literatuur, architectuur en beeldende kunst 1980–2013*, ed. by Ton Bevers, Bernard Colenbrander, Johan Heilbron, and Nico Wilterdink, 56–96. Nijmegen: Vantilt.

# Notes on the authors

**Maricel Botha** began lecturing translation as a postgraduate student in 2015 at the University of Pretoria. For the past five years, she has been lecturing in the School of Languages at the North-West University in Potchefstroom, South Africa. Her research interests are power and ideology in African translation and African translation history. Some of her most recent research has involved investigating translation in relation to social exclusion, analysing the translator agency of female Khoesan language translators in colonial South Africa and studying a late 19th-century German-Nama dictionary as an expression of colonial ideology. In 2020, she published a monograph on power and ideology in South African translation history from a systems theory perspective.

**Fruela Fernández** is Senior Lecturer in English Studies at the University of the Balearic Islands. His most recent monograph is *Translating the Crisis: Politics and Culture in Spain after the 15M* (Routledge). He has co-edited *The Routledge Handbook of Translation and Politics* and is the series co-editor for *Critical Approaches to Citizen Media*.

**Paola Gentile** is Assistant Professor of Dutch Translation and Interpreting at the University of Trieste. She has held research positions at KU Leuven and the University of Tartu and she is also a guest research fellow at Stellenbosch University and at Leiden University. She has been working on several research projects, among which: "The imagological importance of translation policy: The transfer of Estonian images through translation" (coordinated by Luc van Doorslaer) and "DLIT: Dutch Literature in Translation" (coordinated by Herbert Van Uffelen). Together with Jack McMartin she is the principal co-investigator of the project: "Cultural policy, international publishers and the circulation of Dutch literature in translation", funded by the Dutch Language Union. She has participated in many national and international conferences and has been invited as guest lecturer to Leuven, Graz, Stockholm, Naples, Tartu and Leiden. She is the review editor for the peer-reviewed journal *Translation in Society* (John Benjamins). Her research interests include the reception of Dutch-language literature in Italy, translation policy, imagology and the sociology of translation.

**Philipp Hofeneder** is currently a postdoctoral researcher at the Karl-Franzens-University in Graz (Austria). He specializes in multilingual and pluriethnic empires such as the Habsburg monarchy, the Russian tsardom and the Soviet Union, and conducts research on translation history and knowledge transfer. In his work he focuses on translation history and how to localize and visualize translation. For more information see: https://homepage.uni-graz.at/de/philipp.hofeneder/

**Bei Hu** is an Assistant Professor of Translation and Interpreting Studies in the Department of Chinese Studies at the National University of Singapore. She received her doctoral degree in translation studies from the University of Melbourne, Australia. Her research area revolves around reception research on translation and interpreting, focusing on ethical issues in high-stakes intercultural communication.

**Selahattin Karagöz** is currently working as a research assistant in Translation and Interpreting Studies at Ege University, İzmir, Turkey. He received his PhD in translation studies from Yıldız Technical University in 2019 with his dissertation "Amateurs, Experts, Explorers: Video Game Localization Practices in Turkey". His research interests cover game localization, translation sociology, production studies and labour in virtual communities.

**Yvonne Lindqvist** is Professor in Translation Studies at the Institute for Interpreting and Translation Studies (IITS), Department of Swedish and Multilingualism, Stockholm University. She is one of the authors of the volume *Northern Crossings. Translation, Circulation and the Literary Semi-Periphery* (2022. Bloomsbury Academic: New York & London). She was a researcher in the research programme Cosmopolitan and Vernacular Dynamics in World Literatures from 2016 to 2021. She works mainly within the Sociology of Translation and World Literature Studies and has published several articles on translation bibliomigrancy of Francophone and Hispanic literature from the Caribbean to the Swedish literary space and on translator consecration and prestige.

**Sofía Monzón Rodríguez** is Assistant Professor of Translation and Interpretation at Utah State University. Her research explores the intersection of literary translation, censorship, and affect. In 2021, she received the Killam Memorial Scholarship to carry out her doctoral project (University of Alberta): "Affective Matters: Translation, Censorship, and the Circulation of Romans-à-Clef from Argentina to Franco's Spain," a work that studied the transatlantic circulation of censored novels via translation in the mid-20th century. Her academic works have been published in *Mutatis Mutandis, Entreculturas, Translation Matters, TranscUltural, Transletters, and Editorial Comares.*

**Sare Rabia Öztürk** is a PhD candidate at Boğaziçi University, Translation and Interpreting Studies. She is engaged in cultural research within the framework of translation, studying instances of inter-cultural transfer in relation to historical context, popular culture and power relations. She also has professional experience in the field of gender studies, working as senior researcher at an organization for women's rights. She carries out her professional and academic studies in Turkish, English and Arabic.

**Anthony Pym** is Distinguished Professor of Translation and Intercultural Studies at the Rovira i Virgili in Tarragona, Spain, Professor of Translation Studies at the University of Melbourne, Australia, and Extraordinary Professor at Stellenbosch University in South Africa.

**Laëtitia Saint-Loubert** obtained a PhD in Caribbean Studies from the University of Warwick. She is a practising literary translator, currently working as an Irish Research Council Postdoctoral Fellow at University College Dublin on a two-year research project entitled "Rethinking Translation Studies from Caribbean Meridians: Towards an Ecosystemic Approach" (2021–2023). Her first monograph, *The Caribbean in Translation: Remapping Thresholds of Dislocation* (Oxford: Peter Lang) was published in 2020, following receipt of the 2018 Peter Lang Young Scholars Award in Comparative Literature. She has translated works by Caribbean writers Michelle Cliff, Elizabeth Nunez, Gisèle Pineau and Roger Parsemain, and is currently working on a collaborative English translation of a Reunionese novel.

**Duygu Tekgül-Akın** is a translation researcher based in Bahçeşehir University, Istanbul. She obtained her BA degree in Translation and Interpreting Studies at Boğaziçi University, then completed an MA in Publishing and Language at Oxford Brookes University and a PhD in Sociology at the University of Exeter. She did postdoctoral research at the University of the Free State. Her areas of interest include the sociology of translation, intercultural communication, cultural and creative industries, and Turkish literature in English translation. Her articles have appeared in *Translation Studies, Translation and Interpreting Studies, Perspectives, Language and Intercultural Communication*, and *The European Journal of Cultural Studies*.

# Index

**A**

agents, 23–25, 32, 34, 37–38, 43–46, 61, 65, 112, 123, 151, 163, 170, 178, 228, 230, 240
agents and objects, 24, 26, 28–30
audiences, 33, 139, 144, 194

**B**

book fairs, 159, 168, 171, 231–32, 240–41

**C**

censorship, 45, 56, 61, 63, 65, 172, 227
centers, 74, 87, 92–93, 151, 207–8, 220
circulation, 13, 29, 43, 45, 56–57, 62, 107, 109–10, 113, 115, 122, 124, 150, 165, 171, 175, 208–9, 212, 214, 219–20, 228, 230
communities, 13, 62, 92, 109–15, 117–18, 121, 123–24, 130–31, 144, 221
constraints, 78, 133, 139, 142, 188–90
consumers, 46, 62, 116, 165, 167, 177
consumption, 18, 64, 111, 114, 116, 143
creoles, 10–11
cultural capital, 109, 113, 123
cultural diversity, 198, 212, 215
cultural expression, 131, 140, 144, 217
cultural images, 167, 172, 176, 184, 226, 228–31, 238
cultural intermediaries, 165–66, 169
cultural intermediation, 164–66, 175, 177–78
cultural mediation, 139, 143, 163, 166, 176–78
cultural mediators, 25, 88, 95, 163–64, 166, 171, 176, 178
cultural production, 65, 89–90, 164, 171, 177, 211
cultural products, 8, 88, 137, 165, 171, 227, 230
cultural transfer, 29, 88, 90, 137, 225

**D**

dissemination, 10, 24–27, 39, 141
distance, 14, 16, 24, 26, 157, 185, 187, 192, 197–98, 200, 211
distribution, 10, 17, 37, 39, 108, 122, 136, 170, 210, 212, 219

**E**

emergence, 24, 26, 28, 69, 71–74, 76, 81–82, 91, 137, 166, 207
entertainment, 134, 136–37, 145
environment, 26, 63, 132–33, 139, 143, 237
exchanges, 5, 10, 69–70, 73, 88, 113, 170, 213, 227
expectations, 116, 183–84, 187–89, 192–93, 195–97, 199–200, 241
reader's, 187–89
explicitation, 185, 187, 192, 195–97, 200, 204

**F**

faithfulness, 185, 187–88, 192–95, 199–200
fields, 72, 78, 80, 94–95, 164, 170–71, 177, 208, 225–26, 240
films, 59, 131, 133–34, 136, 138–39, 142–43, 227, 230
flows, 17, 19, 43, 65, 69, 100, 130–31, 138, 166, 184, 207, 211, 213, 219, 221–22
fluency, 185, 187–88, 192–95, 199–201

**G**

gaming capital, 107, 109–10, 112–15, 117–20, 122–24
globalization, 69, 73, 147, 207

graphics, 108–9, 119

**H**

hegemony, 6, 129
history, 24, 89–90, 94, 98–99, 150, 152, 168, 211

**I**

identity, 11–12, 62, 69–70, 98, 130, 137, 144
ideologies, 62, 135, 201
image building, 163, 226
images, 16, 30, 142, 163, 169, 174, 199, 206, 213, 225–26, 228–31, 233–34, 237–38, 240–41
imagology, 184, 225, 240
import, 47–48, 55–58, 63–64, 227
indigenous, 7, 18, 130–31, 142, 221
indigenous languages, 4, 130–33, 138, 140–41, 143–45
indigenous language translation flows, 144
institutions, 25, 37, 46, 87, 157, 163, 165, 170, 178, 192, 227–28, 230
interaction, 27, 29, 89, 99, 115, 122, 191
intercultural communication, 185, 201
intercultural transfer, 87, 100
interculture, 88, 100, 177
intersection, 87, 92, 150–51, 208
intervention, 13, 108, 110, 189–90, 192, 199, 228

**K**

knowledge, 5, 7–9, 11, 17, 24, 30, 87–88, 90, 92–93, 100, 117–19, 139, 172–73, 175, 197, 212

**L**

language borders, 3, 8, 14, 16
languages
  central, 70, 157, 226, 228, 230

ex-colonial,  129–30, 145
minority,  59, 212, 221
official,  95–96, 98, 170, 219
peripheral,  69–70, 156, 240
literary circulation,  207–9, 214, 218, 220–22, 226, 240
literary markets,  151, 154, 165, 173, 207
localization,  107–9, 111–14, 119, 121–23

## M

maps,  8–9, 12, 28–30, 33, 100
markets,  59, 136, 141, 169, 173–74, 207, 214, 240
meaning,  15, 17–18, 24, 28, 140, 142, 196
mediation,  4, 132, 134–35, 139, 143, 165, 169, 173, 240
mediators,  4, 25, 32, 93, 166
message,  3, 7, 15–16, 72, 134, 193, 198
metaphors,  5, 25, 38, 150, 170
migration,  73, 150, 211
mobility,  23, 32, 187
movements,  15, 17–18, 25, 29, 71, 79, 87–88, 90, 94–95, 99–100, 137, 212
multilingualism,  12, 130, 187

## N

narratives,  15, 17, 44, 62, 142, 144, 150
national contexts,  62, 136, 163, 178
national literatures,  167, 169, 172, 177, 219
networks,  32, 36–37, 45–46, 63, 89, 164, 166, 173–74, 177–78

non-commercial translation practices,  107, 110–11, 113, 116–17, 123–24

## P

paratexts,  62, 74, 114, 119–20, 122–23, 154–55, 183, 225
peripheral cultures,  227, 240
peripheries,  207–8, 226
pidgins,  10–11, 138
power,  87–88, 90–92, 96–97, 133
prizes,  156, 158–60, 167, 229
proximity,  81, 137, 185, 187, 192, 197–98, 200
publishers,  35, 44–45, 47–49, 51–53, 55–56, 59–60, 62–64, 71, 74, 76–82, 151, 163–64, 166–67, 171–77, 213, 218–19, 225, 236–37, 240–41
publishing houses,  49–50, 56, 59, 63–64, 78, 82, 175

## R

reception,  43, 46, 70, 82, 142, 149–50, 159, 171, 184–87, 192, 200–201, 210, 226–27, 229–30, 240–41
region,  12, 87, 90–94, 97–99, 131, 139, 208–10, 212, 215, 219, 221–22
relations,  5, 7, 11–12, 78, 89, 130, 132–33, 135, 143, 163, 169, 171, 228
relationship,  79, 108, 124, 133, 140, 154, 171, 177, 196, 199, 221, 237, 240
relevance,  38, 70, 73–74, 80, 134, 143–45, 178, 210
religion,  87–88, 100, 172

## S

social media,  72, 164, 169, 178, 238
social systems theory,  131–33, 136, 139
society,  4, 13, 62, 131–33, 135–36, 142, 230, 236
sociology,  112, 165, 226
space,  10, 17, 24, 26–29, 90, 100, 112–13, 170, 176, 184, 186, 200, 217, 232
spatial relationship,  24, 29–30
sphere,  7, 108, 130, 135
subtitling,  121, 131, 138–41, 143–44

## T

territory,  96, 212, 232
time,  9, 32, 35, 38–39, 46, 51, 57, 62, 72, 74, 81, 90–91, 93, 100, 116, 121–22, 169, 175, 184, 226
time and space,  90, 100, 184
transfer,  27, 38, 88–96, 100
translation policy,  70, 225–27, 229–31, 235, 240–41
translation reception,  184–89, 192, 200–201
translator interventions,  189–90, 192, 194–95, 200
transnational,  164, 171, 176–78, 207–8, 212
trust,  157, 185, 193, 195, 198, 200–201

## V

visibility,  74, 80, 208, 213, 220, 229, 233, 235–36

## W

women,  4, 13, 17, 77, 176
world literature,  43, 59, 149–50, 153–54, 156, 165